# TALENT
# MANAGEMENT
# TECHNOLOGIES

## A Buyer's Guide to
## New, Innovative Solutions

BY
ALLAN SCHWEYER,
ED NEWMAN
AND PETER DEVRIES

Human Capital Institute Press
Washington, D. C.

AuthorHouse™
1663 Liberty Drive
Bloomington, IN 47403
www.authorhouse.com
Phone: 1-800-839-8640

© 2009 Allan Schweyer, Ed Newman, and Peter DeVries

First published by AuthorHouse 7/15/2009

ISBN: 978-1-4490-0540-5 (sc)

Printed in the United States of America
Bloomington, Indiana

This book is printed on acid-free paper.

Human Capital Institute Press www.humancapitalinstitute.org

authorHOUSE®

# CONTENTS

# INTRODUCTION

*We must all hang together, or assuredly,*
*we shall all hang separately.*
Benjamin Franklin

Talent Management Technologies is part book, part guide. Our intent is to help readers navigate the exciting but often perplexing world of the systems, tools and "solutions" that have been designed to improve the way the workforce is managed and supported in organizations. To gain the most from the technology, we believe it is necessary to understand why a robust market exists for them, how they've evolved and are evolving and how to select them.

The authors represent almost 60 years of combined experience in talent management technology. As pioneers and leaders in the field, we designed some of the earliest talent management technologies and led the organizations that introduced them; we've consulted to hundreds of the world's most respected organizations on the selection, implementation and adoption of the tools; and, as analysts and researchers, we've devoted years to understanding the vendor landscape and the technologies they offer.

The landscape of talent management technology providers is complex, crowded and sometimes contradictory—it is bewildering for the typical HR executive charged with selecting and implementing the right tools. This book and guide is designed to simplify a difficult task. Our first approach to simplification is to eliminate a large percentage of the providers from this publication. At this stage in the evolution of talent management technologies, organizations are best served by narrowing their search and focusing on one of the dozen or so "suite players" in the market. Suite players are vendors that either through home-grown efforts, or through acquisition, are developing full life-cycle solutions. In plain language, they are building integrated technology platforms that allow their customers to do everything from recruiting to off-boarding for the entire workforce (traditional and contingent) using one integrated toolset (Figure 1).

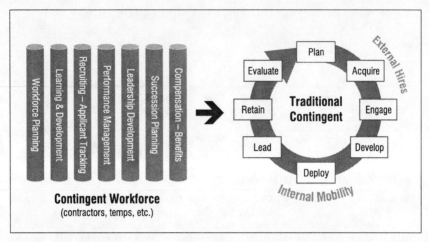

**Figure 1:** From Stove Pipes to Integrated and Holistic Talent Management

While no solutions provider has yet created an end-to-end talent management platform, the solutions described and assessed in this book are making impressive progress. Most organizations approach talent management in a stove piped fashion that resembles the left-side (or before) part of Figure 1. If strategic talent management is being performed at all, it is rarely integrated. Different leaders are responsible for different components (i.e. recruiting and performance management), and information rarely flows between them. Even more isolated are those responsible for the increasingly important contingent, or contract workforce. Despite the fact that most contractors today occupy skilled, professional and even executive positions, their recruitment and management are often left to the same people in the organization that procure pencils and computers.

Integrated talent management represents an opportunity to both streamline and greatly improve HR operations. To date it has been hampered in part by inertia, and the lack of a will to reorganize HR around a talent executive vested with credibility and authority to match any C-level leader in the organization. But integrated talent management has also been restrained by the absence of technology to facilitate and accelerate it. Nonetheless, the tools and solutions described in this book are those that offer the most comprehensive platforms available. The providers of the tools described in this book appear also to be those that are most committed to developing the entire platform as quickly as possible.

We believe that as more organizations explore the benefits of integrated and holistic talent management, the demand for technologies to facilitate it will expand. As this occurs, providers will redouble their efforts and investments to create the platform. In the meantime, we've narrowed our focus in this book and guide to what we call the "suite providers," those that offer several talent management technologies on a single integrated platform. It is our contention that organizations should investigate solutions that help them to improve multiple spokes of the talent lifecycle, depicted in Figure 1, and in an integrated fashion.

Allan Schweyer
May 15, 2009

# CHAPTER 1

# Trends Shaping the Future of Human Resources and Talent Management

By Allan Schweyer

*Forget terrorism. Forget weapons of mass destruction.*
*The next global war will be fought over human capital.*
David Heenan, Author of *Flight Capital*

In 1798, Thomas Malthus wrote: "Population, when unchecked, increases in a geometrical ratio." Essentially, he warned that the population of the world would soon outstrip the planet's capacity to sustain it.[1] Ironically, despite population growth of more than 600 percent since then, concern has recently shifted to focus upon too little population growth in many parts of the world.

Malthus's grim predictions have not materialized, because among the population there has always been a talented core that, through the application of human ingenuity, has so far overcome our major challenges to survival. Scarce talent has similarly driven the growth of our economies and businesses. A more pressing and persistent concern than overpopulation, therefore, is the global undersupply of talent.

Up until the very recent past, the talented few, combined with plentiful and cheap labor, were sufficient to power our economies and prosperity. Today, despite global population growth nearly as steep as it has ever been,[2] and despite recessions, the demand for talent has reached pandemic levels across much of the world. Indeed, as of the publication of this book, the U.S. and most of the world were suffering the worst recession since the Great Depression. Nonetheless, recent studies from Randstad and the National Federation of Independent Businesses, to name a few, revealed that the majority of employers in the U.K. and small business owners in the U.S. were still unable to fill their open positions because of a lack of skilled workers.[3] There is an obvious but important distinction between the thin layer of worldwide talent that can contribute to our increasingly complex, global economy and what is commonly referred to as "labor."

> *The confluence of a bulging aged population*
> *and a shrinking supply of youth is*
> *unlike anything that has happened since*
> *the dying centuries of the Roman empire.*
> Peter Drucker, "The Next Society," *The Economist*, November 1, 2001.

The global market for competent, skilled workers is getting tighter; while at the same time the developed world is shedding as much of the repetitive, "low-end" work as it can. All the while, we raise the bar for talent unrelentingly. In 2000, Thomas Homer-Dixon warned in his thought-provoking book, *The Ingenuity Gap*, "When things happen faster, in greater numbers, and with greater interactive complexity, we need more ingenuity to make the right decisions at the right time."[4] In February, 2008, with the U.S. economy in recession, billionaire investor Warren Buffet said he was bullish on the American economy because, "The world does get better. People get more productive. More human capacity is unleashed over time."[5]

Recessions provide lulls in the global "war for talent," but as French philosopher Auguste Compte said famously, "demographics are destiny." In general, the current birthrates in Western nations are far below replacement levels—meaning that populations (already in decline in Russia, Italy and Spain, for example) will eventually drop in most, if not all western nations. For skilled talent, the problem is far more acute. Using educational attainment as a proxy for talent (albeit an imperfect one), the situation is dire and worsening. Between May 2006 and April 2009, unemployment among four-year college graduates in the United States averaged just over 2 percent,[6] meaning essentially that anyone in the United States with a college degree who wanted a job had one. As of April 2009, the unemployment rate for four-year college graduates stands at just over 4 percent in the U.S. During the last U.S. recession, roughly between 2001 and 2004, unemployment in this group never even approached 4 percent, which is *lower* than the rate economists consider as *full* employment.[7]

With economic recovery, organizations can expect a more intense and more *global* competition for talent than ever. As economies, business, social problems, science and health and security issues become more complex, and as our knowledge and information society becomes more globally integrated and sophisticated, ever greater skills and knowledge are required and in larger numbers. Add to this the demographic realities of an aging workforce nearly everywhere in the world and demand that will continue to come out of developing economies like China and India, and we have the ingredients for a renewed and more serious talent crisis starting early in the next decade.

In an era of "talent" shortages, organizations must renew their management and leadership practices. Many of the most successful organizations in the world, including Toyota, Southwest Airlines and Men's Wearhouse, have learned how to turn ordinary workers into superstars. In doing so, they've insulated themselves against an over-reliance on a thin band of elite talent, often mercenary in attitude.

These organizations and others like them have gained an overwhelming advantage in their ability to hire a more available workforce, at more reasonable rates, and at the same time, gain even greater workforce productivity than their star-chasing competitors.

In this book, we refer to "talent" in the broadest sense. Talent is in equal parts what an employee brings to the job and what his or her employer is able to bring out through effective leadership and the workplace environment. Without a doubt, organizations that can develop, attract, mobilize and retain a committed workforce will be the winners of the future. The talent management executives and teams that lead these efforts will be among the most important and strategic parts of any organization. The question then is what are organizations and the human resources profession in general doing about it?

# Four Critical Trends

*HR today sits smack-dab in the middle of the most compelling*
*battleground in business, where companies deploy*
*and fight over that most valuable of resources—workforce talent.*
Matthew D. Breitfelder and Daisy Wademan Dowling,
"Why Did We Ever Go into HR," *Harvard Business Review*, August 2008.

Where is HR? Has the profession taken advantage of the tremendous opportunity that our nascent "Age of Talent" presents? As the questions surrounding talent, skills, successors, performance and leadership consume more corporate board and "C" suite time, in what direction will the HR profession evolve? There are really just two possibilities—up or out. But which outcome is the more likely?

A good place to start is with the shifts and trends that are likely to shape the workplace in the coming years. The ways in which HR anticipates and responds to these changes will largely determine its future. The first of these trends is demographics. The United Nations cites the aging workforce globally as among the three great challenges facing the world today. Nations in Europe and Asia have already begun the painful process of depopulation, and from the United States to China, the fastest growing segment of the population is the over-50 cohort.

But it is not just an aging workforce that is presenting new challenges; the workforce is being transformed through rapid changes in its makeup—more women, more visible and ethnic minorities, more generations in the workforce and more disparate types of workers—from contingent to virtual. This second trend is accelerating faster than most organizations can respond.

The third sweeping trend that will change the business landscape, and the world, is continued and faster-paced globalization combined with a profound shift in the economy driven by the 2008/09 recession. The threats and opportunities both pose to the global workforce and business are as yet barely understood. For Western workforces, globalization accelerates the imperative for innovation, creativity and productivity. For stewards of talent, it demands a deeper understanding of international economics, laws and culture, as well as a range of new expertise in issues as esoteric as "captive" vs. "third-party" offshoring. The impact of the "Great Recession" is even more speculative. The recession may produce a fundamental shift in our economy and on work itself. Will Americans learn their lesson and never again borrow and spend at the profligate levels of the past? If so, how will this impact the workforce? Will we have permanently higher unemployment rates among lower skilled service and manufacturing workers? If Wall Street and its equivalents around the world no longer attract most of the "best and brightest" into the financial sector, where will the best graduates go? Will they become scientists, entrepreneurs, doctors and academics? Could this lead to a new golden age of discovery and technological breakthrough? Are we seeing an end to, or more emphasis on, famed economist Joseph Schumpeter's ideas of Creative Destruction in the jobs market (the idea that entrepreneurs continuously disturb the status quo, destroying old ways of doing things, including entire companies and industries, but creating new innovative methods, industries and jobs at the same time)?

Finally, as in all other aspects of our lives, technology is impacting talent management profoundly. In just over a decade, the Internet, for example, has radically transformed the manner in which organizations recruit, onboard, retain, develop and even pay their employees. And yet, we've only seen the beginning in terms of the innovations possible from web services and interactive digital technologies, including social networking. The future promises faster and more far-reaching innovation as India, China and other countries add their ingenuity to the mix.

Beyond the Internet, what other world-changing technologies lie right around the corner that will make our workforces more productive and unleash even greater human potential? The only certainty is that there will be more innovation, that it will come in faster cycles and will change our profession each and every time.

These forces will shape the evolution of the HR profession, but HR executives must also shape the trends. A daunting set of skills and knowledge will be required for success. The modern talent management (TM) executive will be multidisciplinary: part economist, demographer, strategist, psychologist, sociologist, salesperson, speaker, leader, coach and consultant. The TM executive will be among the organization's most knowledgeable authorities on globalization, outsourcing, sustainability, corporate social responsibility, talent-related technologies, finance, corporate governance and measurement. Of course, he or she must also be a master of the organization's business and its industry. If this does not sound much like HR, it isn't. It is a tall order for anyone, while exciting at the same time. An executive who can demonstrate these competencies will almost certainly take a well-earned position beside the CEO and will be on par with any senior executive. But advancement is not the point. Increasingly, winning organizations will require world-class Talent Management executives. The best from other parts of the business need to be drawn into these ranks, and this transformation must come soon.

## Trend 1: Demographics

Every day in the United States, 10,000 baby boomers turn 55. By the end of this decade, two experienced workers will leave the U.S. workforce for every inexperienced young one that joins. This is significant in more ways than one. Since the turn of the twentieth century, each new generation of workers has brought more "human capital" to employers (and hence, more productivity) than the generation of workers exiting the workforce—*despite* the imbalance in work experience. This is no longer true. Mass access to higher education began in the 1960s in North America and has continued ever since. Unfortunately, today's 25-year-old male is only marginally better educated than his predecessor of the 1960s and 1970s. Today's generation of workers brings roughly the same level of education as the baby boom generation. Yet the early boomers are leaving with 30–40 years experience, a legendary work ethic and incredible reservoirs of knowledge. The recession, consumer debt and baby boomers' preferences to work longer have kept the mass retirement bubble at bay, but the problem is only deferred, not eliminated. Eventually, the boomer generation must leave the workforce, taking their knowledge and experience with them.

This knowledge deficit could not come at a worse time. Some 85 percent of jobs today require education beyond high school compared with just 61 percent 15 years ago. The trend is only accelerating, yet, in the United States today, less than 70 percent of students graduate high school on time. Many who graduate are the beneficiaries of exaggerated grades and low expectations so much so that they require remedial studies before they can enter university-level courses. As of 2007, only 38 percent of Americans held at least a two-year degree; worse, it is estimated that 60 percent of the jobs in North America already require skills possessed by only 20 percent of the population.

*The greatest HR challenge of the coming decades will be to enhance workforce productivity as the availability of skilled workers declines.*
Watson Wyatt, 2006.

To underscore the importance of workforce productivity gains, especially in an era that promises perpetual talent shortages, consider that since World War II, the U.S. economy has grown eightfold while the labor force has only grown 2–2.5 times. This means that the average worker is about four times as productive now as in 1946. This is partly due to technology but is in greater part due to an increasingly better educated workforce. If the next generation of retirees is replaced by a smaller, less productive cohort, the results will be doubly drastic.

Demographically, the United States is in a much better position through 2030 than other Western nations. The U.S. birthrate, in part due to a much higher  rate among first generation immigrants, is at near-replacement rates (i.e., there are enough people being born to replace those dying), compared with Canada and Europe, where the birthrate is far below replacement rates.

However, the United States is, arguably, in the midst of an education crisis, not only at the primary and secondary levels but also in the university and college systems. As noted above, dropout rates are increasing. High school students opting for math and science tracks are decreasing, and many schools themselves are inflating grades, passing almost everyone and producing legions of graduates who are functionally innumerate and illiterate.

Quality post-secondary education remains America's greatest educational advantage, but today some colleges and universities are complicit in catering to the lowest denominator. Classes and tests are "dumbed down" and passing grades are doled out to anyone who complains loudly enough. Students who do not show up for classes are rarely censored. Obviously this trend produces graduates without the knowledge, skills, abilities or discipline to contribute in the modern workplace.

In the past, North America has made up for labor and talent shortfalls by increasing immigration. The United States and Canada are still magnets for people from all over the world, and neither has lost the ability to attract the best and the brightest. But this advantage is slipping away quickly. Today's stricter immigration laws in the United States are making it more difficult for firms to bring in foreign skilled workers. Moreover, as the Indian and Chinese economies grow (at three or four times the rate of Western economies), more and better opportunities arise in those countries. Far fewer graduates of the famous Indian Institutes of Technology or their equivalents in China are interested in relocating to the West today, and the numbers will only diminish. Moreover, according to experts like Richard Florida and David Heenan, thousands of Indian and Chinese entrepreneurs who built their companies and fortunes in the West in the 1990s are returning home to launch creative new initiatives there.[8]

Whereas the United States had few competitors for global skilled talent in the past, today demographics have changed the game entirely. Many countries are already experiencing the turmoil of shrinking workforces. For Russia, Japan, Italy and Spain the wrenching experience of depopulation has begun or will begin by the end of the decade.[9] For them, attracting young, skilled workers is a matter of national urgency. Much of Western and Eastern Europe face only a slightly milder problem. The competition for talent, especially as the global economy rebounds, will intensify. The United States will be but one competitor.

Global workforce growth, even among developing countries, is already or will soon be in decline. By 2012, China's workforce, which has grown for centuries, will start to reverse. Today only 22 percent of the Chinese population is aged 50 or more. By 2030, that number will jump to 37 percent and by 2050 to 45 percent.

Even more worrisome, in the short term, is the steep decline in worldwide working-age population—a truly bleak picture among developed countries. Combined, the Western economies, including Japan, will see working-age population reductions of more than half. In the developing world, only a few countries—Brazil, India, some

Northern African nations (sub-Saharan African populations are held in check by the AIDS epidemic), and some small countries in the Middle East—will register working age population gains through 2025. By 2050, even India will become an aging society if current trends hold.

The final front in this "perfect storm" is the global, inexorable demand for higher skilled, better-educated talent. As organizations and nations rush to become more creative and innovative (so that they can maintain their higher wages and better standards of living), the demand for talent capable of producing in the global economy is placed under greater and greater stress. Billions of people may reside in Asia and Africa, but the percentage capable of working for a firm that operates in the global economy is tiny. Even university graduates in China, India and Eastern Europe are, in most cases, under-equipped upon graduation to work in the knowledge economy. Simply put, this means that they are not part of the global talent pool.

McKinsey estimates that, over the next 10–15 years, China alone will require 75,000 leaders who can manage in global environments; today there are fewer than 5,000. In India, the situation is similar. In mid-2007, *Business Week* Magazine reported that fewer than eight million of that country's 200 million students make it through high school and even fewer finish college. The article quotes NASSCOM (India's National Association of Software & Services Companies) as stating: "At the nation's 1,200 technical colleges, just 400,000 engineers graduate each year. Among those, only a fourth has the skills to immediately start work at a multinational or major Indian IT firm."[10] In coming years, India will not likely be able to meet its own domestic demand for engineers, let alone supply the West as it has been doing for decades.

To summarize, we are facing everything from declines in workforce growth to outright depopulation in Western nations. At the same time, the young workforce replacing the first waves of baby boomer retirees brings less human capital to the table and therefore (at least theoretically) less productivity to the workforce. Foreign skilled talent, which has been so critical in building the North American economy, is increasingly less likely to emigrate for work. Worse, many thousands of highly skilled and entrepreneurial members of the Indian and Chinese diasporas have decamped and are now applying their creativity and innovations in their countries of origin. For the mobile and virtual global workforce, competition will be intense from all corners of the developed and developing worlds. Already, Poland, for example, is recruiting Asian workers to replace the million-plus young workers who have left that country (mainly for Western Europe) since the fall of the Soviet Union (a trend that has begun to reverse with recession in Western Europe).

The problems above are not insurmountable. However, like the trends described in the next two sections, global demographics represent a serious challenge. The associated problems will almost certainly lead to economic disruption in some nations and the outright demise of thousands of organizations worldwide. To some degree, the economic laws of demand and supply will correct for part of the problem. Smaller working age populations normally result in less demand for goods and services. Obviously, in some sectors, health care for example, steady growth and demand are likely for decades to come. Inevitably, there will also be recessions in the coming decades. These will offer temporary relief, though the cure, in this case, is perhaps worse than the disease, especially where lack of talent might actually be the cause of prolonged recessions in the future, leading to gradually lower standards of living.

Organizations and governments cannot take a laissez-faire attitude toward the aging population phenomena nor the other demographic issues described above. So what can be done? First and foremost, efforts to encourage older workers to delay retirement must be made. This will have a significant impact if even only a small percentage of the baby boom generation remains in the workforce into their late sixties and seventies.

The impact of the recession and unprecedented consumer debt, particularly in the United States, will provide part of the solution— some people will simply have to work longer. For the majority, however, incentives and creative, flexible work options, including phased retirement schemes, will be required.

But organizations must also resign themselves to the fact that they will not have as much talent as they would like. This means investing in labor-saving technologies, more impactful and targeted training and better management to engage the workforce. As has always been the case, any successful measure to increase workforce productivity will lead to immediate (if not sustained) competitive advantage. Outsourcing and off-shoring will almost certainly accelerate, and those organizations that embrace it early and gain experience and deep relationships in developing countries will have the advantage. As will be discussed in more detail below, workforce and succession planning will also take on a new urgency and importance.

## Trend 2: Diversity

Diversity used to mean quotas and targets; it used to center on compliance and focus on gender, race and ethnicity. Today, diversity is a competitive advantage; it is about inclusiveness as opposed to tolerance and affirmative action. It includes most of the population in the sense that it recognizes the differences in talent—from age to lifestyle and from contingent to traditional.

In 2004, Dr Richard Florida unveiled extensive research that compared thriving cities in the United States to those that are stagnant or in decline. Among his findings were that successful cities, including Boston, San Francisco and Austin, have one consistent trait in common—they tend to be more open and more tolerant of talented individuals who are not part of the mainstream culture for whatever reason. Among Florida's more celebrated work is his "Gay Index." By overlaying statistics on the size of the gay population in cities across the United States with data, including unemployment statistics, GDP per capita, and growth, he was able to show a high correlation between cities with larger than average gay populations and success on each of his measures. Florida's point is not that we should deliberately source and hire gay workers, but that talented people, who are different in a variety of ways, are drawn to regions and workplaces that are inclusive and that value a person for the skills and talent they bring rather than whether they conform.

It is clear that the "traditional" North American workforce, whether that means white male or full-time, "on-premises," is only a memory today. Already, more than a quarter of the U.S. workforce is non-white, and almost half is female. By 2050, almost half the U.S. workforce will be racial minorities. What this means for employers is that almost all workforce growth in the United States between now and 2050 will be among the diverse, non-white population. For many sectors, including retail and hospitality, the lack of a diversity strategy is already suicidal. Moreover, the "contingent" or alternative workforce, made up of contract, temporary, remote and part-time workers, already accounts for more than 35 percent of the U.S. workforce and is growing at five times the rate of the traditional workforce.

While "attracting, retaining and managing a more diverse workforce" was considered a significant challenge by almost 70 percent of the 560 respondents to the Human Capital Institute's 2007 study on the state of HR transformation, it was not ranked among their current top five challenges through 2010. This will almost certainly change.

Increasingly, diversity is also about the young, mid-career, boomer and senior generations. We have always had a multigenerational workforce, but, until recently, we have not recognized the importance and advantages of segmenting it and adjusting our messages, benefits and motivators to suit groups that are driven by clearly different factors.

Of course the wise talent manager takes diversity to its ultimate advantage. Today, with the capabilities technology brings and by engaging every manager and supervisor as a talent manager, the work experience can be customized and maximized for each and every worker on a one-to-one basis. This goes beyond individual learning plans and individual performance goals to include individualized retention and engagement initiatives, customized total rewards packages and flexible work arrangements that can maximize the performance and commitment of every contributor.

In many ways, and certainly compared to the more complex demographic challenges outlined above, diversity can be seen as the "low hanging fruit" of talent management issues in the coming years. After all, the main requirement in seizing the opportunity is in understanding the benefits of an inclusive, welcoming culture. These include the advantages of disparate thinking, which have been shown to foster more creativity and lead to faster innovation; the advantage of reflecting customer diversity in the workforce and the advantages in recruiting that come from being known as a great place to work for minorities. Each is collectively worth fortunes to organizations. The solution goes far beyond a campaign of cross-cultural training, however. Diversity for competitive advantage must be quickly embraced by companies today so that antiquated attitudes are changed and the new, inclusive workforce can emerge.

# Trend 3: Globalization & Global Economic Reconstruction

As hackneyed as the term has become, globalization cannot be ignored as a key trend that will continue to change everything. Trade, economies, standards of living, peace, conflict, health, education—everything—is impacted. Among the most publicized disruptions caused by globalization to date is the impact on the workforce. In the 1980s and 1990s globalization resulted in the loss of millions of manufacturing jobs in the West. At the end of the last century, the Internet, Y2K and the dot-com bust contributed to the emergence of the offshore services industry. Suddenly, white collar jobs started moving from the West to India and Eastern Europe. Despite the fact that net job losses have so far been very modest (relative to those lost in manufacturing), the debate has been heated. Yet good or bad, the process of globalization is unlikely to stop or even slow. Therefore, most organizations are compelled to factor globalization into their strategies.

In late 2006, the Human Capital Institute (HCI) and Development Dimensions International (DDI) conducted a survey involving more than 750 talent management leaders. The study revealed that a strong majority foresaw, over the next three years, that trade of knowledge and intellectual capital (86 percent) and goods and services (85 percent) across countries will increase. They also predicted that competition for talent with the skills needed to work across borders would grow fiercer (91 percent).[11]

*Managers will be more virtual and remote. They will have to adapt to an ever-changing workforce ... Outsourcing will continue to increase as will the need for managers to work in a global setting and be flexible enough to handle any situation.*
HCI/DDI Survey Respondent

What our respondents in 2006 did not forecast was the severe recession of 2008/09. Since December 2007 when the recession officially began through April, 2009, over 4.5 million jobs had been destroyed in the United States alone.[12] But this recession offers a true example of our "flat" world. Its near instantaneous spread to every corner of the planet demonstrated the impact of a truly global economy. Companies and economies worldwide were affected negatively and virtually all at once.

Yet, despite the depth of the downturn, talent management challenges remain. The war for talent in general may be in retreat, but the war for talent with specific skills ranges is on. In December 2008, the National Federation of Independent Businesses (reporting on its membership) said that nearly three-quarters of firms wanted to add workers, but there were "few or no qualified applicants for the job openings they were trying to fill."[13] In a late 2008 survey by Ranstad Corporation, more than half of responding companies said that they "are still experiencing skills shortages in spite of the downturn."[14]

In research conducted in 2008 and 2009, HCI learned that many organizations were actually taking an aggressive stance in this recession. More than 25 percent of several hundred survey respondents said that they would, in effect, ignore the recession or get even more aggressive toward hiring top talent. Some countries are taking an opportunistic stance as well. In December 2008, the Canadian government launched a skilled immigration initiative to "get all the skilled people we can to Canada quickly [while the downturn lasts]."[15]

As above, no one can predict the structural changes that will come as a result of this recession. However, it is almost certain that significant and permanent changes to the economy and workforce will result. These changes will affect workers around the world. And while a possible repercussion is protectionism and less globalization, a much more likely outcome is an even greater pace of globalization once the economy improves.

Old mindsets will not succeed in the global economy. Successful workers and business leaders alike must move out of their domestic comfort zones and into a more international or worldly way of thinking. Ultimately, a "global" mindset is necessary. Peter Senge, in his groundbreaking work, *The Fifth Discipline*, defines mindsets as "deeply ingrained assumptions, generalizations or even pictures or images that influence how we understand."[16] Successful global managers broaden their mindset such that they look at a business, an industry or a culture from a global perspective. They can see across multiple geographies and perspectives to focus on the commonalities rather than the differences. Top-performing global managers set themselves apart with the ability to keep the entire worldwide business opportunity in mind.

Part of the success in making the realities of globalization an advantage to an organization in the West is leveraging a virtual workforce. As the competition for critical talent at the lowest cost heats up, organizations must rethink the ways in which they attract, acquire, develop, manage and deploy talent. To begin, one should identify the segments of the workforce that will drive current and future growth and what components of their work need to be done on-site. Given today's economic and demographic realities, more and more talent will be tapped remotely.

The world continues to shrink with greater advancements in technology, while expanding as new business locations and talent pools become viable. The global skilled-labor pool has more than doubled in size in the last 15 years and continues to grow rapidly, though, until very recently, not at a pace fast enough to meet growing demand. The competition for global talent, sure to return quickly, will require organizations to build high-performing *virtual* teams, since moving workers around the world is becoming less practical and less desirable for workers and organizations alike.

Of course, for remote workforce management to succeed, leaders must have the ability to navigate and exploit the complexities of a global business environment. As a starting point, they should understand the capabilities required of global managers. Companies should then select candidates with these competencies while developing existing managers to succeed in a virtual global environment. Managers need to monitor and manage the performance of the remote workforce by instituting simple but effective measurements and processes that are adapted for local and global conditions.

Organizations are also faced with making sure they have the right quality and quantity of global leadership talent. Leaders who are effective when working within the confines of their home country will not necessarily be effective when they have to lead across borders. Underscoring this point is a 2005 Conference Board study in which 97 percent of respondents indicated that general leadership skills are transferable into a global context, but only 50 percent were confident that leaders successful in one setting or region would be equally successful in another.

The impact of globalization will continue to be felt in ways that are impossible to predict. The only certainty is that it will not stop and is likely to accelerate as more economic power shifts east and south. Savvy organizations will see opportunity as more of the world's population become consumers of goods and services. To succeed, however, attitudes, outlooks and mindsets must be adjusted in most organizations. Global leaders must be acquired and/or developed, and remote, virtual teams must be leveraged, either through outsourcing or by developing a workforce overseas. Moreover, HR must get involved in the organization's global strategy, particularly where it impacts the workforce. However, according to HCI research between 2007 and 2009, HR still remains partially or fully on the sidelines in the majority of organizations.

## Trend 4: Technology & Innovation

The pace of technological change and innovation has accelerated steadily since the industrial revolution. A strong case can be made that in the next twenty years, technological breakthroughs, including those that disrupt entire industries and economies, will greatly exceed even the incredible changes we witnessed in the past twenty years. Today, the West is joined by billions of new consumers in the East and South and thousands of brilliant innovators eager to earn their reputations and fortunes on the global stage. Never has the world seen so many people, from all parts of the world, focused on business innovation.

One can think of few trends that have impacted the HR profession more profoundly in the past twenty years than technology. Indeed, technology has made it possible for the Human Resources profession to make its next great transformation. It is common today for us to talk about HR and talent management separately. Included in HR are the repetitive and transactional processes so vital to the smooth operation of organizations. Payroll & benefits administration, claims processing, applicant tracking and screening, time and attendance administration, leave reporting, scheduling and EEOC compliance are but a few of the tasks that have become largely automated in the past few decades. Liberation from manual processing of these and other tasks has given HR the opportunity to change and grow.

Technological change has already gone far beyond the automation of repetitive HR processes. In the 1990s, talent management technologies burst on to the scene, enabling workforce planning, talent acquisition and performance management among other things. Today, it would be difficult to find any mid- to large-size organization that does not use at least some advanced talent management technology.

# The New Role of the HR Leader

Talent management is distinct from human resources, in part because it is the responsibility of leaders across the organization rather than a discipline that can or should reside in just one department. In May 2006, a report from the Economist Intelligence Unit (EIU) and DDI suggested that CEOs from across industries and throughout much of the world are strong believers in taking direct, personal leadership in recruiting, mentoring, succession planning, talent development, performance management and retention. Indeed, seven out of 20 CEOs interviewed for the report said they spend more than half of their time on talent management compared with only four who reported spending less than one-fifth of their time in those pursuits.

CEOs and boards of public companies are paying attention to talent these days for two main reasons. First, there is little room otherwise to differentiate from their competitors. Over the past several decades, industry has been successful in ironing out many of the wrinkles in bringing products and services to market. Production efficiencies and supply chain management combined with globalization have increased competition and reduced margins for most products and many services. The result is that products and processes that were once points of differentiation are now often indistinguishable from supplier to supplier. Even the most advanced products quickly become commodities today unless they offer a design or creative appeal beyond their practical purpose or functionality. Today, intangibles, including constant reinvention, innovation, design creativity, marketing prowess and reputation (through human talent) form the key sustainable advantage for knowledge economy organizations.

Investors and shareholders constitute the second driver. They too have become aware of the importance of hiring and keeping top performers and of maintaining solid succession plans for leaders and those in other critical positions. In 2007, the EIU reported that "human capital risks," related to "loss of key personnel, skills shortages and succession issues" had become the number one risk to global business operations.[17]

Tighter governance rules in many countries mean that boards of directors and CEOs are held responsible for their decisions affecting the health and sustainability of their firms (much of which today rest on the quality and depth of talent). Succession and workforce planning, especially, are areas in which leaders must focus and demonstrate due diligence.

For HR leaders, this is very good news. All 20 CEOs referenced in the EIU/DDI study believe that HR should be responsible for "executing talent management strategy, being custodians of the talent management process and [providing] guidance and fresh thinking about talent management programs." Nineteen of twenty said that their head of HR is part of their "inner circle" of executives, a key person they rely upon to help differentiate the firm on the basis of superior workforce strategy. Indeed, HCI's own poll of over 600 HR managers and executives in August 2007 revealed that more than two-thirds of heads of HR report directly to the CEO.[18]

This is a new and welcome development. HR is finally making headway in becoming a "strategic partner." Traditional HR remains vital, but after decades of hard work and progress, most organizations can now rely on and take for granted efficient and effective processes for payroll and benefits administration. Traditional HR has, in a sense, been a victim of its own success in creating repeatable, dependable administrative processes. Today, most firms outsource payroll and benefits administration, and a growing number are opting to outsource HR in its entirety. One potential benefit is that this should make room for internal centers of excellence in talent management.

However, to the extent that HR has succeeded in administration, it has generally failed thus far at "strategy." Now that CEOs are demanding workforce strategies, including innovative ways to compete—*for and through*—superior talent, the pressure is on HR leaders to perform like their finance, IT, marketing and operations counterparts, who, unlike HR, have for years aligned and integrated their work with the highest corporate goals and objectives. A "transformation" is necessary, but most HR leaders and non-HR leaders alike agree that generally the profession has not progressed as rapidly as needed. An HCI survey of more than 550 HR leaders in 2007 revealed a disappointing self-assessment of HR leaders' skills and knowledge, giving failing grades across a range of eight talent and general management areas from strategic planning to measurement of HR success.

The trends outlined above, along with new attitudes among senior executives, present a tremendous opportunity for HR leaders. This is a golden opportunity for HR to move up the organizational and professional ladder. Clearly, though, HR must change in order to respond to the business challenges confronting organizations today. The art of human resources must quickly evolve into the art and science of human capital management (HCM), or talent management. HR executives with their eyes on a bigger role in the business agree that the reputation of HR is so poor today that the profession must be re-branded.

For those involved in managing talent for competitive advantage, new titles and categories are vital. We should begin seeing more "C"-level human capital and talent management professionals heading highly skilled, business-focused teams in the coming years—categories that began emerging in the late 1990s when the primacy of talent in organizations became widely understood for the first time. HR leaders should start this process by first gaining a solid understanding of their organization's business and then aligning their talent management initiatives toward achieving those goals.

Beyond the name, hardcore change and new skill sets are needed. Modern TM executives must be able to speak in financial terms about the workforce. They must understand the organization's current complement of skills and competencies as well as external local, national and international workforce demographics. They must be able to advise the "C" suite and the board on whether it makes sense to hire, develop or contract temporary talent, and this advice must be presented in financial terms. Talent Management executives must be able to forecast workforce needs aligned with corporate goals, capabilities and objectives.

The modern Talent Management executive is aware that HR is no longer a one-to-many exercise; that there is no one-size-fits-all benefit program, for example. Recruitment, development, performance management and retention will increasingly be ongoing, one-to-one activities that are highly differentiated for the greatest possible impact. Thus, traditional "HR," most often characterized by generic programs, is quickly giving way to the more sophisticated methods of talent management. In order for this to succeed, however, TM executives must enlist the support and active involvement of managers and leaders from all parts of the business.

Another critical skill for today's TM executive is in understanding measurement, data and return on investment (ROI) analysis. Organizations have gone through the discipline of creating measurable processes—a science—around the manufacturing and quality control fields. Unfortunately, this rigor has not yet been applied to the field of human resources.

"The revolution in quality control and manufacturing techniques that has taken place in the last fifteen years was data-driven and systems-driven and statistical-process-control-driven. The U.S. economy has benefited incredibly over the last fifteen years ... by seriously embracing the science of manufacturing and quality control." [19] When Andy Grove, Chairman and Founder of Intel, said these words in a Harvard Business School Press interview in 2003, he was talking about general business strategy and execution.

Jeffrey Pfeffer, a professor of organizational behavior at Stanford University, calls the data-driven approach "Evidence-Based Management." He strongly advocates its application in the field of human capital management. In his book, *Dangerous Half-Truths & Total Nonsense*, Pfeffer says:

> There is compelling evidence that when companies use HR best practices based on the best research, they trump the competition. These findings are replicable in industry after industry, from automobiles to textiles, to computer software to baseball. Yet many companies still use inferior people management practices. The problem isn't just that HR managers know what to do but can't get their companies to do it. Like other leaders, many HR executives hold flawed and incomplete beliefs. They fall prey to second-rate evidence, logic and advice, which produce suspect practices, and in the end damage performance and people.[20]

Despite the admonitions of Pfeffer and other luminaries, HR professionals have for years argued that their discipline is an art rather than a science and that there is no way of measuring the ROI in talent management initiatives. While talent management may indeed be the most esoteric and difficult of sciences, there are more and increasingly credible indicators available today that clearly demonstrate the link between human capital investment, customer satisfaction and profit. To earn credibility, but, more importantly, to continuously measure and improve, TM executives must know and apply these methods in their organizations.

Linda J. Bilmes and W. Scott Gould indicated in their book, *The People Factor:* "There is compelling evidence from the private sector that companies do better—in stock market performance, customer satisfaction and innovation—when they invest strongly in their workforce ... research has not only established a linkage between the people factor and performance but has also revealed a strong *consensus* about which specific factors help organizations to achieve better results."[21]

HR's transformation is also dependent on its leaders having a deep understanding of the organization's business and industry. A talent management division must know corporate plans and objectives and the competitive landscape. It must have deep knowledge of the organization's current talent pool and capabilities and have a good understanding of local, national and international talent pools. It must know the company's competitive advantages and differentiators, the comparative costs of training versus recruiting and where use of the contingent workforce is warranted. It must be able to build a compelling business case to close talent gaps in the most effective manner possible. In short, the TM executive must possess a level of strategic thinking on a par with the CEO and an ability to execute that strategy.

The harsh reality today, however, paints a depressing picture. USC Marshall School of Business professors Ed Lawler and Susan Mohrman found recently that, despite all the talk of HR becoming more strategic, in the 10 years between 1995 and 2004 it actually progressed very little toward a reduced focus on administration and a greater allocation of time toward strategic planning. HCI's own research in 2007 suggests some progress in this area, but it is difficult to argue that a lot has changed in the profession in the past few decades, despite the fact that the "C" Suite and the board now recognize the importance of top talent and the difference that world class talent management can bring.

Ideally, talent management will evolve in much the same way that the finance function has grown into a decision science separate from accounting, or marketing has evolved as a strategic discipline separate from sales. Most HR executives and their teams have a long way to go. Unfortunately, the past three years of unprecedented opportunity for the profession have been more squandered than seized upon. If the profession is to evolve and lead organizations into our "Age of Talent," radical change and transformation are required quickly—our businesses and economies are depending upon it.

# ENDNOTES

[1] Thomas Malthus, *An Essay on the Principles of Population*, (London: Oxford University Press, 1999 first published in 1798).

[2] Malthus, *An Essay on the Principles of Population*.

[3] National Federation of Independent Businesses, Randstad Human Capital Survey, December, 2008.

[4] Thomas Homer-Dixon, *The Ingenuity Gap*, (New York: Random House, 2000).

[5] "Buffet: No Economic Bailout Necessary," *The National Post*, February 7, 2008.

[6] www. bls.gov.

[7] http://www.colorado.edu/Economics/courses/econ2020/section5/full-employment.html, University of Colorado Department of Economics.

[8] David Heenan, *Flight Capital*, (Mountain View, CA: Davies-Black Publishing, 2005) and Richard Florida, *The Flight of the Creative Class*, (New York: Harper Collins, 2007).

[9] Depopulation and Ageing in Europe and Japan: The Hazardous Transition to a Labor Shortage Economy, 2002 (www.globalageing.org).

[10] www.businessweek.com/globalbiz, 2007.

[11] Talent Management in Motion: Keeping Up with an Evolving Workforce, The Human Capital Institute And Development Dimensions International, 2006.

[12] Employment Situation Review, U.S. Bureau of labor Statistics, March 6, 2009.

[13] National Federation of Independent Businesses, December, 2008.

[14] Randstad study of 355 UK Companies, December, 2008.

[15] Globe and Mail, December 15, 2008.

[16] Peter Senge, *The Fifth Discipline*, (New York: Doubleday, 1990).

[17] Innovation: Transforming the Way Business Creates, EIU, May, 2007, (www.eiu.com).

[18] Survey of over 600 HR Managers and Executives, The Human Capital Institute, August, 2007.

[19] Harvard Business School interview with Andy Grove, April 20,2003 (http://news.com.com/Andy+Grove+on+the+confident+leader/2009-1069_3-997426.html).

[20] Jeffrey Pfeffer and Robert I. Sutton, *Dangerous Half-Truths & Total Nonsense: Profiting from Evidence-Based Management*, (Boston: Harvard Business School Press, 2006).

[21] Linda J. Bilmes and W. Scott Gould, *The People Factor*, Washington, D.C.: Brookings Institution Press, 2009.

# CHAPTER 2

# Technology and Talent: Today's Market and How We Got There

By Ed Newman

*Never before in history has innovation offered promise of so much to so many in so short a time.*
Bill Gates

Over the past two decades, the evolution of HR and the more recent emergence of the talent management mindset occurred hand-in-hand with corresponding advancements in technology. Today, technology solutions play a central role in determining how well organizations identify, attract and retain talent. Companies apply new solutions to fix broken processes, break open isolated silos of information and put the right data into the right hands at the right time. They are looking for more than features and functions in their solutions; they are looking for technology that delivers real impact to the business.

Of course, technology alone cannot solve business challenges. Just as important are the processes that enable talent operations. "Best Practices" have become the rallying cry for a host of new strategic approaches—some practical, some not-so-practical. Unfortunately, best practices only go so far. They reflect the successes of the past and the present, but they are no guarantee of success in the future. Competing for talent is a game of one-upmanship. If a new process or technology helps beat the competition to the critical talent, you can be certain that your competitor will be hard at work on the "next practice" that will trump your strategy. As a result, talent solutions will continue to evolve.

The emergence of talent management systems has been driven by the willingness of technology providers to evolve their products and boost their promises to companies hungry for the next best thing. Buyers boost their expectations for what their systems should do, and providers deliver more advanced solutions. The spiral of innovation will not end, but the nature of that innovation may change.

So, what does technology have to do with the emerging talent mindset and how will it shape talent operations tomorrow? The answer requires a perspective on how the technology developed in the past, where it is today and the forces that will push development in the future. A good place to start is to look at how businesses utilized application software and systems when they first started being developed for the HR function.

# In the Beginning:
# The Emergence of
# the Niche Application

It wasn't until the eighties and early nineties that companies began working with large-scale application software packages for talent acquisition. These packages were designed to support Human Resources by automating many of the tasks that were previously handled by pen and paper, phone calls and bulletin boards. The main driver for adopting these software packages was efficiency. Early software applications promised to automate manual processes and deliver tremendous improvements in productivity while reducing operational costs.

The emergence of enterprise applicant tracking systems (ATS) occurred in the early 1990s. One of the main challenges for the recruiting function at the time was the need to sort through thousands of inbound resumes and match them to open positions. It was a recruiter's ritual to bring home a stack of resumes, sit in front of the television and, in between bites of dinner, sort those resumes into hot, warm and cold piles. Typically, the recruiter would assign a cryptic code in the upper right-hand corner so that the secretary (as they were known back then) could put them in the appropriate file. Not only was this method time-consuming and inefficient, but accuracy and consistency were serious problems. No two recruiters would have the same coding system, which made the likelihood of retrieving resumes in the future unlikely.

It was fitting, then, that the information and activity-intensive resume sorting function would be the first to spawn a niche software product. The process was ripe for improvement. In answer to that need, the industry saw the emergence of the first two ATS players: Resumix and Restrac. They provided the first large-scale niche software products to support a segment of HR. The main goal of the ATS was to take the vast amounts of candidate resume information off of paper and put it into the system—and then use that data to match candidates to job requisitions. The main point of comparison between the two providers revolved around how fast their solutions could scan and process resumes. By automating the task of matching resumes to requisitions, these products addressed a unique need for overwhelmed recruiters, and the early ATS solution occupied a lucrative niche in the enterprise technology market.

Applicant tracking was a function that was at once large enough to merit further growth for the companies that provided applicable solutions and, at the same time, small enough to escape the focused attention of the large ERP solutions providers. ERP providers such as PeopleSoft and SAP did provide HRMS products with applicant tracking capabilities, but companies frequently implemented a different ATS to perform front-end recruiting functions.

For ERP providers, applicant tracking was a relatively small module. It generated little in the way of licensing fees, and it was generally seen as a necessary part of a much larger platform. ERP providers were not inclined to devote resources to developing deep functionality to compete with ATS capabilities. Instead, they supported their clients' desire to adopt dedicated ATS systems by forming integration relationships with ATS companies. Restrac became an extension of PeopleSoft, while Resumix became integration partners with SAP.

By forming relationships with major ERP providers, the two pioneering niche players paved the way for the development of other niche products that could be created as a "bolt on" to the HRMS. The development of the niche product and the subsequent relationships with large players revealed an important point for the market: in spite of a corporation's investment of millions of dollars in the core HRMS platform, there was a willingness to pay more for highly specialized functionality. This opened the door for more innovation and the development of the better mousetrap.

The next significant step in the evolution of talent systems occurred in the late 1990s with the emergence of the Web as a venue for developing and distributing applications. With a new medium for distribution, the ATS market expanded rapidly. The number of providers grew dramatically, and the industry saw the introduction of the first Application Service Providers (ASP). The defining feature of the ASP model (now known as "Software as a Service", or SaaS) is that the software is hosted entirely by the vendor. The customer's users simply access the system through a Web browser. Clients would no longer need to buy servers and install infrastructure to implement a new solution.

HireSystems (later BrassRing, which was then acquired by Kenexa) was one of the first to offer the ASP model. The early experience of these ASP solutions revealed a fundamental problem. How could companies scan and process resumes if none of the hardware or software was onsite? Even though many companies were starting to post jobs on their Web sites and receive electronic resumes, a large percentage of recruiting information remained in the form of paper and fax resumes.

Mark Dane, founder of HireSystems, provided an answer to the problem by developing an innovative approach: a virtual assembly line. The client would ship (or direct applicants to submit their) resumes to the HireSystems processing center. The center scanned the resumes and distributed data online to an army of verification specialists. These specialists worked from anywhere, and their job was to validate the data. This function was called the Factory. It was truly a first of its kind and extremely effective.

Through its well-designed and distributed function, HireSystems was able to process resumes at a fraction of the cost of an in-house operation. Shortly thereafter, new applications appeared. These solutions allowed customers to quickly launch an online career center where applicants could create user accounts. When an application was submitted, the data would be integrated directly into the ATS. Hire.com (now owned by Authoria) and Pure Carbon (now owned by Workstream) were the pioneers that created the first career portals. In essence, they worked as an addition to the ATS.

These career portal solutions played a remarkable role in the marketplace. Basically, they were niche products serving as bolt-ons to niche wares. This was a viable model at the time, but the market would soon evolve as the larger ATS players expanded their capabilities. The market for niche portal and scanning products dried up as the ATS solutions, such as Taleo (then Recruitsoft), PeopleClick and Vurv (then Recruitmax), began to deliver career site functionality as a core capability. As the ATS market grew and expanded, solutions providers evolved to offer deeper and focused functionality, including pre-screening, approval workflow and offer management, to name a few.

By 2001, there were more than 100 ATS solution providers. At least 10 of them were competing for large enterprise business in the

Fortune 500. With software delivered over the Web, many believed that companies could easily switch vendors and that there would be major turnover from one platform to the next. However, it did not take long to realize that companies did, in fact, need to make significant investment in their solution in order to ensure that it lasted long enough to deliver the returns they sought. Soon, it became evident that there were too many vendors. The market would either begin to see failures or consolidations. Only time would tell.

# A Broader Talent Mindset and the Comprehensive Platform Vision

Over the last 10 years, the focus on talent has broadened considerably. It is no longer good enough to simply hire more people, faster and at a lower cost. Acquiring the right quality talent, assessing and managing performance and retaining and developing people has become the new priority.

With this shift toward a Talent Management mindset, the solutions market has responded in kind. It was this movement combined with the expansion and success of the ATS market that spurred the emergence of Web-based Learning and Development (eLearning), Succession Planning and Performance Management systems. Very similar to the manner in which their predecessors drove the growth of the ATS market, providers of these types of solutions gained market share by offering deeper functionality than the core modules of the ERP solutions.

Over time, talent-focused solutions continued to proliferate. At the pace the market was putting out new products, it soon became possible for a company to end up with a solution consisting of four or five different loosely integrated niche products and large amounts of redundant data. It became evident to most observers that something had to give, and, once again, they began to predict major consolidations in the market.

As proliferation continued, companies wrestled with the challenge of making the niche products work together. Eventually, a new vision emerged: the single comprehensive talent management platform. According to this vision, companies would one day be able to manage everything from recruiting to performance management, workforce planning and all HR functions through one complete talent management suite.

ATS providers quickly adopted the terminology and called themselves Talent Management Systems. They changed their names; Recruitsoft became Taleo, and Recruitmax became Vurv, in order to minimize the emphasis on recruiting and create a broader image. They began developing plans to grow, acquire or partner to deliver the functionality needed to support the other talent management areas. Similarly, the providers of performance management, succession planning and learning and development solutions made comparable moves.

While niche players were making strides toward the comprehensive talent management suite, ERP solution providers could no longer ignore this growing marketplace, because the move toward broader talent management posed a threat. Within the sector, Peoplesoft was the most aggressive in marketing its recruiting solution and the most advanced in functionality. While not as deep in functionality or flexible in terms of meeting business requirements, ERPs made a noticeable gain in market share—a gain that was mainly due to the economic climate.

During the post 9/11 downturn, HR functional leaders no longer had the budget or autonomy to make technology purchase decisions. CIOs and IT executives became the driving authorities regarding these investments. Policies were implemented in some organizations that mandated use of the ERP module if it met 80% of the business requirements—no questions asked. However, ERP providers still faced a challenge. They needed to enhance functionality in each of the talent management disciplines to stay competitive with the niche providers and retain market share. The challenge remains today. If the solutions do not meet business requirements, eventually the functional leaders will make their case for something different.

What is very interesting about the evolution of the talent management solutions market is that, like history, it is set to repeat itself. As niche providers converge to offer the talent management suite, they are taking on a functionality base that is so broad that it will be very challenging to keep it deep and flexible enough to compete in the individual disciplines. Essentially, they will find themselves in the same situation that ERPs have experienced in the past, and they will once again open the door for new niche solutions that have deep functionality in particular areas.

# Understanding the Market and the Drivers that Shape It

The industry continues to move quickly, with solutions providers reaching toward that proverbial ideal vision of the complete end-to-end talent management suite. While bringing that vision to reality is a tall order, the intent that drives it is very practical. Providers are striving to meet the needs of a customer who, today, will not only have one single driving issue, but a myriad of related needs, all while struggling to meet talent goals.

Eventually, the market will produce a comprehensive suite that can be fully implemented in a large enterprise. It is not a matter of *if;* rather, it is a question of *when* it will happen. Today, there are solutions that do span the gamut, but most would agree that it would be a stretch to call them "best-of-breed" in each functional area. Then there is the challenge of supporting the large complex enterprise.

There are two reasons that today's solutions are coming up short. First, even if each component of a system is best in its class, it is unlikely that those components are integrated to the point that their total value to the company is greater than the sum of their parts. Second, for larger companies, no two talent operations are exactly alike. A solution that is "best" for one company may be completely inappropriate for another.

The providers of technologies and services who are reaching for this vision of a comprehensive solution are confronted with the need to develop the deepest of capability in each of the niche segments, cover the broadest set of functional areas and get the solution to market as fast as possible. There are two fundamental approaches being taken to achieve this goal. First, companies may simply decide to grow organically, applying resources to build new functionality on their own. The second approach is expansion through acquisition. Companies are acquiring other providers in an effort to expand their range of functionality to new areas or deepen their presence in a particular area. This approach is leading to two market-shaping forces, horizontal consolidation and vertical consolidation. These approaches—organic growth, horizontal consolidation and vertical consolidation—will go a long way toward determining what our talent systems choices look like in the future.

# Organic Growth: Companies Expand Capabilities from Within

Organic growth represents the most basic approach for expanding the capabilities of a talent system. The vendor simply expands its internal resources to build new modules. The organic build methodology gives the vendor the ability to create a solution that is extremely well-integrated to its existing products or platform. It will have the same look and feel as the vendor's existing solution and will often share some of the functionality.

The biggest challenge with this approach is speed to market. It is difficult enough for a talent solutions provider to allocate the resources needed to incorporate feature enhancements into an existing product. Building out a complete new solution takes that challenge to a new level. As with any new release, the features in a newly-built function are usually basic, and plenty of work is usually deferred to subsequent releases. This struggle to deliver compelling new functionality is the same challenge faced by larger HRMS providers.

SuccessFactors and Taleo are recent examples of companies who have taken the organic development approach. On one end of the spectrum, SuccessFactors has been taking the performance management and succession management market by storm. In late 2007, the company ventured to the pre-hire side of the equation, releasing its first version of recruiting management. On the other end, Taleo has had a very strong foothold in the talent acquisition market. In early 2008, the company ventured into post-hire functionality with the release of its first edition of performance management. These two cases are examples of vendors from opposite ends of the talent continuum moving toward the middle.

When evaluating a talent management suite vendor that is growing organically, it is important for the buyer to consider priorities. If the priority is talent acquisition, for example, it would make sense to strongly consider the platform that was founded on recruiting functionality. Recruiting is a very dynamic function, and large enterprises generally require a large degree of flexibility, which is typically only available in very mature product offerings. If succession planning and employee development are most important, a solution may be sufficient even if its talent acquisition module is light in functionality.

# Acquisition:
# Balancing "Best-in-Class" with
# the Challenge of Integration

Because the demand for new and improved capabilities is growing quickly, technology and service providers are feeling competitive pressure to expand capabilities more quickly and more thoroughly than internal development will allow. These pressures can be addressed through the second means of adding functionality: acquisition. Through the acquisition of niche providers, the vendor can buy a deeper functionality in a particular segment without the delays associated with internal development. Additionally, the acquiring company usually inherits an installed base of customers and the associated revenue that they bring.

There are drawbacks to the acquisition approach. Even the most well-orchestrated addition of complimentary products and services may take some time to jell into an offering that provides meaningful value to customers. The challenge here lies in the integration of the product and the customer base. If the customer base was not entirely satisfied with the original vendor, it can be very difficult to win those customers as the acquiring firm.

There also may be issues from a product perspective. Depending on the compatibility of the technical infrastructure, the acquiring firm might find it necessary to rewrite a good portion of the product. Nevertheless, a variety of companies are actively pursuing this approach. A few examples of this horizontal consolidation include Vurv (before being acquired by Taleo) and Authoria. Vurv expanded from its roots as a recruiting technology to focus on what it once referred to on its Web site as "managing the entire employee lifecycle." Toward that end, Vurv acquired several companies, including People Business Network (workforce optimization and analysis), InScope (competency management) and KnowledgePoint (performance management). In turn, Vurv was acquired by Taleo in July, 2008, further underscoring the dynamic nature of the talent solutions market.

Authoria began in 1997 with a focus on Web-enabled employee benefits. Since then, the company has acquired AIM (performance management, compensation and succession planning) and Hire.com (recruiting software). In each case, the direction toward a complete talent management platform is clear. The acquisition approach fueled significant growth for both companies.

For companies considering solutions from vendors that have grown through acquisitions, examining how well those acquired parts work together will be important. When evaluating such a talent management suite vendor, it will be very important to understand the business requirements relative to the integration of processes and seamless flow of data from one application to the other.

# Vertical Consolidation

In addition to horizontal acquisition, the market for talent solutions is also feeling impact from companies as they acquire their competitors who provide similar functionality. This has been a long time coming. Over the last decade, the proliferation of niche solutions has led to predictions that vertical consolidation was on the way. There were simply too many different players in the market.

Despite the predictions, however, change in the market has been slow to arrive. One of the reasons that consolidation has taken so long is that the span of functionality has continued to grow within ATS products. Each vendor had unique differentiators to offer. Today, they are beginning to catch up with each other, and it is becoming more difficult for providers to stand out with distinct offerings.

One reason that a company may acquire others offering similar functionality is to broaden its target market. Taleo is a good example of this approach in action. Originally, the company was established with a focus on Fortune 500 customers, but the market for smaller businesses represented a growth opportunity. To address the opportunity, Taleo acquired Recruitforce.com and maintained it as a separate product to reach out to smaller businesses. For similar reasons, Kenexa acquired WebHire and BrassRing. At the time of acquisition, both of these products were maintained as distinct offerings, enabling Kenexa to focus on different market segments.

Taleo's acquisition of Vurv represented the beginning of a new direction in talent systems—namely, companies with a similar focus came together to truly reduce the choices in the market. The market will continue to see more examples of vertical consolidation as the number of distinct providers balances with demand.

# Making the Comprehensive Talent Platform a Reality

The solutions market has recognized the value represented by the vision of the talent management suite. Larger vendors have felt the pressure to make that vision a reality by broadening their capabilities. They are either building out new functionality by applying internal resources to achieve organic growth, or they are acquiring the smaller players to deepen their functionality. While the vision is compelling, there is a feeling that the solutions market has fallen behind initial expectations in putting together that suite.

The challenges to achieving a comprehensive platform stem from business realities. The main issue is that in order for the suite to provide real value, companies have to be aligned to accommodate it. Companies continue to align their talent processes across the talent continuum. They are moving in the right direction, but more work remains.

One notable issue for larger companies is that information and processes often remain in silos. While much is made of the need to break silos and make information and processes accessible across the organization, the silos are there for a reason. Pockets of information, along with associated processes and people who bring those processes to life, are coordinated to address very specific business functions. As a result, they have very specific needs.

To deliver effective functionality as a true comprehensive platform, a solution must have the flexibility to meet the varying needs of those silos. For some functions, vendors may be able to claim they have the maturity, depth and flexibility to address varying needs across the enterprise—but they cannot claim such depth across all talent functions. For the complex enterprise with multiple distinct organizations, processes and varying requirements, vendors are still striving to address their complexity. A realistic solution today is to simplify and provide a system that may not meet every single requirement of every individual part of the enterprise.

While the market may not yet be able to provide a truly comprehensive suite to the complex enterprise, another type of customer may represent an earlier path to realization. That customer is the smaller organization with less complex recruiting and talent management needs. Smaller businesses do not have as much variance across departments, and, therefore, the functional requirements for each segment of talent management can be met more easily. With the larger technology providers expanding their offerings, new names, traditionally associated with the old-guard, large enterprise, are now within the budgetary reach of organizations with 50, 500 or 5,000 employees.

Today, smaller organizations have a choice of perfectly functional packaged solutions that will meet their recruiting needs. In the near future, they will very likely become the proving ground for the more complete talent management suite. Once it is shown that providers can deliver the functionality that is needed, and that these companies can align processes to accommodate the suite, larger enterprises will want to do the same.

What does the trend toward consolidation mean for those who are considering their technology options? The answer, in a nutshell, is "keep an open mind." The comprehensive talent management suite is a vision that has driven change in the market over the past decade, and it is a vision that will continue to shape the way companies look at talent systems well into the future.

CHAPTER 3

# The Future Possibilities of Talent Management Technology

By Ed Newman

*Trying to predict the future is like trying to drive down
a country road at night with no lights
while looking out the back window.*
Peter Drucker

With an appreciation of the history of the talent management technology market and its current trends, it is appropriate to discuss what might come next. Large-scale prognostication is commonplace in most areas of business. It is tempting to make a sweeping educated prediction, because when any part of the prediction comes true, the prognosticator can then tout his or her clairvoyance to all who will listen. Unfortunately, such predictions represent only part of the story. A general understanding of what *will* happen can lead to more informed decisions, at least in theory, but considering what *should* happen is just as important. Success is more likely for those who understand both.

What will happen? We can look to the history of talent management and of the evolution of talent acquisition systems to help understand the direction of the industry. What should happen? We can look at the fundamental challenges faced by companies as they compete for talent. This can help us better understand where talent management and related technology should grow stronger and how it should change in the future.

# What Will Happen

As mentioned in the previous chapter, the history of talent management applications centers around the struggle between the need for breadth (solutions that cover all key talent operations) and the need for depth (the ability to provide best-of-breed functionality in each area of operation). All of this is driven by a push toward the creation of a suite of talent management applications.

Today, solutions providers find themselves in a conundrum. They need to build functionality that meets the demands of their clients and prospects, but, at the same time, they need to go to market with new innovations as quickly as possible. They would like to build features and functions that meet the specific requirements of many potential customers, but they must draw a line somewhere to launch the product. As a solutions provider expands into more functional areas within talent management, this conundrum multiplies.

It is very evident that in the near future we will see more consolidation among niche vendors as well as continuing horizontal expansion across the talent management spectrum. As specialty vendors broaden their footprint, they are creating the opportunity for the emergence of new categories of niche products. These products will focus on one particular area of functionality and build deeper and more flexible features than what exists in the larger and now broader platforms. New categories such as workforce planning, e-reference checking and search engine optimization are reflecting this trend today. The largest explosion has been the emergence of tools that focus on the front end of the talent life cycle in the area of sourcing and candidate generation. Internet data mining and social networking sites have been at the forefront.

Having spent the better part of 20 years working with software applications that support talent management, I've seen the progress that has been made. We have gone from resume processing and job matching to candidate self-service interview scheduling and online pre-screening and assessments. We are on the verge of connecting talent acquisition to performance management and succession planning. The concept of a resume database has expanded well beyond just the candidates who apply to jobs posted on company Web sites. It now includes third-party job board databases, association Web sites and social networking sites. In fact, the database of accessible candidates now includes the record of any person who can be identified by a flip search, an x-ray, a spider or a Google search.

Training classes and certification programs are offered that run from days to weeks to teach recruiters and researchers about the various nooks and crannies that can be exploited to find candidates. These techniques fuel the never-ending quest for the passive candidate. It seems that new Web sites arise every week claiming to have found the key that unlocks access to the places passive candidates are hiding.

While the variety of innovations and emergence of new features continues to multiply, nearly all of that innovation to date has been developed to address the most common and recurring objective for talent acquisition—that is, finding the best talent. Talent solutions providers and the companies that buy them continue to focus on the goal of accessing the largest quantities of data possible and then using technology to filter down to the relevant few pieces of information with the expectation that the selected few will be the best. This is leading to a sense of frustration. The more "efficient" the technology becomes, the more information we have to filter, and yet we still cannot quantify a better result.

All of us enjoy a great new gadget, but we shouldn't lose sight of the fact that technology solutions promising efficiency through automation are simply tools that can be leveraged by people. There have been many recent technological advancements that are now categorized as Web 2.0 tools offering a level of interactive capabilities. However, it seems that no matter what new tools may emerge, people continue to use them in the same way as in the past. There is a predisposition toward the idea of gathering and sifting larger and larger amounts of data in search of the gold nugget. In effect, we focus on turning anything we find into a resume database, or a way to seek out people we might otherwise not be able to find. The fundamental issue is, while the tools and technology have evolved, we have not yet perfected the way in which we use them.

# What Should Happen

While technological innovation will certainly continue, even in the face of economic turmoil, the driving need in talent management today is a change in the underlying model for how the technology is used.

## The Issues

There are three characteristics of the current use of talent management technology that are preventing us from achieving our full potential.

1. *A Reactive Mindset:* We strive to use technology to become more efficient, but there is a fundamental flaw in this quest. Our focus has been on leveraging new tools to become more efficient in filling requisitions. Basically, we are trying to be more efficient in being reactive.

2. *Unsustainable Predatory Networking:* Over time, companies have adopted increasingly aggressive recruiting tactics, sometimes referred to as "predatory recruiting." This is sometimes characterized as poaching. Often there is little exchange of value between the recruiter and the talent pool. Predatory networking is not as sustainable as cultivating candidate networks over time. Being a hunter is not a bad thing, and good recruiters with strong business acumen can actually pull it off. When companies try to expand this capability to all recruiters, however, there are those who will use less tact in the process. As a result, the underlying trust is lost. Like Captain Ahab boarding a whale watching tour, eventually he will get thrown off the boat.

3. *Manager Self Service:* There has been a move, among companies and the solutions that they adopt, to emphasize manager engagement and in the process make managers more accountable for the recruiting process—but giving them the tools for self-service will not necessarily achieve better results. Talent organizations tend to get managers involved by giving them an online requisition form and automated approval workflow. Then the manager is asked to

update the status of candidates so that the talent organization can track cycle times. Is this how managers should spend their time? In what part of the process should managers be engaged?

## Changing the *More is Better* Mentality

One of the basic goals of talent management is to have the right people in the right roles at the right time. In this age of talent, the focus on quality of hire has been increasingly important, and many technological solutions aim to help increase the quality of employees. If we take a hard look at the process for hiring new talent, however, that fundamental flaw of the *more is better* mentality starts to show.

Most companies follow a similar process for filling positions with a series of steps that require speed and efficiency. As talent organizations, we are driven by time pressure through each step, because we are working in a very competitive labor market. We create and approve the requisition. We post the position and search for candidates. As quickly as possible, we filter through all of the candidate data that has been generated to pull out the best, and then we phone screen for basic information. Then we present these candidates to the managers and ask them to quickly make a decision before we lose the candidate to the competition. Our hope is that the tools we used to generate these candidates will help us select higher quality talent. The question is, *how do we measure quality?*

Measuring the quality of hire has been somewhat elusive, but several methods have emerged as best practice. The most common method is to measure retention. The assumption is that if the new hire is still on board after a year, then quality must be good. Another approach is to review the first performance rating, and then a third approach is to conduct post-hire surveys either 30, 60, or 90 days after hire.

The underlying challenge in all of these methods is that one cannot really ascertain the quality of hire until becoming familiar with the person on the job. Culture fit, chemistry with the manager and employee engagement are very important elements in determining quality. Even if we have the best assessment and screening tools, there is nothing like having first-hand knowledge of how a person behaves in a work situation. This is the reason that employee referrals are commonly viewed as being the source of the highest quality candidates.

If someone on our team knows the candidate and believes the candidate will fit into the culture, the result is likely to be a quality hire. In short, *knowing the candidate* is the key to a successful hire. It may seem obvious, yet it is a commonly overlooked fact in our race to expand candidate databases and accelerate our filtering and sorting capability.

The idea of knowing the candidate also offers a better way of applying innovation and shifting away from a "more-is-better" mentality. New Web 2.0 tools and technology offer much more interactive capabilities, and it is time we start using them to have real interactions—to get to know more people. Rather than using the tools to funnel more people to our managers, talent organizations need to teach hiring managers how to use these tools to get to know potential hires. Toward that end, the relationship between HR and hiring managers *should* evolve. This can begin with the development of a new role in HR with respect to the hiring manager. In essence, HR can take on the role of the "Talent Coach."

## Defining a New Role for HR

Based on our new mentality regarding the source of quality, the key to reaching quality talent is the ability to cultivate networks in which we get to know the people involved. We want to know much more than what's on the resume. We want to know about work styles preferences, professional motivations and interests, problem-solving capabilities and overall personality. It is also just as important for the candidate to get to know us, our work environment, the job content and the quality of our management. By developing a reciprocal knowledge between our internal resources and external candidates, we can create a cultural fit that will significantly impact employee engagement and retention. Gaining this type of knowledge requires many interactions. Growing a network requires building relationships, and that takes time. It also needs to be a constant process so that talent pipelines are being developed and managed regardless of the business climate.

Secondly, the vitality of the network depends on the quality of the interactions and the ability to provide value to all involved. Some possible interactions include getting together at conferences, breakfast meetings with a guest speaker, a social event such as a baseball game, online meetings or webinars or discussion forums on topics of interest. It means hiring managers will be spending time engaging in networking activities to develop a pipeline of talented people and, in the process, acquire in-depth knowledge of their behaviors in a professional environment. This is a much better investment of the manager's time than updating an applicant tracking system with interview notes. The network will take work to maintain, so bigger is not necessarily better. Based on current social network theory, 20-35 people is a reasonable size for such a network. As a group grows larger, the dynamic can change, such that soon we are managing acquaintances instead of relationships.

Since the desired goal of this activity is to have the hiring manager feel like he or she *knows* this network of valuable candidates, then it follows that this activity must be led by the hiring manager. This is where the role of HR will need to change. In the traditional role, a recruiter within the HR function takes on the requisition, identifies and gets acquainted with candidates and then hands the most likely candidate off to the hiring manager. Even with the largest candidate database and the most powerful and efficient processes for evaluating candidates, this is a reactive process. In the new or desired situation, the responsibility of getting to know potential candidates and then identifying the right people for the job will fall to the manager, with a continuous cycle of activity occurring before a requisition is ever created.

The new role for HR, then, will be to function as a talent coach. Not all hiring managers are well-versed in networking interactions. Our mission will be to assist the manager in developing and maintaining the network and to create a culture within the company of a talent mindset—i.e. one that understands talent acquisition as an ongoing process of relationship-building, rather than a requisition-based *hunting* process.

As a Talent Coach, there are very specific activities associated with reaching out to the talent market. Notably, there is the obvious parallel with the idea of sourcing. Of course we are not sourcing for an open position; rather we are sourcing for participants in the network. For HR, that entails a variety of activities, including:

- **Identifying prospects to be introduced into the manager's network**—The Talent Coach will need to seek out new and varied places for connecting with talent. The "old boy network" will not suffice over time. The challenge will be to look beyond the limited resources of known networks to reach out to new sources of talent. In addition to coaching the managers on how to systematically look for potential talent, we can be proactive and invite specific prospects into the network to ensure a diverse population.

- **Providing the tools for managing the network**—The ability to reach out to a wider range of people is the chief benefit of the recent spate of social networking technologies. They are evolving quickly, and the way people are adopting them is rapidly maturing into an accepted, and expected, point of interaction across all aspects of business. A solution such as LinkedIn is a proven business-oriented networking tool commonly used by managers and candidates alike—but the tried-and-true is subject to change, as Twitter, Facebook and the myriad of social networking tools shape the social networking environment. The Talent Coach will have to do more than simply provide the tools; he or she will have to understand the technology involved, including new tools and innovations as they arise.

- **Attending industry events with the manager**—For HR, as well as the hiring manager, the ability to connect with more people also depends on networking opportunities such as industry events and conferences. By attending as well as creating such events, the Talent Coach is taking an active role in helping the manager forge valuable relationships with candidates. This is an important manifestation of the much-talked-about "talent mindset" that is taking hold in many organizations today. Attending or holding such events might not have been the job of HR in the past, but it is becoming increasingly important today and will be essential in the future. In effect, building networks is everyone's job, and it is a mission that is no longer constrained by traditional silos of responsibility.

- **Communicating with network members on a continuous, systematic basis**—Periodic communication with all members of the network is important for keeping everyone engaged. Without a conscious and scheduled effort, communication may erode or become inconsistent. When this happens, the network's value will be greatly diminished. The Talent Coach can play a significant role by driving systematic periodic communication, ensuring that interactions continue to add value, monitoring the size of the network and introducing new members as needed. The Talent Coach can ensure that the network continues to provide its most important function—enabling managers to "know" the candidates.

## Establishing the Role of Talent Coach

Creating the Talent Coach role can be as informal as one recruiter spending some time with a manager to show him or her how to register on LinkedIn and join some groups. While fostering a talent mindset across the company may be a broad and gradual process, it is possible to take some formal action to design and implement talent coaching as a way of doing business. To launch such a program will require the following three main steps: identifying and educating participants in the network building effort; establishing the process and tools and setting goals and identifying metrics for success. Each of these steps includes a number of activities, all aimed at building on the overall effort and engaging participants.

*Step I—Identify and Educate Hiring Managers*
The first step will be identifying the managers to be involved in the process. These will be managers who are involved in hiring critical talent. Then look at the overall hiring goals and demographics to determine what size and number of networks need to be established. Once the network goals are established, the criteria can be developed for inviting participants into the network. Finally, with the criteria in place and a targeted group of people identified, a focused effort will be needed to educate managers on networking basics and protocol.

*Step II—Establish Tools, Opportunities and Communications*
The network-building process will be driven by continuous communication between hiring managers and others within the network (this is the source of real value to those in the network). A good starting point in identifying the types of interactions that will be most successful is to interview those managers who are naturally inclined to engage in this activity—i.e. interview leaders who already operate as talent scouts. Another important activity is to

determine the tools to be used for managing the information. Finally, create opportunities to provide relevant and meaningful content to participants. This can include newsletters, press releases and possible "centers of expertise" within the company. As the strategy takes shape, a calendar of events will become important. This can include attendance at trade shows, sports/entertainment events, association meetings and other relationship-building activities.

*Step III—Establish Goals and Metrics*

As with nearly all corporate initiatives, the success of the talent network effort requires clear goals and a means of measuring progress and success. The final major step in creating the initiative, then, is the establishment of goals for network production, number of hires and number of referrals. To support these goals, planners will need to determine the type of data needed and the method of capturing that data. There is no exact science to networking activity, so there is a need to monitor results and make adjustments as appropriate.

# Taking it to the Next Level: Measure, Manage and Improve

The basic elements for building candidate networks are available today. The actual networking—that is, interaction with those in the network and providing real value—will always be the job of HR and the hiring manager. Technology can enable that activity, but it cannot replace it. What technology can do, however, is exponentially extend the reach of managers and HR in building networks. In addition, thanks to innovations and research in the field of social networking, the ability to "measure" a network has also come into play.

It is widely accepted that the stronger the network the better results, but how do we measure the strength of a person's network today? The proverbial Rolodex of years past was largely replaced with the Outlook contact folder as an indicator of network strength. Today, we may be more likely to consider LinkedIn connections, yet there will always be the simple anecdotal references. People inherently understand who is "really well connected." These references indicate the importance of having a network, but they are not measurable.

To develop metrics for measuring, managing and improving the network, an understanding of current network theory can help. Network theory concerns itself with the study of graphs as a representation of either symmetric relations or, more generally, of asymmetric relations between discrete objects. Typically, the graphs of concern in network theory are complex networks, examples of which include the World Wide Web, the Internet, gene regulatory networks, metabolic networks, social networks and epistemological networks.

A fundamental concept behind network analysis is the idea of "social capital." Various commentators have written about the concept of social capital since the early 20th century. They can be boiled down to two main approaches. First, there is the idea of social capital as the value of one's social networks and the level of trust and value that they provide to members. Keys to value can range from volume of interaction to the "distances" between connected relationships (i.e. a tight network or clique would have more value if/when it can have meaningful connections to others outside of its group). The second idea, espoused by the international non-government organization, "The Social Capital Foundation," promotes social capital as the propensity and ability to create networks, rather than the outward result of the networks themselves.

For someone in the world of talent management, both definitions have relevance. The second idea, building the propensity and ability to create networks, is a direct precedent to HR's need to "build and foster the talent management mindset." To a large degree, that mindset is predicated on the commitment from those in the organization to cultivate quality candidates. The first idea, that social capital is the actual result of network-building activity, is also important to the process. By this definition, social capital can be measured.

While it is beyond the scope of this publication to prescribe a step-by-step process for quantifying the value of a network, it is useful to understand some key ingredients in the social capital equation. Chief among these is the idea that the social network consists of many "nodes." These nodes represent individuals in the network.

The value of those nodes is reflected in two main qualities: Betweenness and Closeness. Betweenness is the extent to which a node is directly connected only to those other nodes that are not directly connected to each other. In other words, a person with great "betweenness" value is one who is an intermediary or bridge between otherwise unrelated groups. The other quality is of closeness. This reflects how well-connected the individual is within his or her associations. In other words, how far up or down the "grapevine" is this person in accessing information?

Key points of analysis in the network include the esoteric-sounding term known as "Eigenvector centrality." This is a measure of the importance of a node within the network. It assigns relative scores to all nodes in the network based on the principle that connections to nodes having a high score contribute more to the score of the node in question. Other points of importance are "structural holes." These are static holes that can be strategically filled by connecting one or more links to bring together other points. This relates directly to ideas of social capital: namely, if you link to two people who are not connected, you can benefit from their communication and thus create value.

The study of these ideas and of larger network relationships reveal complexities that are beyond our control in the talent management organization today, but they also reveal important insights. From these insights, it is possible to create a system of measuring effectiveness on the talent acquisition process. Important lessons to understand are:

- The shape of a social network helps determine a network's usefulness to its individuals.
- Tighter networks can be less useful to their members.
- More open networks are more likely to introduce new ideas and opportunities to their members.
- A group of friends who only do things with each other already share the same knowledge and opportunities—cliques.
- It is better for individual success to have connections to a variety of networks rather than many connections within a single network.
- Individuals can exercise influence or act as brokers within their social networks by bridging two networks that are not directly linked.

What can we do to apply these ideas to the networks built by HR and the hiring manager? Applying innovations in theory and network visualization technology, it will be possible to address several critical needs. First, we can identify gaps or structural "holes" in the network, and establish targets for filling those holes. These gaps represent people who would provide great value in connecting previously unconnected groups. We can also identify internal resources in key positions in the network to develop retention and succession strategies. Finally, we can assess the value of the overall network and create a new metric for the dashboard: "Recruiting Capital." Objectives can then be assigned based on the goal of increasing the recruiting capital of the network.

## New Applications

Technology continues to evolve in the area of social networking in general, as well as in networking for the HR and talent acquisition function. New solutions and services include microsites or Talent Community Portals. By establishing a community, a company can bring together employees and external candidates in a venue that includes discussion forums, blogs, tools and information, and, most importantly, a growing network of "known" and, therefore, higher quality candidates.

Along this line, there is niche market evolving for functionality that sits on top of, or outside of, the traditional career site. This can provide more interactive functionality for candidate contacts. One example is Jobs2Web, a self-described "Recruitment Marketing Platform." This company focuses on applications that enable posting of Web 2.0 solutions such as LinkedIn and Facebook. Most notable, however, is that it provides applications for helping companies build talent communities and automates much of the "housekeeping" interaction of introducing people to the community and facilitating repeat visits and interaction.

Another example is Climber.com, which provides the means for companies to create microsites, actively market job postings and "automatically build networks of candidates." Ning is a site devoted to helping anyone to build a social network about anything.

The solutions around social network creation will continue to evolve rapidly. Whether examples such as these grow stronger, fade, or pave the way for more advanced solutions, it is important to remember that the heart of a coherent network is the value it provides, and that depends on interaction. In the talent environment, that interaction will require consistent and meaningful participation from the hiring manager.

On the analysis side, applications are emerging that provide increasingly sophisticated capabilities for tracing the growth of networks, assessing their value and identifying those critical "bridges" between groups that represent key relationships. One example, Touchgraph, has become well known for its Facebook browser, which enables people to view and browse their networks visually. A variety of applications are arising today focusing on network visualization and analysis. Another notable provider, Orgnet.com, offers solutions that have been used to "map and measure" networks in business organizations as well as community, government and non-profits. With the rise of social network media, the use for and availability of practical network analysis tools will continue to grow over time.

# Moving Forward:
# Human Interaction Remains Key

Over the past two decades, HR and Talent organizations have experienced a steady stream of innovation in the tools they have available. Talent acquisition and talent management are gaining recognition as strategic components to business performance. Newspaper classifieds and paper resumes are replaced by technologies that can reach millions of people instantly, and we can now process thousands of candidates more quickly than ever before. The "funnel mentality" continues to drive the way we approach talent acquisition. The main focus has been to put more candidates into the funnel, filter them as quickly as possible with improved tools and processes and quickly arrive at the ideal few at the end of the funnel before our competition does the same.

Thanks to the rise of new tools for building and maintaining the social network, there is an opportunity to evolve that fundamental thinking. The tools are changing, and we need to change the way we use them. For all the innovation that has occurred, the ability to secure the right talent boils down to an ideal that is as relevant today as it was in 1950: "Hire who you know." Social networking tools enable managers to do a better job of reaching new people and managing networks, but when it comes to "knowing" the candidate, even the most advanced technologies cannot replace human effort. Getting to know people requires participation. Ultimately it will be up to the manager to participate in the network and foster the interaction that gives it real value. This interaction is the key to keeping people engaged in the network and for supporting it as a sustainable source of quality candidates.

One particular concern for talent leaders is that this shift in emphasis to manager-based candidate networks requires a change in strategy and resources. A different model would drive investment of the recruiting budget. With that in mind, effecting such a change will require careful planning at the outset. No single application is ideal in all situations, so planners must be selective in identifying the tools they use, and in where and how they use them. What is the right application? Where does it make sense? These questions will depend on the unique needs and propensities of the organization and of the individual hiring manager. Finally, the ability to measure will be crucial in the ongoing effort at building candidate networks. Measurement enables organizations to understand progress, support adoption and buy-in for the approach and focus efforts at improvement over time. While human interaction is the basis for value, technology will continue to play a key role in the way that companies track and measure their candidate networks.

The focus on hiring manager-driven candidate networks reflects one of the ways that technology "should" evolve in the world of talent management. Meanwhile, technology providers will continue to develop solutions in a never-ending quest for functionality that is both broad and deep. Ultimately, the selection of any solution will be driven by the needs of the company. Even in a changing economy, talent will still drive corporate survival and success. The competition for talent will never end. With that in mind, technology will continue to play a critical part in the equation. As always, technology provides the potential for competitive advantage, but real success will be determined by how an organization puts that technology to work.

CHAPTER 4

# Selecting a Talent Management Systems Vendor: Insights for Making the Right Choice

By Peter DeVries

A primary objective of this book is to profile the leading talent management suite solutions currently in use by enterprise organizations. The solutions profiled here represent major players in the industry, namely those with the greatest market share of Fortune 1000 and Global 1000 customers. Market visibility, stability, a commitment to innovation and customer service are key qualities in this group.

Since 2002, the Newman Group (TNG) has produced annual reports on talent acquisition technology. As the market has expanded to encompass all aspects of talent management, the scope of TNG's evaluations have expanded also. A team of experienced consultants from The Newman Group created the framework for evaluation used in this book, based on critical functional and strategic criteria. This framework encompasses five key modules offered by vendors: Talent Acquisition, Performance Management, Compensation Management, Succession Planning and Learning Management.

Using this framework, the team conducted product demonstrations with over a dozen vendors, applying these criteria to develop objective evaluations that are relevant to the real-world demands of talent management in enterprises and other mid-to-large size organizations. Each module offered by the vendors was reviewed separately. Some suite vendors that were considered for review but declined to participate include the following:

- Oracle
- SAP
- Kronos
- Authoria
- SumTotal

# Talent Management Systems Vendor Selection Overview

As HR leaders have begun to focus on a more comprehensive approach to Talent Management, the marketplace for technology supporting these initiatives has exploded. Many vendors no longer focus on single aspects of talent management, such as talent acquisition or performance management. Instead, they offer suites of modules to help address an organization's overall talent management needs. Selecting the right technology to help an organization meet its talent management goals may seem daunting, but the rewards, in terms of operational effectiveness and overall strategic impact, are worth the effort. Choosing the right solution, however, requires substantial work and a thoughtful and methodological selection process.

A good way to approach vendor selection is to first understand the types of mistakes that are commonly made in the process. Mistakes made during selection can have a long-term impact on the success or failure of the implementation of the chosen technology. They include:

- **Gut reactions**: Making a decision based on emotion (a "gut feeling") rather than a set of well-defined requirements that have been prioritized to support business goals.
- **Vendor-first planning**: Meeting with a vendor before the organization's business requirements have been defined (even worse—meeting with a vendor to help define your requirements!)
- **Over-reliance on RFP**: Trying to select (or eliminate) a vendor based solely on RFP responses.
- **Forgetting about the User**: Excluding usability testing in the selection process and users from the selection process.
- **Supplier Bias**: Selecting a single preferred supplier based on emotion, past relationships or casual referrals.
- **Lack of Stakeholder Input**: Excluding other business stakeholders (such as IT, procurement, etc.) from participating in the evaluation process in a meaningful way.
- **Lack of Support**: Failing to obtain or achieve buy-in from sponsors due to an inability to justify the value proposition.

So what can you do to avoid the pitfalls that are commonly made in selecting a Talent Management System? It is critical to conduct a thoughtful, methodological and consistent evaluation process of your organization's needs. A vendor selection process can be divided into three key phases: 1. Internal Needs Assessment; 2. Detailed Vendor Analysis and 3. Finalization of the Selection. What follows are recommendations for each phase to help ensure the right solution for the organization.

## Phase One: Internal Needs Assessment

A successful selection process hinges on a meaningful evaluation of the organization. The key to vendor selection is not tied to the understanding of all of the available systems in the market, but rather to the comprehension of the needs of the business and how these needs support the organization's overall goals. This is why the first phase in the selection process, the Internal Needs Assessment, is so crucial. The Internal Needs Assessment phase includes three components: (1) assembling the selection team; (2) defining the requirements and (3) setting key criteria for vendor selection.

An effective assessment begins with the development of the right selection team. The first step is to ensure that an executive sponsor or champion is in position to guarantee alignment with strategic goals and mitigate funding issues. This will help prevent the implementation from stalling once the selection is complete. It is also important to include other stakeholders, such as IT or procurement, in the selection process. They may help identify unique requirements, but, more importantly, early inclusion gives these participants a stake in the success of the project, which will be a key factor during implementation. Being able to leverage these resources as project champions during the implementation can greatly simplify change management.

Once the project team has been determined, work can begin to define the organization's requirements. Reviewing current process documentation is a great place to start the analysis. Key documents to review may include:
- Current-state process maps
- A copy of all related talent management policies
- Any forms or correspondence used in the process

- A list of any SLAs currently in place
- A catalog of current integration points within the existing talent management systems
- Copies of all reports being used within talent management

Review of this documentation will provide a solid base for facilitating a business process discovery session. It will also help provide structure for this session. Focus on each step in the talent management process to reach a necessary understanding of the current business process and its limitations. Additionally, define desired best practices for future processes with the new system. Remember, this is not only an opportunity to define requirements for a new system, but also a chance to identify any opportunities to improve business processes.

After the process and needs discovery work is completed, the project team must consolidate the information into a matrix of functional requirements. One of the most important aspects of this process is to ensure the evaluation criteria is structured and weighed to facilitate a fact-based, non-emotional assessment. Consolidate all of the requirements into a matrix that will help define "wants" versus "needs" in a new system. By creating a consolidated requirements matrix and weighting the requirements, it can be determined whether a piece of new and cutting-edge functionality meets a "need" or a "want" and whether or not this should be a critical point on which to base the selection.

In addition to functional requirements, there are several other areas that should be included in the requirements summary. These include:

- *Technical*: Key considerations in this category should include platform, distribution models, integration points, security and technical implementation services.
- *Cost*: Defining cost can be an elusive task. It is often difficult to arrive at an apples-to-apples comparison between vendors. Develop a cost matrix and estimated budget and work with service provider finalists to map their costs into the matrix. It is important to understand the total cost of ownership, which includes both the initial and ongoing costs, as well as the cost of associated vendor services required to deliver a complete solution. Pricing models, consulting and training fees, maintenance schedules and payment schedules are some of the key points of consideration when evaluating cost.
- *Services*: The ability to deliver a solution with a new provider depends largely on the initial success with implementation, initiation

of service and alignment with internal resources. If these steps are not executed correctly, user adoption is jeopardized. This category should also include expected Service Level Agreements for system availability and issue resolution.

- *Vendor viability*: The vendor profile category is a representation of a vendor's viability and is an essential criteria given today's economic climate. This is one area of due diligence that an organization's corporate legal or procurement team can support. Key viability criteria include the vendor's cash position, revenue and profit growth, management track record and workforce stability.

- *Vendor vision*: Indicators of vendor vision include market share, commitment to the space, leading-edge services or technology and market understanding. Does the vendor have a vision for the future? Is the vendor a pioneer in the space or a follower? What are the extended services offerings or development plan, and how are releases rolled out? How well does the vendor's corporate culture and communication style mesh with the organization's? Will the vendor be a good long-term partner with a focus on service? Does the company share the same corporate values as the organization?

These criteria are by no means exhaustive. Individual lists will need to be developed based on the organization's unique needs. Remember, the more time spent defining and weighting the organization's requirements, the easier it will be to select the best solution for the company.

## Phase Two: Detailed Vendor Analysis

Once time has been spent "evaluating yourself" and defining the requirements, the next step is to move into a detailed analysis of vendors. Determine which vendors to evaluate in this phase, with a target of 10 or less.

Some organizations find that sending out a targeted Request for Information or a questionnaire helps identify which vendors are obvious mismatches for their requirements. This type of document should include unique essay questions that require the vendor to understand the organization's specific business needs, rather than a simple list of requirements or "Yes/No" questions. Be realistic and detailed about the expectations. Target five to 10 questions for this round.

When reviewing the vendors' responses, it is helpful to create an evaluation form that allows each participant to score each question and response. Create an evaluation matrix, which is a quick way of capturing every evaluator's scores. Summarize the scoring and comments for each question in this matrix. Then evaluate the information in the matrix to help make a decision about which vendors will move forward in the process.

Once the responses to the Request for Information are evaluated, enough knowledge should have been collected to narrow the target group to three to five vendors. At this point, a deeper evaluation process can begin. The Request for Proposal can be issued, and vendor demonstrations and introduction meetings can be scheduled. This is the time to get the procurement team involved if they are not already participating in the process. This step includes both written responses to the detailed RFP, as well as onsite demos. Evaluate the vendor responses and demonstrations against the weighted functionality matrix developed in Phase One.

The vendor demonstration process is one of the few times that everyone on the organization's team has an opportunity to gain a shared understanding of the vendor's capabilities and to have a voice in the selection. Areas of focus during demonstrations typically include an overview of the vendor company, a functional product demonstration and a technical demonstration/discussion.

Prior to the demonstration, create a presentation script that focuses on the organization's talent management processes (based on the work completed in Phase One). Review the demonstration script with the vendors prior to the sessions to ensure that they have all of the information needed to highlight their product's strengths and how it can be used to support the company's strategic goals. Extensive collaboration on schedules, agendas, demo scripts, expected discussion points, logistics and facilitation are critical to the success of the demo event. At the end of a successful demo, the evaluation group will have a clear understanding of the vendors and their capabilities.

If one vendor doesn't rise to the top—and they rarely do—then the next step is a "bake off" between finalists. Think of this as a test drive of the potential solution. The most success at this step can be assured by convening a team that includes all end user constituents and by spending dedicated time going through a usability study. The vendor should facilitate a hands-on product walkthrough and allow time for users to put the services and system through their paces. Once again, have the evaluation team assess the vendor's product based on the services/functionality matrix that has been created. Schedule adequate time to debrief with the team after the vendor has left to select the final vendor.

## Phase Three: Finalization of the Selection

Now that the vendor to be engaged has been identified, it's time to finalize the selection process and negotiate a contract. Based on the company's procurement process, it may be necessary to present a final recommendation to the executive sponsor (or a steering committee). This presentation typically includes a summary of the selection process, as well as a business justification for the recommendation. By following the consistent vendor selection methodology outlined in this chapter, the recommendation can easily be documented and justified.

Once receiving final sign-off from the leadership team, begin contact negotiations with the selected vendor. While these negotiations can take time, the contract is the cornerstone and one of the most important components of vendor management. How an organization manages the contract negotiations can set the tone for the relationship moving forward and can directly impact the success of technology implementation.

Contract negotiations can set a rocky foundation for a vendor relationship, particularly when members of the team are guilty of the following lines of thinking:

- "I'm going to squeeze every ounce out of them for the money I'm spending."
- "They should be grateful for the brand—let some other customer pay them the big bucks."
- "I don't care if they have to hire an army to support us; they can do it at their own expense."

Many contract negotiations sessions end up including these kinds of discussions, especially when there is a set budget dictating the contract. But setting this kind of tone in the discussions can lead to animosity and resentment on both sides of the relationship, which could result in the vendor's performance merely meeting expectations that otherwise would have been exceeded. It is always in a company's best interest to avoid this level of contract debate and focus on the longer-term relationship.

Spend some time thinking about how your organization can support the vendor in return for establishing an ongoing partnership. Determine your organization's ability or willingness to be involved in press releases, case studies, speaking engagements or references. With the Talent Management Systems market crowded with competitors, willing customers who can serve as references are cornerstones to success for most vendors.

## Laying the Foundation for Success

The upfront investment made in structuring and executing a methodological vendor selection process will establish a solid foundation for a successful implementation of the selected technology. By evaluating the organization's talent management processes, HR is not only able to identify its requirements for a new technology but is also able to identify opportunities to improve or streamline the process. It will also ensure the critical executive buy-in for the new system, as well as establish a sense of ownership among key stakeholders, both of which will only help as the system is implemented. As a result, HR can help the organization to realize long-term value with its new talent management system.

Finally, to achieve continuous returns on investment, it is important to always keep in mind the key strategic objectives of the organization and its HR leadership. Use these objectives to build success metrics for the talent management system. It is important to consistently measure performance against these metrics. This will allow optimization of the alignment of people, process and technology over time and ensure that the system is always aligned with the organization's business goals. These will prove to be critical steps in the journey towards developing the infrastructure, processes and organizational change the company will need in order to evolve and achieve its talent management goals in the coming years.

# Buyer's Guide to Talent Management Technologies

To access the On-Line Buyer's Guide, please visit:
**http://tmtech.hci.org.**
Please note that this site will be launched in Fall 2009,
with updated information and new suppliers.

# ADP

## Company Information (provided by ADP)

**Company Name:**      ADP Pre-Employment Services is a division of ADP, Inc.

**Corporate URL:**      www.virtualedge.adp.com

**Main Phone:**      (215) 504-5400

**Headquarters Address:**      5 Caufield Place, Newtown, PA 18940

**Type of Business or Areas of Focus
(i.e. ATS, Compensation, Consulting, Etc.):**
ADP offers the VirtualEdge® Talent Lifecycle Software platform that automates and streamlines the exempt and non-exempt hiring process in a software-as-a-service (SaaS) model.

**Number of Employees:**      170

**Year Founded:**      1998

**Stock Symbol:**      ADP

## Company Description and History:

VirtualEdge is a market-leading, robust recruitment solution that is 100 percent purpose-built to deliver the breakthrough solutions to transform the way you work. Offering a smart, intuitive and fully personalized platform for performance, our software enables power recruiting professionals to optimize the flow of talent throughout the organization, while significantly improving productivity and fundamentally impacting the overall talent capital of the business.

Founded in 1998, VirtualEdge was acquired by ADP to complement a suite of pre-employment services, establishing it as an end-to-end provider of talent acquisition solutions including recruitment automation, background screening, tax credit screening and I-9 compliance services.

## Products/Services/Solutions:

### 1. VE Professional

VE Professional automates and streamlines requisition-centric workflow for the exempt and non-exempt workforce. VE Professional streamlines and automates key tasks within the recruitment process from creating and posting a job requisition, to making an offer and initiating pre-hire activities.

### 2. VE High Volume

VE High Volume provides an automated hiring solution for position-centric workflow that combines applicant tracking, pre-screening, assessment, drug and background testing, tax credit capture, interview scheduling and payroll integration into one system. This robust solution distributes all hiring activities to give unprecedented real-time access and control over this vital process and generates substantial savings.

### 3. VE Pilot

VE Pilot provides a platform to identify high performing candidates through robust search tools. Candidate relationship management tools are available to develop strong, pre-need relationships with these prospects to support future hiring requirements.

### 4. VE Salute

VE Salute provides the underlying catalyst that automates and streamlines all the onboarding tasks previously performed manually by multiple company stakeholders; thus bringing all essential activities and reporting metrics into one centralized, online portal on-demand. By utilizing a dynamic self-serve portal and having a process in place that is constant and reliable, organizations gain control and increase efficiency. VE Salute enables the transfer of knowledge to new hires to give them the power to perform. Corporate compliance is guaranteed through automation of dissemination and data collection required with enrollment forms, employment agreements and corporate documents.

## Additional Notes/Comments:

VirtualEdge recruitment solutions are a critical component in ADP's initiative to offer market-leading, Pre-Employment Services. In addition to the above-mentioned solutions, additional strategic solutions are offered, including background screening, employment tax credit screening and electronic I-9 compliance.

## Author's ADP Functionality Matrix

| Function | Function Description | Response |
|---|---|---|

Talent Acquisition

| Requisition Management & Posting | | |
|---|---|---|
| Multiple requisition forms allowed (Example: hourly, internal transfer, business unit specific, reoccurring, sourcing, college) | More than one requisition form/template can be configured in a client's database to accommodate variance in business units or type of recruiting. (Example: A user from the Manufacturing group can enter a requisition and only see and populate fields that are applicable to Mfg. A different user from the Services group can enter a requisition and only see the fields designated for a Services requisition within the same database.) | No |
| Data Segregation | Ability to segregate requisitions and candidates by hire type (executive, HR, etc.) or organization. | Yes |
| Requisition approval routing workflow and approval status indicator | Select a list of approvers; route for approval via email. Approvals should be able to be sent in parallel or sequentially. | Yes |

| Function | Function Description | Response |
|---|---|---|
| Approval status tracking | The status of the approval process is tracked and displayed real-time on the requisition in the application as well as in the subsequent emails that go to the second and third approver, etc. | Yes |
| Pre-defined approval routing lists | Lists of approvers can be created, saved, and/or assigned to a user or requisition, or defined by the organizational structure automatically. | Yes |
| Approvals can take place directly from an email | When approving a requisition, the approver can take action directly from the email notification without having to log into the application. | Yes |
| Pre-qualifying questions based on position/job needs, including weighting to filter for top candidates | Questions developed, defined and delivered to a candidate in the online application process tied directly to the job posting/requirements, including weighting to filter for top candidates. | Yes |
| Knock-out questions | Ability to establish certain questions to be disqualifiers, where if the candidate does not answer correctly, the process is ended. | Yes |
| Job posting scheduling | Check a box to select the appropriate career site(s) for the job to appear. Scheduling of start and end dates of posting to any given site to allow for staggered posting. | Yes |
| Advanced job descriptions - Formatting and Spell Checking | Ability to edit and format job descriptions and marketing messages with MS Word like functions for Bolding, Underlining, and Spell Checking. | No |

| Function | Function Description | Response |
|---|---|---|
| Electronic job board relationship management (facilitation of job positing to all e-media providers) | Ability to identify and post job opportunities to an unlimited number of electronic job boards and other end destinations. Ability to multi-select boards and push positions out to the market. | Yes |
| **Candidate Experience** | | |
| Unlimited Career Site portals | Ability to establish an unlimited number of integrated career sites for different purposes - such as college recruiting, location - specific kiosks, or for a specific job family like Sales or Engineering. Determine if there are additional costs per Career Section. | Yes |
| Online profile form(s) defined by the client | Data collection form(s) that can be pushed to a candidate to gather needed information for relationship management and interested resume submissions. Customers can tailor the form to their specification, adding or removing fields. | Yes |
| User-defined secure login user name and password | User-created login and password authentication for accessing profile and career management activities. | Yes |
| Candidate login optional | Candidate can submit resume and apply to jobs without establishing a password-protected user account. | No |
| Resume submission via upload of file - Candidate | Candidate can browse hard drive for formatted resume and upload to candidate resume repository. | Yes |
| Resume submission via upload of file - Recruiter/Manager | Recruiter/Manager can browse hard drive for formatted resume and upload to candidate resume repository. | Yes |
| Resume builder functionality | Ability for candidates without a formal resume to submit one via a "Resume Builder." | Yes |

| Function | Function Description | Response |
|---|---|---|
| Extraction of data from resume to create profile | Extraction engine behind the text or uploaded resume for population of fielded data in the candidate profile. | Yes |
| Candidate-defined Job Agents | Candidates can establish job search parameters and be notified when jobs are posted which meet their preferences. | Yes |
| Candidate status check | Candidates can login to check the status of their resume submissions. | Yes |
| Ability to upload attachments | | Yes |
| Ability for candidate to save a submission as a draft | | Yes |
| Candidate self-withdrawal | Ability for candidates to remove themselves from consideration for a position. | No |
| Conceptual search for the candidate when searching for jobs | Candidates can use "free form" language to search for jobs. | Yes |
| **Sourcing/CRM** | | |
| Specific job referral and general referrals | Employees can submit a resume as a general referral or to a specific job. | Yes |
| Notifications to the referring employee and the referred candidate | Email notifications are automatically sent to the employee making the referral and to the candidate who was referred. | Yes |
| Referral status check | Employees can review a list of candidates they have referred and check their status. | Yes |
| Tracking steps and status searches | Recruiters can search for candidates based on their tracking steps and status against requisitions. | Yes |

| Function | Function Description | Response |
|---|---|---|
| Keyword search against free form text and fielded data | Keyword search against text records from candidate and fielded data in the same search. | Yes |
| Search criteria high-lighted for relevance in record review | Search results with indicators for criteria matching and relevance in the results. | Yes |
| Configurable search results list | The column headers that are displayed in a search results list can be configured with different data elements from the candidate record. (Example: Education, Work History, Phone Number). | No |
| Ability to search file attachments | Keyword searching will search the resumes that have been submitted as file attachments as well as text fields. | No |
| Ability to create "overnight" searches | | No |
| Conceptual search engine to match resumes | Ability to use the requisition's job description or a large text phrase to find matching resumes using a conceptual search or natural language search engine. Conceptual searches should also be able to be conducted with fielded search. | Yes |
| "More like this" searching | Ability to take a resume and conduct a search to find other resumes that are similar to it (more like it). | Yes |
| Library of candidate correspondence/ communication templates | Ability for clients to create a library of correspondence templates that can be sent to candidates at the user's discretion. | Yes |
| Editable correspondence at the user level | Users can make edits to the correspondence at the time of generation and distribution. | Yes |

| Function | Function Description | Response |
|----------|---------------------|----------|
| Agency Portal | Functionality designed for the management of third-party staffing agencies. Includes the ability to push requisitions to one or more suppliers and receive agency resume submissions. | Yes |
| Contingent Labor Management | Functionality designed specifically for the requisition and management of contract labor including the distribution of job requirements to multiple vendors, submission and review of resumes, tracking of assignment, time reporting and billing. | No |
| Candidate Pool Generation (Leads/ Prospective Candidates) | Able to enter limited candidate information (less required fields than regular candidate profile without comprising the configuration of the candidate profile) and develop target candidate pool for key skills. | Yes |
| Marketing Campaigns (Leads/Prospective Candidates) | Include proactive candidate pool in messaging, advertising campaigns or special event invitations. This should include the ability to send emails to thousands of candidates (as necessary). | Yes |
| Sending resumes to a manager | Ability to send a "Formatted Resume" to a Hiring Manager. | Yes |
| **Assessment and Interview Management** | | |
| Customer defined workflow steps and status | Customer can set up steps and status for tracking candidates through their recruiting process, with ability to tailor it for required and desired steps. | Yes/No |
| Customer can define multiple process workflows (Example: employee referral, internal transfers, etc.) | Ability to create multiple applicant workflows (set of tracking steps & status) to be selected at the requisition level. | No |

| Function | Function Description | Response |
|---|---|---|
| Workflow triggered alerts | Alerts can be set up in the system to drive the next step in the process or to function as reminders. | Yes |
| Ability to create a "tree-structure" workflow (i.e. step A can be followed by step B, C, D or E) | | Yes |
| Volume hiring updates | The ability to change the status for a group of candidates to hire in a single step (e.g. mass hiring in one step). | Yes |
| Integrated Assessments | Ability to store and/or integrate validated assessment tools into the recruiting workflow for certain jobs. | Yes |
| Assessment Triggers | Ability for Assessment to automatically be presented to a candidate based on responses to pre-screening questions or other data in his/her profile. | Yes |
| Assessment on demand | Ability to push an online assessment to a candidate on demand via email link. | Yes |
| Interview team member history | Ability to select and record a list of interviewing team members for a requisition. | Yes |
| Interview team notifications | Ability to send an email notification (including a calendar meeting request) to the interview team members when scheduling the interview within the system (including interview packets, resumes, etc. when sending the email request). | Yes |
| Storage of interviewer comments | Ability to configure an online interview feedback form to capture the comments from each interviewer. | Yes |

| Function | Function Description | Response |
|---|---|---|
| **Offer Management and Onboarding** | | |
| Interviewer attachments | Ability to include attachments to the interviewer notifications (e.g. interview guidelines, interview schedule, resume, etc.) | Yes |
| Approval routing and status tracking | Select a list of approvers, route for approval via email. In addition, the status of the approval process is tracked and displayed real-time on the Offer in the application as well as in the subsequent emails that go to the second and third approver, etc. | Yes |
| Pre-defined approval routing lists | Lists of approvers can be created, saved, and/or assigned to a user or requisition. | Yes |
| Approvals can take place directly from an email. | When approving an Offer, the approver can take action directly from the email notification without having to log into the application. | Yes |
| Offer letters can be generated by merging fields into letter templates. | Data can be merged from the candidate record, the requisition and the offer terms into offer letter templates. | Yes |
| Offer letters can be edited at the user level. | Users can make edits to the offer letter at the time of generation and distribution. | Yes |
| Specific Onboarding Module | Does the product offer a specific Onboarding module, allowing clients to define required notifications at hire and send notifications through the system? (e.g. provisioning, IT for user account setup, new hire, manager checklist, etc.) | Yes |
| Onboarding Documentation Management | Electronically provide new hire paperwork and track completion of key documents (I-9, Non Disclosures, Benefits Paperwork.) | Yes |

| Function | Function Description | Response |
|---|---|---|
| **Global Capabilities & Compliance** | | |
| EEO Compliance data collection | Configurable notification and collection of EEO compliance information at variable points in the process. | Yes |
| Global - in country data collection based on regulations | Configurable data requests based on in-country requirements. Example: Germany, martial status, number of children. | Yes |
| Ability to present Career Sections in Multiple Languages | Ability to present Career Sections in Multiple Languages. | Yes |
| Ability to present the Recruiter and Manager Portals in multiple languages | Ability to present the Recruiter and Manager Portals in multiple languages. | Yes |
| Data Segregation by country, region or predefined type | Data Segregation, i.e. preventing users from a particular country or location from seeing candidates who are in another country or location. | Yes |
| OFCCP Compliance tools to enable search and applicant declaration | Functionality consistent with the new OFCCP definition of Internet Applicant (record keeping for searches, candidate submissions, etc.) | Yes |
| Privacy Policy acknowledgements | Ability to require that candidates agree with the privacy policy before they submit. | Yes |
| Compliance with Data Privacy | Ability for customers to remove a candidate's data at that candidate's request. | Yes |

| Function | Function Description | Response |
|----------|--------------------|----------|
| Tax Credit Screening & Processing | Provides automatic Tax ID and SSN validation. Automatically transmits request to conduct tax credit screening for WOTC, WTW and more through to screening partners and displays those results within the Candidate profile for review and processing upon hire. | Yes |
| **Reporting & Integration** | | |
| Standard reports are delivered with the system | System is delivered with a minimum of 10 standard reports. | Yes |
| Ad-hoc reporting capability | System is delivered with an ad-hoc report-writing tool so that clients can create their own reports as needed. | Yes |
| Reporting Security | Ability to enable field-level security and access to report creation, output and distribution. | Yes |
| Reporting Distribution | Ability to generate scheduled reports and distribute through email. | No |
| Real-Time Reporting | Ability to report on data in the application in real time (not based on a refresh of data in a reporting environment). | Yes |
| HRIS Integration | Ability to create bi-directional integrations from an HRIS to the ATS. | Yes |
| Integration - Client Self-Service Tools | Ability for clients to create their own integration touchpoints as needed (and make them operational). | Yes |
| Integration - API Capability | Ability to allow clients to create integrations through APIs. | Yes |

# Cornerstone

## Company Information (provided by Cornerstone)

**Company Name:**          Cornerstone OnDemand, Inc.

**Corporate URL:**         www.cornerstoneondemand.com

**Main Phone:**            (310) 752-0200

**Main Email:**            info@cornerstoneondemand.com

**Headquarters Address:**  1601 Cloverfield Blvd., Suite 620,
                           Santa Monica, CA 90404

**Type of Business or Areas of Focus:**
Integrated talent management systems and allied services.

**Number of Employees:**   155

**Year Founded:**          1999

**Stock Symbol:**          Privately held

## Company Description and History:

Cornerstone OnDemand helps organizations empower their people and optimize workforce productivity with a comprehensive suite of integrated talent management solutions for learning, compliance, performance, compensation and succession management, as well as robust reporting and analytics. Cornerstone also provides more than 30,000 pre-integrated training titles.

The Company's multi-tenant, multi-user software-as-a-service (SaaS) architecture provides customers with rapid deployments, minimal IT costs, greater flexibility, proven reliability and a lower total cost of ownership.

Cornerstone's triple-digit growth has been supported by a market-leading customer retention rate. Leading enterprises such as Aon, Bank of the West, Flextronics, Pearson, Randstad, Ticketmaster and Trend Micro count on Cornerstone to help them achieve organizational excellence and competitive advantage.

The company was founded in 1999 as CyberU, a provider of online learning and learning technology for consumer and corporate markets. By 2001, the company had expanded its product and service offerings into a totally on-demand learning and performance management system and quickly became a market leader. The company is headquartered in Santa Monica, California, and has international offices in London, Paris, Munich and Tel Aviv.

## Products/Services/Solutions:

### 1. Cornerstone Integrated Talent Management Suite

Designed by HR executives from the world's leading companies, the Cornerstone OnDemand Talent Management Suite is a fully-integrated, self-configurable talent management system. Cornerstone is delivered via the software-as-a-service model.

Cornerstone approaches the broad employee lifecycle, addressing multiple areas of talent management:

- Enterprise social networking
- Learning management
- Employee performance management
- Succession and workforce planning
- Analytics and reporting

Cornerstone is offered as a set of bundled modules. The entire suite can be rolled out for a full talent management platform, or individual modules can be implemented to provide strategic point solutions.

### 2. Cornerstone Connect
### (part of the integrated Cornerstone OnDemand Suite)

Cornerstone Connect brings together the best of Enterprise 2.0 technologies with the latest in social networking to enable effective workplace collaboration, improve employee performance and drive innovation from customer and partner communities.

By encouraging collaboration and making it easy to join communities of practice, Cornerstone Connect fosters social (informal) learning, organizational memory, professional networking and better communication across its customers' employee base and the extended enterprise.

Cornerstone delivers a complete social networking and workplace communities platform. This includes communities of practice, rich user profiles, expertise location, tag clouds, rating/sharing content, knowledge management, blogs, wikis, podcasts, RSS feeds and much more.

### 3. Cornerstone Learning
### (part of the integrated Cornerstone OnDemand Suite)

Cornerstone OnDemand incorporates one of the most comprehensive and powerful learning management systems available today. Offered as separate e-learning, instructor-led training, learning content and compliance management modules or as a complete system, Cornerstone's learning management tools provide administration, reporting and delivery functionality to meet the needs of even the most advanced enterprise.

Cornerstone supports a wide range of learning activities and provides real-time tracking through the user's personalized learning transcript. Clients use Cornerstone Learning to deliver and track a wide range of training modalities.

### 4. Cornerstone Performance/Succession
### (part of the integrated Cornerstone OnDemand Suite)

Cornerstone's employee performance management (EPM) system provides state-of-the-art tools to direct and measure performance at the individual, departmental and organizational level. This includes support for cascading, SMART-based goals; development planning; competency management; 360-degree, 180-degree and self assessments and performance reviews.

Inside Cornerstone's Succession Planning module, companies will find a wealth of tools to help identify and promote high-potential employees, allocate resources, find needed skills, build highly efficient teams, examine talent pools and create enterprise-wide succession plans.

## Additional Notes/Comments:

- **Developed by Cornerstone:** Cornerstone developed ALL modules of the integrated talent management suite in-house and in collaboration with clients
- **Software-as-a-Service:** Cornerstone is among the largest pure-play Software-as-a-Service vendors across all industries, with close to 1,300,000 subscribers and an average engagement of approximately 10,000 per organization. Cornerstone has proven to be fast, agile and responsive. The size of our company and the on-demand nature of our service translate into rapid development and global deployment.
- **Consulting Services.** Cornerstone has invested deeply in consulting services. The company has built out sophisticated offerings to help clients maximize their investment in EPM products.
- **Client Success:** Cornerstone has always invested heavily in servicing clients. This is imperative as a core premise of the SaaS model: that the very nature of the ongoing licensing model provides strong incentives to deliver world-class customer care. These efforts have paid off with a 97% client retention rate for 2007 and approximately 93% for the history of the company.

# Author's Cornerstone Functionality Matrix

| Function | Function Description | Response |
|---|---|---|

## Performance Management

| Performance Dashboard | | |
|---|---|---|
| Dashboard configuration | Ability to configure dashboard based on user preference. | Yes |
| Create and display reports | Display reports that can be generated (i.e. review completion progress, goal progress). | Yes |
| Create and display charts and graphs | Display available charts and graphs that are available to show planning actions. | Yes |

| Function | Function Description | Response |
|---|---|---|
| Display help and reference tools | Display and view help and reference tools that can be selected by link or mouse hover. | Yes |
| **Employee Information Review (Data Import from HRIS/LMS)** | | |
| Import and display employee information | Display name, address, phone, email, location, photo, education (typically pulled from HRIS). | Yes |
| Import and display employee position information | Display current job title, job summary, job family, job level/grade, job code, FLSA, shift, status (FT/PT) (typically pulled through HRIS). | Yes |
| Create and display work history | Display created previous work history (i.e. name of company, job title, responsibilities/duties, employment dates). | Yes |
| Create and display years in management | Display created years of management experience (manually entered or via integration). | Yes |
| Create and display years in industry | Display created years of experience in industry (primarily entered manually). | Yes |
| Import, create and display employee language(s) | Display employee languages (i.e. read, written, fluent) (primarily entered manually). | Yes |
| Import, create and display employee affiliations | Display employee affiliation memberships. | Yes |
| Import, create and display employee certifications | Display employee certifications and dates. | Yes |

| Function | Function Description | Response |
|---|---|---|
| Import, create and display employee licenses | Display employee licenses and dates (usually a text box) - important to include expiration dates (could be for transportation, professional licenses, healthcare licenses, etc.) | Yes |
| Import and display organizational information | Display company name, company division, company department (typically imported from HRIS). | Yes |
| Import and display management hierarchy information | Display multiple levels of management names and information (i.e. Executive Management, Division Head, Department Head, Direct Manager, Employee). | Yes |
| Import and display direct reports | Display name and information of employee direct reports. | Yes |
| Import and display matrix manager hierarchy information | Display multiple levels of matrix management names and information (i.e. Employee has dotted line reporting relationships). | Partial |
| Import and display multiple manager hierarchy information | Display multiple levels of numerous management names and information (i.e. Employee reports to more than one manager directly). | Yes |
| Organizational Chart View | Organizational information can be displayed in an Org Chart view (note how this is displayed visually). | Yes |
| Organizational Change Requests | Due to potential errors within HRMS, manager has the ability to request an employee change in hierarchy (i.e. manager name, organization, location, job role); changes can be configured to require approval. | Yes |

| Function | Function Description | Response |
|----------|---------------------|----------|
| Import and display employee current and past compensation | Display employee's past and current base salary, bonus, equity, commission, etc. | Yes |
| Import and display employee most recent performance measures | Display employee's current competencies, goals, skills, projects, performance rating, development plan, personal improvement plan. | Yes |
| Import and display employee previous performance measures | Display employee's previous competencies, goals, skills, projects, performance rating, development plan, personal improvement plan. | Yes |
| Complete and display employee training | Display employee's completed and assigned training (i.e. mandatory/development). Note if there is any integration with LMS. | Yes |
| External Identifier | Ability to have an external identifier field to bring in content on goals from a third-party application (i.e. description, start date, critical, public goal) - can be configured to be read-only for imports. | Yes |
| UDFs | Available user-defined fields for employee profile. | Yes |
| **Career Planning / Personal Development (Employee)** | | |
| Create and display future career plan scenarios | Display multiple future career plans (vertical, horizontal, both). Where does the employee want to go next? (lateral, promotion, etc.) | Yes |
| Select and display positions, job families and organizations/divisions of interest | Display selected positions and organizations of interest from import of job list and organization list (mentorships and cross-training). Gives the employee the opportunity to identify a position, job-family or organization of interest. | Yes |

| Function | Function Description | Response |
|---|---|---|
| Create and display training requests | Display developmental training requests (entered by an employee or manager). This could be an integration point to the LMS. | Yes |
| Create and display executive/professional requests | Display various executive/professional requests (i.e. executive coaching, cross training, job shadowing, speaking engagements, writing submittals, managing people, presentations, mentoring, apprenticeships). | Yes |
| Create and display organization affiliations and/or conferences/seminars | Display employee organization/affiliation or conference/seminar requests to join or attend. | Yes |
| Select and display competency development | Display selected desired competencies (entered by employee). | Yes |
| Create self-asses job readiness | Display selected self-readiness from list of options (i.e. Now, 0-3 months, 3-6 months, 6-9 months, 9-12 months, 12 months +). | Yes |
| Display position Gap % | Display gap % of employee readiness to ideal position as well as required training, license(s), education, certification(s) - this could be automatically calculated by the system (key differentiator). This is a gap analysis on the underlying competencies (most recent performance rating vs. competencies required for next position). | Yes |
| Select and display willingness to relocate | Display selected willingness to relocate (i.e. yes, no, maybe, comments). | Yes |

| Function | Function Description | Response |
|---|---|---|
| Display career pre-requisites | Display required training, education, certification(s), license(s) for position of interest. | Yes |
| Submit develop-ment requests for approval | Submit development self assessments to direct manager for review, feedback and approval (areas where the develop-ment needs to occur, as well as specific courses, conferences to help meet these development areas). Could be an inte-gration point with LMS. | Yes |
| **Career Development (Manager)** | | |
| Create or select and display employee training goals | Display created or selected employee completed training, assigned training (mandatory/development), scheduled training and employee training requests. This is the manager identifying training goals for an employee. | Yes |
| Competency Devel-opment | Display assigned professional/leadership competencies. | Yes |
| Create and display executive/profes-sional assignments | Display various executive/professional recommendations (i.e. executive coach-ing, cross training, job shadowing, speaking engagements, writing submit-tals, managing people, presentations, mentoring, apprenticeships). | Yes |
| Create and display organization affilia-tions and/or confer-ences/seminars | Display employee organization/affiliation or conference/seminar recommenda-tions. | Yes |
| **Individual Goal / Self Assessment (Employee)** | | |
| Select, create and display individual development goals | Display selected or created completed training, improvement competencies, executive coaching, promotion, cross training. | Yes |

| Function | Function Description | Response |
|---|---|---|
| Select competency development | Display selected development competencies. This is where the employee selects competencies wanted to develop for career on the annual review. | Yes |
| Submit goal/competency assessment for approval | Submit manual or automatic goal/competency assessment to direct manager. | Yes |
| Solicit and display feedback | Select employees (i.e. managers, matrix managers, peers) to solicit performance feedback (i.e. 360, peer review, business review) and display results. | Yes |
| Create and display self-performance notes | Display created performance notes (i.e. kudos) throughout the review cycle (manually entered by employee or can solicit feedback throughout project). | Yes |
| Create and display self-goal assessment progress | Display created self-goal progress (i.e. quantitative % of completion, qualitative to include customer satisfaction, timeline to include start/completion date). | Yes |
| Submit goal/competency review for approval | Submit manual or automatic goal/competency assessment to direct manager and higher levels. | Yes |
| UDFs | Available user-defined fields for employee goals. | Yes |
| **Review Process (Employee and Manager)** | | |
| Select and display competencies | Display selected professional or leadership competencies. | Yes |
| Select and display goals/objectives | Display selected goals/objectives (i.e. quantitative and/or qualitative). | Yes |
| Select and display goal alignment | Display selected goal alignment to company, organization, department and/or manager goals (cascading goals). | Yes |

| Function | Function Description | Response |
|---|---|---|
| Select or create and display projects | Display selected or created projects. | Yes |
| Select and display project alignment to goals | Display selected project alignment to company, organization, department and/or manager goals. | Yes |
| Select or create and display skills | Display selected or created company, organization, department, employee skills. | Yes |
| Create and display employee performance notes | Display created performance notes (positive or negative) throughout the review cycle. These are notes created by the manager. | Yes |
| Solicit and display feedback | Select employees (i.e. managers, matrix managers, peers) to solicit performance feedback (i.e. 360, peer review, business review) and display. Pay particular attention to how this feedback is gathered and entered into the system. | Yes |
| Create and display employee goal assessment review | Display created employee goal progress (i.e. quantitative % of completion, qualitative to include customer satisfaction, timeline to include start/completion date) - this is the manager entering the assessment. | Yes |
| Performance review filtering | Manager can filter performance review information based on approval status, assigned to, author/owner, manager, employee, organization, location, job field, job role, review cycle, review group, review group owner, overall rating; filtering can be cumulative. | Yes |
| Batch activities | Manager can take group actions on multiple employees simultaneously. | No |
| UDFs | Available user-defined fields for employee competencies. | Yes |

| Function | Function Description | Response |
|---|---|---|
| **Workflow** | | |
| Review cycles | Ability to configure multiple review cycles and tie to various reviews. | Yes |
| Review groups | Ability to define review recipients based on dates, job function, organization, job code, etc. | Yes |
| Workflow Order | Ability to configure order of workflow (i.e. self-assessments can be configured to be completed first). | Yes |
| Notifications | Ability to push reviews to employees and managers. | Yes |
| Reminders | Ability to send reminders to employees and managers via email (manual and automatic). | Yes |
| Acknowledgements | Ability to send auto-acknowledgements triggered by event/activity. | Yes |
| Next Level Approval | Ability to auto/manually route to multiple levels of approval. | Yes |
| Configurable work-flow | Ability to configure various steps of the review process, ability to: make review steps mandatory; have manager override ability; display/hide visual graphic work-flow diagram. | Yes |
| Auto/Manual Pro-gression | Ability to automatically or manually prog-ress through the review process. | Yes |
| Review form | Exportable and printable review form. | Yes |
| **System Admin** | | |
| Review sections | Ability to configure multiple review sec-tions, including goals, competencies, comments, rating models, etc. | Yes |

| Function | Function Description | Response |
|---|---|---|
| Configurable rating models | Does it configure and display alpha and numeric values? Can values be rounded (up/down/both), value ranges, number of decimals (1-5)? | Yes |
| Comments | Displayed and available in individual review sections and overall review? Be configured to be mandatory and ability to be overridden by management? | Yes |
| Goals | Ability to link organizational, divisional, departmental, individual goals into sections and ability to display goal progress. | Yes |
| Competencies | Ability to link competencies into sections. | Yes |
| Weightings | Ability to weigh employee performance based on goals and competencies. | Yes |
| **Search Functionality** | | |
| Basic Employee Search | Basic search by employee name (i.e. first or last name or a combination of both). | Yes |
| Job/Position Basic Search | Basic search by job role or position title, etc. | Yes |
| Competency Basic Search | Basic search by competency name. | Yes |
| Advanced Search | More detailed search capabilities that combine various search criteria or fields - may include optional weighting to determine which employees are retrieved in a search as well as each person's rank in the search results. | Yes |
| Succession Planning Search | Search functionality that dynamically generates the criteria used to match employees who would make good succession candidates with a specific position profile (could have various levels of "fit"). | Yes |

| Function | Function Description | Response |
|----------|---------------------|----------|
| **Employee View / Navigation / Help / Other** | | |
| List View | Display employee goals, business goals or projects; the list mode is a list of items with information on key dates and progress. | Yes |
| Card View | Display employee goals, business goals or projects using the card mode; the card mode provides details on one item at a time and offers the possibility of editing progress. This can also include employee photos as well. | Yes |
| Timeline / Gantt | Display employee goals, business goals or projects using the timeline mode; the timeline mode provides a timeline view of an item's start and due dates. | No |
| Org Chart | Managers can access and manage information on their direct reports for all functionalities activated; the organizational chart will provide key data (i.e. risk of loss or most recent performance rating) for each of the manager's direct reports. | Yes |
| Mini Org Chart | Displays a single analytic data point at a time; the manager can drill down into all layers of his organization and can view key metrics (i.e. performance reviews, goals, succession). | Yes |
| Graphs | Graphical display of various information (i.e. Gap Analysis, goal progress, review completion progress). | Yes |
| Help Links | Online help, FAQs, customer support, product version. | Yes |
| Attach Documents | Ability to attach reference documents to various sections within the system. | Yes |

| Function | Function Description | Response |
|---|---|---|
| Browser capabilities | Supported by general Internet access (works with standard browsers: IE, Safari, Mozilla, Opera). | Yes |
| Mouse-Over Hover | Additional tooltips or descriptions that display when user hovers the mouse pointer over various graphics or words within the system. | Yes |
| Web 2.0 | Ability to utilize Web 2.0 functionality, i.e. social networking. | Yes |
| **Security** | | |
| Logging In | Various login options (i.e. manual, SSO, LDAP). | Yes |
| File Transfer | Various file transfer protocol (i.e. FTP, sFTP, vendor-specific transfer import/export tool). | Yes |
| Encryption | Various data encryption ability (i.e. PGP) | Yes |
| Roles / Permissions | Configurable list of permission-based roles with detailed access rights to various organizations, levels, etc. Typically employees only view within their own organization hierarchy. | Yes |
| Integration | Ability to integrate organizational data i.e. HRIS/ATS/ LMS and employee data including competencies, training, development plans, etc. | Yes |
| **Reporting** | | |
| Standard reports are delivered with the system | System is delivered with a set number of standard reports. | Yes |

| Function | Function Description | Response |
|---|---|---|
| Ad-hoc reporting capability | System is delivered with an ad-hoc report-writing tool so that clients can create own reports as needed. | Yes |
| Advanced Value metrics | Data analysis of employee review process status, goal progress by hierarchy. | Yes |
| Reporting Security | Ability to enable field-level security and access to report creation, output and distribution. | Yes |
| Reporting UDFs | Ability to report user-defined fields. | Yes |
| Exporting reports | Reports can easily be exported to other applications (i.e. .xls, .pdf, .txt). | Yes |

## Succession Planning

| Succession Planning (Manager - Planning of Individual Talent Matched to Critical Roles) | | |
|---|---|---|
| Create and display critical roles for today | Display critical job roles (i.e. title, level, location, division, organization). | Yes |
| Create and display critical roles for future | Display critical job roles (i.e. title, level, location, division, organization) for future (workforce planning-like tools). | Yes |
| Calculate and display performance rating | Performance rating is automatically averaged from various sections of the performance review and displayed (current and past). | Yes |
| Calculate and display performance ranking | High potential employees will be automatically ranked according to order of fit with critical role (i.e. 9-box grid, numeric ranking, high performer, high potential). Can be ranked by position, organization, etc. | Yes |
| Multi-dimensional matrix | Matrix that can be configured up to various # of cells (i.e. 9-box, 12-box, 16-box, 25-box); text within grid is configurable. | Yes |

| Function | Function Description | Response |
|---|---|---|
| Various dimensions of matrix | Matrix displays employee performance, potential, number of succession plans an employee is on, years in management, years in industry. | Yes |
| Navigation from multi-dimensional matrix | Manager can select an employee within the matrix and navigate to employee information (i.e. Performance review, talent profile, employee goals, career plan). | Yes |
| Display employee comparisons | Display comparison of multiple high potential employees according to fit to critical role (i.e. # of employees to compare, comparable data, fit gap analysis, ranking analysis, bench strength). | Yes |
| Create and display role readiness | Manager can create and display high potential employee role readiness (i.e. now, 0-3 months, 3-6 months, 6-9 months, 9-12 months, 12+ months). | Yes |
| Create and display retention risk | Manager can create and display high potential employee retention/loss/flight risk (i.e. high, medium, low, comments). | Yes |
| Create and display role willingness | Manager can create and display high potential employee role willingness (i.e. yes, no, comments). | Yes |
| Create and display willingness to relocate | Manager can create and display high potential employee willingness to relocate (i.e. yes, no, maybe, comments). | Yes |
| Create and display willingness to travel | Manager can create and display high potential employee willingness to travel (i.e. none, 25-50%, 50-75%, 75-100%). | Yes |
| Create and display interest in international assignment | Manager can create and display high potential employee interest in international assignment (i.e. yes, no, maybe). | Yes |

| Function | Function Description | Response |
|---|---|---|
| Create and display interim replacement for critical role | Manager can create and display high potential interim replacement for critical roles. | Yes |
| Display of gap analysis | Automatically calculate and display high potential employees' fit gap analysis to the next position and ranking analysis of employee to that next position. | Yes |
| UDFs | Available user-defined fields for succession planning. | Yes |
| **Succession Pooling (Manager - Planning of a Talent Pool for Critical Roles)** | | |
| Display high potential pool | Display nominated and/or approved high potential pool (i.e. employee information, designated nominators, designated approvers, approvals, rejections, role readiness, rejection comments). | Yes |
| Calculate and display performance rating | Performance rating is automatically averaged from various sections of the performance review and displayed (current and past). | Yes |
| Calculate and display performance ranking | Pool of high potential employees will be automatically ranked according to order of fit with critical role (i.e. 9-box grid, numeric ranking, high performer, high potential). | Yes |
| Display employee comparisons | Display comparison of multiple high potential employees according to fit to critical role (i.e. # of employees to compare, comparable data, fit gap analysis, ranking analysis, bench strength). | Yes |
| Create and display role readiness | Manager can create and display high potential employee role readiness (i.e. now, 0-3 months, 3-6 months, 6-9 months, 9-12 months, 12+ months). | Yes |

| Function | Function Description | Response |
|---|---|---|
| Create and display retention risk | Manager can create and display high potential employee retention/loss/flight risk (i.e. high, medium, low, comments). | Yes |
| Create and display role willingness | Manager can create and display high potential employee role willingness (i.e. yes, no, comments). | Yes |
| Create and display willingness to relocate | Manager can create and display high potential employee willingness to relocate (i.e. yes, no, maybe, comments). | Yes |
| Create and display willingness to travel | Manager can create and display high potential employee willingness to travel (i.e. none, 25-50%, 50-75%, 75-100%). | Yes |
| Create and display interest in international assignment | Manager can create and display high potential employee interest in international assignment (i.e. yes, no, maybe). | Yes |
| Create and display interim replacement for critical role | Manager can create and display high potential interim replacement for critical roles. | Yes |
| Display of gap analysis | Automatically calculate and display high potential employees' fit gap analysis to position and ranking analysis of employee to position. | Yes |
| UDFs | Available user-defined fields for succession pooling. | Yes |
| **Workflow** | | |
| Succession approval workflow | Ability to define or edit approvers, add/remove users and roles, ability to change the approval order, ability to reject with comments. | Yes |
| Nominations for succession pool | Ability to nominate, reject and enter comments on nominated HiPo employees. | Yes |

| Function | Function Description | Response |
|---|---|---|
| **Reporting** | | |
| Standard reports are delivered with the system | System is delivered with a set number of standard reports. | Yes |
| Ad-hoc reporting capability | System is delivered with an ad-hoc report-writing tool so clients can create their own reports as needed. | Yes |
| Advanced Value metrics | Data analysis of high performers / high potential employees, identified gaps, critical roles. | Yes |
| Reporting Security | Ability to enable field-level security and access to report creation, output and distribution. | Yes |
| Reporting UDFs | Ability to report user-defined fields. | Yes |
| Exporting reports | Reports can easily be exported to other applications (i.e. .xls, .pdf, .txt). | Yes |

## Compensation Management

| Function | Function Description | Response |
|---|---|---|
| **Compensation Dashboard** | | |
| Dashboard configuration | Ability to configure dashboard based on user preference. | Yes |
| Create and display a compensation worksheet | Display a compensation worksheet that will provide individual and org planning status and detail. | Yes |
| Create and display reports | Display reports that can be generated, i.e. budget usage by merit, bonus, equity, adjustment and percent of planning completed. | Yes |
| Create and display charts and graphs | Display charts and graphs that are available to display planning actions. | Yes |

| Function | Function Description | Response |
|---|---|---|
| Import and display allocation guidelines | Display compensation allocation guidelines for merit, bonus, equity and adjustments - also refer to the time allocation/ workflow to complete this process. | Yes |
| Import and display eligibility guidelines | Display employee eligibility guidelines for planning, i.e. FT, PT, commission, LOA, new hire, etc. Guidelines are input by compensation department. | Yes |
| Display help and reference tools | Display and view help and reference tools that can be selected by link or mouse hover. | Yes |
| **Compensation Budget** | | |
| Import and display multiple aggregate planning budget by org | Display multiple approved allocated budget by diverse business groups on all pages (usually imported from financial system). | Yes |
| Import and display aggregate merit budget by org | Display approved allocated merit budget by diverse business groups on all pages. | Yes |
| Import and display aggregate bonus budget by org | Display approved allocated bonus by diverse business groups on all pages. | Yes |
| Import and display aggregate equity budget by org | Display approved allocated equity budget by diverse business groups on all pages. | Yes |
| Import and display aggregate adjustment budget by org | Display approved allocated adjustment budget by diverse business groups on all pages. | Yes |
| **Employee Information Review** | | |
| Import and display employee Information | Display name, location, photo, org, direct manager (typically imported from PM tool). | Yes |

| Function | Function Description | Response |
|----------|---------------------|----------|
| Import and display employee position | Display current job title, job code, level/grade. | Yes |
| Import and display employee prior compensation planning period data | Display current hourly rate, annual rate, bonus percent, bonus amount, equity allocation, total compensation. | Yes |
| Import and display employee prior performance rating | Display prior performance rating. | Yes |
| Import and display new employee performance rating | Display new performance rating. | Yes |
| Import and display employee's position salary range | Display employee's salary range. | Yes |
| Import and display % salary penetration based on position salary range | Display percentage of penetration that employee's salary falls within the range. | Yes |
| Promotion | | |
| Display position information | Ability to select and display job titles, job codes, job level/grades. | Yes |
| Import and display corporate promotion guidelines | Ability to display promotion guidelines per position including salary range and percent increase guidelines. | Yes |
| Promotion amount | Ability to enter promotion percent or amount. | Yes |
| Auto-calculate promotion amount | System to auto-populate promotion amount based on percent increase. | Yes |
| Ability to calculate hourly rate | System to auto-populate new hourly rate based on promotion increase. | No |

| Function | Function Description | Response |
|---|---|---|
| Ability to auto-calculate annual rate | System to auto-populate new annual rate based on promotion increase. | Yes |
| Promotion approval chain | TBD. | |
| Develop documentation | Ability to document the promotion justification. | Yes |
| **Adjustment** | | |
| Import and display adjustment guidelines | Ability to display adjustment allocation guidelines, including salary range and percent increase guidelines. | Yes |
| Adjustment allocation | Ability to enter and submit an adjustment percent or amount. | Yes |
| Auto-calculate hourly amount | System to auto-populate new hourly rate based on adjustment percent increase. | No |
| Auto-calculate adjustment amount | System to auto-populate new annual rate based on adjustment percent increase. | Yes |
| Adjustment approvals | | Yes |
| Develop documentation | Ability to document the adjustment justification. | Yes |
| **Merit** | | |
| Import and display promotion guidelines | Ability to display merit allocation guidelines, including salary range and percent increase guidelines. | Yes |
| Performance based recommendations | Merit allocation can be based on performance rating. | Yes |
| Merit allocation | Ability to enter and submit a merit percent or amount. | Yes |

| Function | Function Description | Response |
|---|---|---|
| Import and display proration of merit based on hire date | System to auto-calculate merit increase based on hire date, i.e. less than one year would be calculated by months employed. | Yes |
| Auto-calculate hourly amount | System to auto-populate new hourly rate based on merit percent increase. | Yes |
| Auto-calculate adjustment amount | System to auto-populate new annual rate based on merit percent increase. | Yes |
| Merit approvals | | Yes |
| Develop documentation | Ability to document the merit justification. | Yes |
| **Bonus** | | |
| Import and display bonus allocation guidelines | Ability to display bonus allocation guidelines. | Yes |
| Performance-based recommendations | Bonus allocation can be based on performance rating. | Yes |
| Bonus allocation | Ability to enter and submit a bonus percent or amount. | Yes |
| Bonus adjustment | Auto-Proration of bonus based on hired or leave, i.e. severance date. | Yes |
| Bonus approvals | Ability to obtain appropriate approvals (workflow to select appropriate approvers). | Yes |
| Develop documentation | Ability to document the merit justification. | Yes |
| **Equity** | | |
| Import and display equity allocation guidelines | Ability to display equity allocation guidelines. | Yes |

| Function | Function Description | Response |
|---|---|---|
| Performance-based recommendations | Equity allocation can be based on performance rating. | Yes |
| Equity allocation | Ability to enter and submit equity percent or amount. | Yes |
| Equity allocation adjustment | Auto-Proration of equity allocation based on hire date. | Yes |
| Equity approvals | | Yes |
| Develop documentation | Ability to document the merit justification. | Yes |
| **Other** | | |
| Ability to assign a delegate | Ability to assign a delegate to complete compensation planning, i.e. Admin. | Yes |
| Employee Filter | Ability to sort by employee name or data, i.e. first name, last name, employee ID, etc. | Yes |
| Employee Search | Ability to search throughout the tool by employee name or data, i.e. first name, last name, employee ID, etc. | Yes |
| Revert or change functionality | Ability for planning administrators to revert or change submitted data. | Yes |
| Collaborative workflow | Ability for managers, compensation, and HR Partners to collaborate on various compensation workflows. | Yes |
| Display out-of-guideline entries | Ability to display out-of-guideline entries made within adjustments, merit, bonus, equity. | Yes |
| **Reporting** | | |
| Standard reports are delivered with the system | System is delivered with a set number of standard reports. | Yes |

| Function | Function Description | Response |
|---|---|---|
| Ad-hoc reporting capability | System is delivered with an ad-hoc report-writing tool so that clients can create their own reports as needed. | Yes |
| Advanced Value metrics | Data analysis of comp gaps based on roles, hierarchy. | Yes |
| Reporting Security | Ability to enable field-level security and access to report creation, output and distribution. | Yes |
| **Security** | | |
| Logging In | Various login options (i.e. manual, SSO, LDAP). | Yes |
| File Transfer | Various file transfer protocol (i.e. FTP, sFTP, vendor-specific transfer import/export tool). | Yes |
| Encryption | Various data encryption ability (i.e. PGP). | Yes |
| Roles / Permissions | Configurable list of permission-based roles with detailed access rights to various organizations, levels, etc. Typically employees only view within their own organization hierarchy. | Yes |
| Integration | Ability to Integrate organizational data with appropriate org system, i.e. HRIS/Payroll, employee data including employee salaries, levels, performance rating, etc. | Yes |
| Reporting UDFs | Ability to report user-defined fields. | Yes |
| Exporting reports | Reports can easily be exported to other applications (i.e. .xls, .pdf, .txt). | Yes |

| Function | Function Description | Response |
|----------|---------------------|----------|

## Learning Management

| Content Management and Delivery | | |
|--------------------------------|---|---|
| Application Simulation | Client content owners can create application simulations for use in training (i.e. "Show Me"/"Try Me" Flash-type simulations). | No |
| Assign learning content based employee data | Learning content can be assigned to employees based on their job function or organizational data (not specific to position, but job family or organization). | Yes |
| Catalogs | Employees can search through and browse course catalogs to identify courses in which they are interested. | Yes |
| Competency Management - Third-Party Defined | Courses and learning plans can be built around competencies, driven by integration with a third-party vendor. | Yes |
| Competency Management - Customer-Defined | Courses and learning plans can be built around competencies as determined by the customer. | Yes |
| Offline Capabilities | Learning content can be downloaded for completion even if the user is not connected to the Internet/network. Can also upload results. | No |
| Employee Profile Management | System can house employee profiles that can be used for learning plan assignment, development plan creation and management (could be integration point). | Yes |
| External Content Integration | Employees can access, review, and register for courses in systems and online portals that are integrated with the LMS. | Yes |

| Function | Function Description | Response |
|---|---|---|
| Internal Content Authoring | WYSIWYG (what you see is what you get) editor is built into the system for creation of learning materials within the system by client content owners. | No |
| Learning Plans | Customer can create learning plans for employees. Employees can manage their progress, review schedules, register for courses and access online courses from plans. Collaboration with employees and managers to create this learning plan (and appropriate workflow). Could be an integration point from PM tool. | Yes |
| Multiple Languages | System supports multiple languages for global implementations. | Yes |
| PowerPoint Conversion | System allows for uploading of PowerPoint files as learning content. | Yes |
| Repository | Digital repository for management of draft and active content is available in the system. Content managers would use this functionality (and allows for collaboration). | Yes |
| Scheduling | Users can book resources, locations and structures from within the system. This is an integration point as well. | Yes |
| Single Sign-On | Standard SSO capability for integration with client intranet. | Yes |
| Version Control | Content owners have the ability to manage content versioning. | Yes |
| Virtual Classrooms | System provides virtual classroom functionality for live, remote learning sessions. | Yes |

| Function | Function Description | Response |
|---|---|---|
| **Testing and Tracking** | | |
| General Assessments | System allows for creation of assessments that aren't tied to particular training content. Could be tied to competencies. | Yes |
| Content Test Completion | Users can complete tests online as assigned. Could be offline as well. | Yes |
| Content Test Creation | System allows for creation of tests for learning content. | Yes |
| Polling | Polling can be conducted through one or more channels (e.g. Content, User Home Page Interface, etc.). | Yes |
| Test Completion Tracking | User test completion status and rates can be tracked. | Yes |
| Test Score Tracking | User test scores can be stored and tracked. | Yes |
| **Reporting** | | |
| Ad-hoc reporting capability | System is delivered with an ad-hoc report-writing tool so that clients can create their own reports as needed. | Yes |
| Data analysis | System provides functionality for advanced data analysis and dashboarding. | Yes |
| Reporting Security | Ability to enable field-level security and access to report creation, output and distribution. | Yes |
| Standard reports are delivered with the system | System is delivered with a minimum of 10 standard reports. | Yes |

| Function | Function Description | Response |
|---|---|---|
| **Integration** | | |
| Employee Profile Integration | System allows for employee profile integration with other talent management solutions (e.g. Performance, Succession, Compensation, Recruitment, etc.). | Yes |
| Integration | Ability to allow clients to create integrations through APIs, XML, flat files, etc. | Yes |
| **Web 2.0 Features** | | |
| Blogs | System allows for creation of blogs for content delivery. | Yes |
| Forums | System allows for creation and maintenance of forums to capture user-generated content and enable collaborative learning activities. | Yes |
| Other Collaborative Learning Tools | Additional collaborative learning tools are available. | Yes |
| Podcasting | System allows for creation of podcasts for content delivery. | Yes |
| RSS Feeds | System allows users to identify content "tracks" that they wish to monitor on a regular basis and displays updates in an RSS-like format. | Yes |
| Wikis | System allows for creation and maintenance of wikis to capture user-generated content and enable collaborative learning activities. | Yes |
| **User Communication** | | |
| Completion Date Reminders | Users can be notified when they are approaching a target content completion date. | Yes |

| Function | Function Description | Response |
|---|---|---|
| Completion Reminders | Users can be reminded to complete content that has been saved in progress. | Yes |
| Content Notifications | Users can be notified when new content is added to their learning plan or a track in which they are interested. | Yes |
| Manager Notifications | User managers and/or learning administrators can be notified when certain activities are completed. | Yes |
| Workflow | System allows for creation of workflow to communicate user status to content and people managers. | Yes |

# Halogen

## Company Information (provided by Halogen)

**Company Name:**            Halogen Software

**Corporate URL:**           www.halogensoftware.com

**Main Phone:**              (613) 270-1011

**Main Email:**              info@halogensoftware.com

**Headquarters Address:**    495 March Rd., Suite 500,
                             Ottawa, ON K2K 3G1

**Type of Business or Areas of Focus:**
Talent Management Software (Employee Performance Management, Compensation Management, Succession Planning, Learning Management).

**Number of Employees:**     170

**Year Founded:**            2001

**Stock Symbol:**            Privately-held

## Company Description and History:

Founded in 2001, Halogen Software is recognized as a market leader by industry analysts including Gartner, Bersin and IDC, and endorsed by thousands of HR professionals around the world. Halogen provides powerful, award-winning performance and talent management solutions that follow industry best-practices, yet are easy to implement and use.

Halogen's fully integrated web-based solutions allow organizations to quickly automate and streamline their performance management, compensation management, succession planning and learning and development programs. Managers, HR and executives gain fingertip access to the key performance data they need to drive decision making. And Halogen's simple and highly flexible applications give HR full control—so there is never a need to rely on the vendor, incur additional service fees, or wait in line, to get things done right. Industry-specific applications that meet the unique needs of Healthcare, Financial Services and Professional Services organizations come complete with specific content, features and implementation programs to ensure success.

As testament to their customer focus, Halogen is also consistently recognized by the industry and its customers for exceptional implementation and support services and has won multiple awards for its corporate leadership and product innovation, including HR Technology Product of the Year.

## Products/Services/Solutions:

### 1. Halogen eAppraisal

Halogen eAppraisal™ offers organizations a convenient and cost-effective way to develop their critical talent and align organizational goals—year-round. Halogen eAppraisal is a simple to use, flexible and feature-rich employee performance appraisal web application that replaces today's time-consuming paper or spreadsheet-based processes. Feature complete, it has everything an organization needs to automate and simplify employee performance management process, as well as align and develop workforce to drive bottom-line success. The optional Multi-Rater Module makes it convenient to gather and analyze feedback from peers, direct reports, other supervisors on particular competencies or an employee's overall performance.

### 2. Halogen eCompensation

Establishes pay-for-performance and allocates pay increases across the entire organization with ease. Halogen eCompensation™ greatly simplifies and automates the entire compensation management process. It provides all levels of management with secure, easy-to-use tools that manage compensation budget flow down and make distributing merit-based compensation, including base salary, variable pay, bonuses and stock options, a breeze. Fully-integrated with Halogen eAppraisal™, it allows an organization to automatically incorporate employee performance appraisal scores into the compensation adjustment process so it can truly pay for performance.

### 3. Halogen eSuccession

Practical, effective succession planning with immediate results. Halogen eSuccession™ makes it easy and affordable for organizations of all sizes to implement effective succession planning, today. It follows the *Talent Pool Model*—a proven best practice approach to succession planning. It helps establish a larger number of "promoteable" employees, who are more likely to stay loyal and whose skills are better aligned with the organization's strategic plans. Its unique and highly efficient staged approach allows organizations to start today, gathering the information they need while conducting performance appraisals, to enable an understanding of retention risks and workforce potential.

### 4. Halogen eLMS

A learning management system that closely links training with an organization's bottom line success. Halogen eLMS™ melds breakthrough thinking in employee performance management with proven best practices in learning management. Halogen eLMS is a revolutionary, enterprise-class learning management solution that addresses the needs of companies of all sizes. By tying development planning to employee performance assessments, training and development teams can deliver the right instruction at the right time and tangibly measure the resulting performance improvements to validate the effectiveness of those programs.

### 5. Halogen e360

Get broader, richer 'multi-rater' feedback without the processing headaches. Flexible, easy to implement, and simple to use, Halogen e360™ provides all the features needed to conduct Web-based 360-degree feedback assessments. With point and click simplicity, HR administrators can configure the 360-degree evaluation process workflow any way they like. It allows managers or the subjects themselves to select the raters and decide who gets to see the reports. Powerful graphical reporting capabilities make it easy to see results at a glance. It provides the needed insight without the processing demands of traditional 360-degree feedback systems.

## Author's Halogen Functionality Matrix

| Function | Function Description | Response |
|---|---|---|

### Performance Management

| | | |
|---|---|---|
| **Performance Dashboard** | | |
| Dashboard configuration | Ability to configure dashboard based on user preference. | Yes |
| Create and display reports | Display reports that can be generated (i.e. review completion progress, goal progress). | Yes |
| Create and display charts and graphs | Display charts and graphs that are available to feature planning actions. | Yes |
| Display help and reference tools | Display and view help and reference tools that can be selected by link or mouse hover. | Yes |
| **Employee Information Review (Data Import from HRIS/LMS)** | | |
| Import and display employee information | Display name, address, phone, email, location, photo, education (typically pulled from HRIS). | Yes |
| Import and display employee position information | Display current job title, job summary, job family, job level/grade, job code, FLSA, shift, status (FT/PT) (typically pulled through HRIS). | Yes |
| Create and display work history | Display created previous work history (i.e. name of company, job title, responsibilities/duties, employment dates). | Yes |

| Function | Function Description | Response |
|---|---|---|
| Create and display years in management | Display created years of management experience (manually entered or via integration). | Yes |
| Create and display years in industry | Display created years of experience in industry (primarily entered manually). | Yes |
| Import, create and display employee language(s) | Display employee languages (i.e. read, written, fluent) (primarily entered manually). | Yes |
| Import, create and display employee affiliations | Display employee affiliation memberships. | Yes |
| Import, create and display employee certifications | Display employee certifications and dates. | Yes |
| Import, create and display employee licenses | Display employee licenses and dates (usually a text box) - important to include expiration dates (could be for transportation, professional licenses, healthcare licenses, etc.) | Yes |
| Import and display organizational information | Display company name, company division, company department (typically imported from HRIS). | Yes |
| Import and display management hierarchy information | Display multiple levels of management names and information (i.e. Executive Management, Division Head, Department Head, Direct Manager, Employee). | Yes |
| Import and display direct reports | Display name and information of employee direct reports. | Yes |
| Import and display matrix manager hierarchy information | Display multiple levels of matrix management names and information (i.e. Employee has dotted line reporting relationships). | Yes |

| Function | Function Description | Response |
|---|---|---|
| Import and display multiple manager hierarchy information | Display multiple levels of numerous management names and information (i.e. Employee reports to more than one manager directly). | Yes |
| Organizational Chart View | Organizational information can be displayed in an Org Chart view (note how this is displayed visually). | No |
| Organizational Change Requests | Due to potential errors within HRMS, manager has the ability to request an employee change in hierarchy (i.e. manager name, organization, location, job role); changes can be configured to require approval. | Yes |
| Import and display employee current and past compensation | Display employee's past and current base salary, bonus, equity, commission, etc. | Yes |
| Import and display employee most recent performance measures | Display employee's current competencies, goals, skills, projects, performance rating, development plan, personal improvement plan. | Yes |
| Import and display employee previous performance measures | Display employee's previous competencies, goals, skills, projects, performance rating, development plan, personal improvement plan. | Yes |
| Complete and display employee training | Display employee's completed and assigned training (i.e. mandatory/development) - Note if there is any integration with LMS. | Yes |
| External Identifier | Ability to have an external identifier field to bring in content on goals from a third-party application (i.e. description, start date, critical, public goal) - can be configured to be read-only for imports. | No |

| Function | Function Description | Response |
|----------|---------------------|----------|
| UDFs | Available user-defined fields for employee profile. | Yes |
| **Career Planning / Personal Development (Employee)** | | |
| Create and display future career plan scenarios | Display multiple future career plans (vertical, horizontal, both). Where does the employee want to go next? (lateral, promotion, etc.) | Yes |
| Select and display positions, job families and organizations/divisions of interest | Display selected positions and organizations of interest from import of job list and organization list (mentorships and cross-training) - gives the employee the opportunity to identify a position, job-family or organization of interest. | No |
| Create and display training requests | Display developmental training requests (entered by an employee or manager) - this could be an integration point to the LMS. | Yes |
| Create and display executive/professional requests | Display various executive/professional requests (i.e. executive coaching, cross-training, job shadowing, speaking engagements, writing submittals, managing people, presentations, mentoring, apprenticeships). | Yes |
| Create and display organization affiliations and/or conferences/seminars | Display employee organization/affiliation or conference/seminar requests to join or attend. | Yes |
| Select and display competency development | Display selected desired competencies (entered by employee). | Yes |
| Create self-asses job readiness | Display selected self-readiness from list of options (i.e. Now, 0-3 months, 3-6 months, 6-9 months, 9-12 months, 12 months +). | No |

| Function | Function Description | Response |
|---|---|---|
| Display position Gap % | Display gap % of employee readiness to ideal position as well as required training, license(s), education, certification(s) - this could be automatically calculated by the system (key differentiator). This is a gap analysis on the underlying competencies (most recent performance rating vs. competencies required for next position). | Yes |
| Select and display willingness to relocate | Display selected willingness to relocate (i.e. yes, no, maybe, comments). | Yes |
| Display career pre-requisites | Display required training, education, certification(s), license(s) for position of interest. | Yes |
| Submit development requests for approval | Submit development self- assessments to direct manager for review, feedback and approval (areas where the development needs to occur, as well as specific courses, conferences to help meet these development areas). Could be an integration point with LMS. | Yes |
| **Career Development (Manager)** | | |
| Create or select and display employee training goals | Display created or selected employee completed training, assigned training (mandatory/development), scheduled training and employee training requests. This is the manager identifying training goals for an employee. | Yes |
| Competency Development | Display assigned professional/leadership competencies. | Yes |

| Function | Function Description | Response |
|----------|---------------------|----------|
| Create and display executive/professional assignments | Display various executive/professional recommendations (i.e. executive coaching, cross training, job shadowing, speaking engagements, writing submittals, managing people, presentations, mentoring, apprenticeships). | |
| Create and display organization affiliations and/or conferences/seminars | Display employee organization/affiliation or conference/seminar recommendations. | Yes |
| **Individual Goal / Self-Assessment (Employee)** | | |
| Select, create and display individual development goals | Display selected or created completed training, improvement competencies, executive coaching, promotion, cross training. | Yes |
| Select competency development | Display selected development competencies - this is where employees select competencies they want to develop for their career on the annual review. | No |
| Submit goal/competency assessment for approval | Submit manual or automatic goal/competency assessment to direct manager. | Yes |
| Solicit and display feedback | Select employees (i.e. managers, matrix managers, peers) to solicit performance feedback (i.e. 360, peer review, business review) and display results. | Yes |
| Create and display self-performance notes | Display created performance notes (i.e. kudos) throughout the review cycle (manually entered by employee or can solicit feedback throughout project). | Yes |
| Create and display self-goal assessment progress | Display created self-goal progress (i.e. quantitative % of completion, qualitative to include customer satisfaction, timeline to include start/completion date). | Yes |

| Function | Function Description | Response |
|----------|---------------------|----------|
| Submit goal/competency review for approval | Submit manual or automatic goal/competency assessment to direct manager and higher levels. | Yes |
| UDFs | Available user-defined fields for employee goals. | No |
| **Review Process (Employee and Manager)** | | |
| Select and display competencies | Display selected professional or leadership competencies. | Yes |
| Select and display goals/objectives | Display selected goals/objectives (i.e. quantitative and/or qualitative). | Yes |
| Select and display goal alignment | Display selected goal alignment to company, organization, department and/or manager goals (cascading goals). | Yes |
| Select or create and display projects | Display selected or created projects. | Yes |
| Select and display project alignment to goals | Display selected project alignment to company, organization, department and/or manager goals. | Yes |
| Select or create and display skills | Display selected or created company, organization, department, employee skills. | Yes |
| Create and display employee performance notes | Display created performance notes (positive or negative) throughout the review cycle. These are notes created by the manager. | Yes |
| Solicit and display feedback | Select employees (i.e. managers, matrix managers, peers) to solicit performance feedback (i.e. 360, peer review, business review) and display. Pay particular attention to how this feedback is gathered and entered into the system. | Yes |

| Function | Function Description | Response |
|---|---|---|
| Create and display employee goal assessment review | Display created employee goal progress (i.e. quantitative % of completion, qualitative to include customer satisfaction, timeline to include start/completion date) - this is the manager entering his/her assessment. | Yes |
| Performance review filtering | Manager can filter performance review information based on approval status, assigned to, author/owner, manager, employee, organization, location, job field, job role, review cycle, review group, review group owner, overall rating; filtering can be cumulative. | Yes |
| Batch activities | Manager can take group actions on multiple employees simultaneously. | Yes |
| UDFs | Available user-defined fields for employee competencies. | Yes |
| **Workflow** | | |
| Review cycles | Ability to configure multiple review cycles and tied to various reviews. | Yes |
| Review groups | Ability to define review recipients based on dates, job function, organization, job code, etc. | Yes |
| Workflow Order | Ability to configure order of workflow (i.e. self-assessments can be configured to be completed first). | Yes |
| Notifications | Ability to push reviews to employees and managers. | Yes |
| Reminders | Ability to send reminders to employees and managers via email (manual and automatic). | Yes |

| Function | Function Description | Response |
|---|---|---|
| Acknowledgements | Ability to send auto-acknowledgements triggered by event/activity. | Yes |
| Next Level Approval | Ability to auto/manually route to multiple levels of approval. | Yes |
| Configurable work-flow | Ability to configure various steps of the review process, to make review steps mandatory, to have manager override ability, to display/hide visual graphic workflow diagram. | Yes |
| Auto/Manual Progression | Ability to automatically or manually progress through the review process. | Yes |
| Review form | Exportable and printable review form. | Yes |
| **System Admin** | | |
| Review sections | Ability to configure multiple review sections, including goals, competencies, comments, rating models, etc. | Yes |
| Configurable rating models | Does it configure and display alpha and numeric values? Can values be rounded (up/down/both), value ranges, number of decimals (1-5)? | Yes |
| Comments | Displayed and available in individual review sections and overall review. Can they be configured to be mandatory and ability to be overridden by management? | Yes |
| Goals | Ability to link organizational, divisional, departmental, individual goals into sections and ability to display goal progress. | Yes |
| Competencies | Ability to link competencies into sections. | Yes |
| Weightings | Ability to weigh employee performance based on goals and competencies. | Yes |

| Function | Function Description | Response |
|---|---|---|
| **Search Functionality** | | |
| Basic Employee Search | Basic search by employee name (i.e. first or last name or a combination of both). | Yes |
| Job/Position Basic Search | Basic search by job role or position title, etc. | Yes |
| Competency Basic Search | Basic search by competency name. | Yes |
| Advanced Search | More detailed search capabilities that combine various search criteria or fields - may include optional weighting to determine which employees are retrieved in a search as well as each person's rank in the search results. | No |
| Succession Planning Search | Search functionality that dynamically generates the criteria used to match employees who would make good succession candidates with a specific position profile (could have various levels of "fit"). | Yes |
| **Employee View / Navigation / Help / Other** | | |
| List View | Display employee goals, business goals or projects; the list mode is a menu of items with information on key dates and progress. | Yes |
| Card View | Display employee goals, business goals or projects using the card mode; the card mode provides details on one item at a time and offers the possibility of editing progress. This can also include employee photos as well. | No |
| Timeline / Gantt | Display employee goals, business goals or projects using the timeline mode; the timeline mode provides a timeline view of an item's start and due dates. | Yes |

| Function | Function Description | Response |
|----------|---------------------|----------|
| Org Chart | Managers can access and manage information on their direct reports for all functionalities activated; the organizational chart will provide key data (i.e. risk of loss or most recent performance rating) for each of the manager's direct reports. | No |
| Mini-Org Chart | Displays a single analytic data point at a time; the manager can drill down into all layers of his organization and can view key metrics (i.e. performance reviews, goals, succession). | No |
| Graphs | Graphical display of various information (i.e. Gap Analysis, goal progress, review completion progress). | Yes |
| Help Links | Online help, FAQs, customer support, product version. | Yes |
| Attach Documents | Ability to attach reference documents to various sections within the system. | Yes |
| Browser capabilities | Supported by general Internet access (works with standard browsers: IE, Safari, Mozilla, Opera). | Yes |
| Mouse-Over Hover | Additional tooltips or descriptions that display when user hovers mouse pointer over various graphics or words within the system. | Yes |
| Web 2.0 | Ability to utilize Web 2.0 functionality, i.e. social networking. | No |
| **Security** | | |
| Logging In | Various login options (i.e. manual, SSO, LDAP). | Yes |

| Function | Function Description | Response |
|---|---|---|
| File Transfer | Various file transfer protocol (i.e. FTP, sFTP, vendor-specific transfer import/export tool). | Yes |
| Encryption | Various data encryption ability (i.e. PGP). | Yes |
| Roles / Permissions | Configurable list of permission-based roles with detailed access rights to various organizations, levels, etc. Typically employees only view within their own organization hierarchy. | Yes |
| Integration | Ability to integrate organizational data i.e. HRIS/ATS/ LMS and employee data including competencies, training, development plans, etc. | Yes |
| **Reporting** | | |
| Standard reports are delivered with the system | System is delivered with a set number of standard reports. | Yes |
| Ad-hoc reporting capability | System is delivered with an ad-hoc report writing tool so that a client can create own reports as needed. | No |
| Advanced Value metrics | Data analysis of employee review process status, goal progress by hierarchy. | Yes |
| Reporting Security | Ability to enable field-level security and access to report creation, output and distribution. | No |
| Reporting UDFs | Ability to report user-defined fields. | Yes |
| Exporting reports | Reports can easily be exported to other applications (i.e. .xls, .pdf, .txt). | Yes |

| Function | Function Description | Response |
|---|---|---|

## Succession Planning

| Succession Planning (Manager - Planning of Individual Talent Roles) | | |
|---|---|---|
| Create and display critical roles for today | Display critical job roles (i.e. title, level, location, division, organization). | No |
| Create and display critical roles for future | Display critical job roles (i.e. title, level, location, division, organization) for future (workforce planning-like tools). | No |
| Calculate and display performance rating | Performance rating is automatically averaged from various sections of the performance review and displayed (current and past). | Yes |
| Calculate and display performance ranking | High potential employees will be automatically ranked according to order of fit with critical role (i.e. 9-box grid, numeric ranking, high performer, high potential) - can be ranked by position, organization, etc. | Yes |
| Multi-dimensional matrix | Matrix that can be configured up to various # of cells (i.e. 9-box, 12-box, 16-box, 25-box); text within grid is configurable. | No |
| Various dimensions of matrix | Matrix displays employee performance, potential, number of succession plans an employee is on, years in management, years in industry. | No |
| Navigation from multi-dimensional matrix | Manager can select an employee within the matrix and navigate to employee information (i.e. Performance review, talent profile, employee goals, career plan). | Yes |

| Function | Function Description | Response |
|---|---|---|
| Display employee comparisons | Display comparison of multiple high potential employees according to fit to critical role (i.e. # of employees to compare, comparable data, fit gap analysis, ranking analysis, bench strength). | Yes |
| Create and display role readiness | Manager can create and display high potential employee role readiness (i.e. now, 0-3 months, 3-6 months, 6-9 months, 9-12 months, 12+ months). | Yes |
| Create and display retention risk | Manager can create and display high potential employee retention/loss/flight risk (i.e. high, medium, low, comments). | Yes |
| Create and display role willingness | Manager can create and display high potential employee role willingness (i.e. yes, no, comments). | No |
| Create and display willingness to relocate | Manager can create and display high potential employee willingness to relocate (i.e. yes, no, maybe, comments). | No |
| Create and display willingness to travel | Manager can create and display high potential employee willingness to travel (i.e. none, 25-50%, 50-75%, 75-100%). | No |
| Create and display interest in international assignment | Manager can create and display high potential employee interest in international assignment (i.e. yes, no, maybe). | No |
| Create and display interim replacement for critical role | Manager can create and display high potential interim replacement for critical roles. | No |
| Display of gap analysis | Automatically calculate and display high potential fit gap analysis of employee to next position and ranking analysis of employee to that next position. | Yes |
| UDFs | Available user-defined fields for succession planning. | Yes |

| Function | Function Description | Response |
|----------|---------------------|----------|
| **Succession Pooling (Manager - Planning of a Talent Pool for Critical Roles)** |||
| Display high potential pool | Display nominated and/or approved high potential pool (i.e. employee information, designated nominators, designated approvers, approvals, rejections, role readiness, rejection comments). | Yes |
| Calculate and display performance rating | Performance rating is automatically averaged from various sections of the performance review and displayed (current and past). | Yes |
| Calculate and display performance ranking | Pool of high potential employees will be automatically ranked according to order of fit with critical role (i.e. 9-box grid, numeric ranking, high performer, high potential). | Yes |
| Display employee comparisons | Display comparison of multiple high potential employees according to fit to critical role (i.e. # of employees to compare, comparable data, fit gap analysis, ranking analysis, bench strength). | Yes |
| Create and display role readiness | Manager can create and display high potential employee role readiness (i.e. now, 0-3 months, 3-6 months, 6-9 months, 9-12 months, 12+ months). | Yes |
| Create and display retention risk | Manager can create and display high potential employee retention/loss/flight risk (i.e. high, medium, low, comments). | Yes |
| Create and display role willingness | Manager can create and display high potential employee role willingness (i.e. yes, no, comments). | No |
| Create and display willingness to relocate | Manager can create and display high potential employee willingness to relocate (i.e. yes, no, maybe, comments). | No |

| Function | Function Description | Response |
|----------|--------------------|----------| 
| Create and display willingness to travel | Manager can create and display high potential employee willingness to travel (i.e. none, 25-50%, 50-75%, 75-100%). | No |
| Create and display interest in international assignment | Manager can create and display high potential employee interest in international assignment (i.e. yes, no, maybe). | No |
| Create and display interim replacement for critical role | Manager can create and display high potential interim replacement for critical roles. | No |
| Display of gap analysis | Automatically calculate and display high potential employees' fit gap analysis to position and ranking analysis of employee to position. | Yes |
| UDFs | Available user-defined fields for succession pooling. | Yes |
| **Workflow** | | |
| Succession approval workflow | Ability to define or edit approvers, add/remove users and roles, ability to change the approval order, ability to reject with comments. | Yes |
| Nominations for succession pool | Ability to nominate, reject and enter comments on nominated HiPo employees. | Yes |
| **Reporting** | | |
| Standard reports are delivered with the system | System is delivered with a set number of standard reports. | Yes |
| Ad-hoc reporting capability | System is delivered with an ad-hoc report-writing tool so that a client can create own reports as needed. | No |

| Function | Function Description | Response |
|---|---|---|
| Advanced Value metrics | Data analysis of high performers / high potential employees, identified gaps, critical roles. | Yes |
| Reporting Security | Ability to enable field-level security and access to report creation, output and distribution. | Yes |
| Reporting UDFs | Ability to report user-defined fields. | Yes |
| Exporting reports | Reports can easily be exported to other applications (i.e. .xls, .pdf, .txt). | Yes |

## Compensation Management

| Compensation Dashboard | | |
|---|---|---|
| Dashboard configuration | Ability to configure dashboard based on user preference. | No |
| Create and display a compensation worksheet | Display a compensation worksheet. that will provide individual and org planning status and detail. | Yes |
| Create and display reports | Display reports that can be generated, i.e. budget usage by merit, bonus, equity, adjustment and percent of planning completed. | Yes |
| Create and display charts and graphs | Display charts and graphs that are available to feature planning actions. | Yes |
| Import and display allocation guidelines | Display compensation allocation guidelines for merit, bonus, equity and adjustments - also refer to the time allocation/workflow to complete this process. | Yes |
| Import and display eligibility guidelines | Display employee eligibility guidelines for planning, i.e. FT, PT, commission, LOA, new hire, etc. Guidelines are input by compensation department. | Yes |

| Function | Function Description | Response |
|---|---|---|
| Display help and reference tools | Display and view help and reference tools that can be selected by link or mouse hover. | Yes |
| **Compensation Budget** | | |
| Import and display multiple aggregate planning budget by org | Display multiple approved allocated budget by diverse business groups on all pages (usually imported from financial system). | Yes |
| Import and display aggregate merit budget by org | Display approved allocated merit budget by diverse business groups on all pages. | Yes |
| Import and display aggregate bonus budget by org | Display approved allocated bonus by diverse business groups on all pages. | Yes |
| Import and display aggregate equity budget by org | Display approved allocated equity budget by diverse business groups on all pages. | Yes |
| Import and display aggregate adjust-ment budget by org | Display approved allocated adjustment budget by diverse business groups on all pages. | Yes |
| **Employee Information Review** | | |
| Import and display employee Informa-tion | Display name, location, photo, org, direct manager (typically imported from PM tool). | Yes |
| Import and display employee position | Display current job title, job code, level/grade. | Yes |
| Import and display employee prior compensation plan-ning period data | Display current hourly rate, annual rate, bonus percent, bonus amount, equity allocation, total compensation. | Yes |

| Function | Function Description | Response |
|---|---|---|
| Import and display employee prior performance rating | Display prior performance rating. | Yes |
| Import and display new employee performance rating | Display new performance rating. | Yes |
| Import and display employee's position salary range | Display employee's salary range. | Yes |
| Import and display salary penetration % based on position salary range | Display % of penetration that employee's salary falls within the range. | Yes |
| **Promotion** | | |
| Display position information | Ability to select and display job titles, job codes, job level/grades. | No |
| Import and display corporate promotion guidelines | Ability to display promotion guidelines per position including salary range and percent increase guidelines. | No |
| Promotion amount | Ability to enter promotion percent or amount. | No |
| Auto-calculate promotion amount | System to auto-populate promotion amount based on percent increase. | No |
| Ability to calculate hourly rate | System to auto-populate new hourly rate based on promotion increase. | No |
| Ability to auto-calculate annual rate | System to auto-populate new annual rate based on promotion increase. | No |
| Promotion approval chain | TBD. | No |

| Function | Function Description | Response |
|----------|--------------------|----------|
| Develop documentation | Ability to document the promotion justification. | No |
| **Adjustment** | | |
| Import and display adjustment guidelines | Ability to display adjustment allocation guidelines, including salary range and percent increase guidelines. | Yes |
| Adjustment allocation | Ability to enter and submit an adjustment percent or amount. | Yes |
| Auto-calculate hourly amount | System to auto-populate new hourly rate based on adjustment percent increase. | Yes |
| Auto-calculate adjustment amount | System to auto-populate new annual rate based on adjustment percent increase. | Yes |
| Adjustment approvals | | Yes |
| Develop documentation | Ability to document the adjustment justification. | Yes |
| **Merit** | | |
| Import and display promotion guidelines | Ability to display merit allocation guidelines including salary range and percent increase guidelines. | Yes |
| Performance-based recommendations | Merit allocation can be based on performance rating. | Yes |
| Merit allocation | Ability to enter and submit a merit percent or amount. | Yes |
| Import and display proration of merit based on hire date | System to auto-calculate merit increase based on hire date, i.e. less than one year would be calculated by months employed. | Yes |

| Function | Function Description | Response |
|---|---|---|
| Auto-calculate hourly amount | System to auto-populate new hourly rate based on merit percent increase. | Yes |
| Auto-calculate adjustment amount | System to auto-populate new annual rate based on merit percent increase. | Yes |
| Merit approvals | | Yes |
| Develop documentation | Ability to document the merit justification. | Yes |
| **Bonus** | | |
| Import and display bonus allocation guidelines | Ability to display bonus allocation guidelines | Yes |
| Performance based recommendations | Bonus allocation can be based on performance rating. | Yes |
| Bonus allocation | Ability to enter and submit a bonus percent or amount. | Yes |
| Bonus adjustment | Auto-Proration of bonus based on hired or leave, i.e. severance date. | Yes |
| Bonus approvals | Ability to obtain appropriate approvals (workflow to select appropriate approvers). | Yes |
| Develop documentation | Ability to document the merit justification. | Yes |
| **Equity** | | |
| Import and display equity allocation guidelines | Ability to display equity allocation guidelines. | Yes |
| Performance-based recommendations | Equity allocation can be based on performance rating. | Yes |

| Function | Function Description | Response |
|---|---|---|
| Equity allocation | Ability to enter and submit equity percent or amount. | Yes |
| Equity allocation adjustment | Auto-Proration of equity allocation based on hire date. | Yes |
| Equity approvals | | Yes |
| Develop documen-tation | Ability to document the merit justification. | Yes |
| **Other** | | |
| Ability to assign a delegate | Ability to assign a delegate to complete compensation planning, i.e. Admin. | Yes |
| Employee Filter | Ability to sort by employee name or data, i.e. first name, last name, employee ID, etc. | Yes |
| Employee Search | Ability to search throughout the tool by employee name or data, i.e. first name, last name, employee ID, etc. | Yes |
| Revert or change functionality | Ability for planning administrators to revert or change submitted data. | No |
| Collaborative work-flow | Ability for managers, compensation and HR Partners to collaborate on various compensation workflows. | Yes |
| Display out-of-guideline entries | Ability to display out-of-guideline entries made within adjustments, merit, bonus, equity. | Yes |
| **Reporting** | | |
| Standard reports are delivered with the system | System is delivered with a set number of standard reports. | Yes |

| Function | Function Description | Response |
|---|---|---|
| Ad-hoc reporting capability | System is delivered with an ad-hoc re-port-writing tool so that clients can create their own reports as needed. | No |
| Advanced Value metrics | Data analysis of comp gaps based on roles, hierarchy. | No |
| Reporting Security | Ability to enable field-level security and access to report creation, output and distribution. | Yes but not field-level |
| **Security** | | |
| Logging In | Various login options (i.e. manual, SSO, LDAP). | Yes |
| File Transfer | Various file transfer protocol (i.e. FTP, sFTP, vendor-specific transfer import/ex-port tool). | Yes |
| Encryption | Various data encryption ability (i.e. PGP). | Yes |
| Roles / Permissions | Configurable list of permission-based roles with detailed access rights to vari-ous organizations, levels, etc. Typically employees only view within their own organization hierarchy. | Yes |
| Integration | Ability to integrate organizational data with appropriate org system, i.e. HRIS/Payroll, employee data, including employee salaries, levels, performance rating, etc. | Yes |
| Reporting UDFs | Ability to report user-defined fields. | Yes |
| Exporting reports | Reports can easily be exported to other applications (i.e. .xls, .pdf, .txt). | Yes |

| Function | Function Description | Response |
|---|---|---|

## Learning Management

| Content Management and Delivery | | |
|---|---|---|
| Application Simulation | Client content owners can create application simulations for use in training (i.e. "Show Me"/"Try Me" Flash-type simulations). | No |
| Assign learning content-based employee data | Learning content can be assigned to employees based on their job function or organizational data (not specific to position, but job family or organization). | Yes |
| Catalogs | Employees can search through and browse course catalogs to identify courses in which they are interested. | Yes |
| Competency Management – Third-Party Defined | Courses and learning plans can be built around competencies, driven by integration with a third-party vendor. | Yes |
| Competency Management - Customer Defined | Courses and learning plans can be built around competencies as determined by the customer. | Yes |
| Offline Capabilities | Learning content can be downloaded for completion even if the user is not connected to the Internet/network. Can also upload results. | Yes |
| Employee Profile Management | System can house employee profiles that can be used for learning plan assignment, development plan creation and management (could be integration point). | Yes |
| External Content Integration | Employees can access, review and register for courses in systems and online portals that are integrated with the LMS. | Yes |

| Function | Function Description | Response |
|---|---|---|
| Internal Content Authoring | WYSIWYG (what you see is what you get) editor is built into the system for creation of learning materials within the system by client content owners. | No |
| Learning Plans | Customer can create learning plans for employees. Employees can manage their progress, review schedules, register for courses and access online courses from plans. Collaboration with employees and managers to create this learning plan (and appropriate workflow). Could be an integration point from PM tool. | Yes |
| Multiple Languages | System supports multiple languages for global implementations. | Yes |
| PowerPoint Conversion | System allows for uploading of PowerPoint files as learning content. | Yes |
| Repository | Digital repository for management of draft and active content is available in the system. Content managers would use this functionality (and allows for collaboration). | Yes |
| Scheduling | Users can book resources, locations, and structures from within the system. This is an integration point as well. | Yes |
| Single Sign-On | Standard SSO capability for integration with client Intranet. | Yes |
| Version Control | Content owners have the ability to manage content versioning. | Yes |
| Virtual Classrooms | System provides virtual classroom functionality for live, remote learning sessions. | No |

| Function | Function Description | Response |
|---|---|---|
| **Testing and Tracking** | | |
| General Assessments | System allows for creation of assessments that aren't tied to particular training content. Could be tied to competencies. | Yes |
| Content Test Completion | Users can complete tests online as assigned. Could be offline as well. | Yes |
| Content Test Creation | System allows for creation of tests for learning content. | No |
| Polling | Polling can be conducted through one or more channels (e.g. Content, User Home Page Interface, etc.). | No |
| Test Completion Tracking | User test completion status and rates can be tracked. | Yes |
| Test Score Tracking | User test scores can be stored and tracked. | Yes |
| **Reporting** | | |
| Ad-hoc reporting capability | System is delivered with an ad-hoc report-writing tool so that clients can create reports as needed. | No |
| Data analysis | System provides functionality for advanced data analysis and dashboarding. | Yes |
| Reporting Security | Ability to enable field-level security and access to report creation, output and distribution. | Security based on position within the organization |
| Standard reports are delivered with the system | System is delivered with a minimum of 10 standard reports. | Yes |

| Function | Function Description | Response |
|---|---|---|
| **Integration** | | |
| Employee Profile Integration | System allows for employee profile integration with other talent management solutions (e.g. Performance, Succession, Compensation, Recruitment, etc.). | Yes |
| Integration | Ability to allow clients to create integrations through APIs, XML, flat files, etc. | Yes |
| **Web 2.0 Features** | | |
| Blogs | System allows for creation of blogs for content delivery. | No |
| Forums | System allows for creation and maintenance of forums to capture user-generated content and enable collaborative learning activities. | No |
| Other Collaborative Learning Tools | Additional collaborative learning tools are available. | No |
| Podcasting | System allows for creation of podcasts for content delivery. | No |
| RSS Feeds | System allows users to identify content "tracks" that they wish to monitor on a regular basis and displays updates in an RSS-like format. | No |
| Wikis | System allows for creation and maintenance of wikis to capture user-generated content and enable collaborative learning activities. | No |
| **User Communication** | | |
| Completion Date Reminders | Users can be notified when they are approaching a target content completion date. | Yes |

| Function | Function Description | Response |
|----------|---------------------|----------|
| Completion Reminders | Users can be reminded to complete content that has been saved in progress. | Yes |
| Content Notifications | Users can be notified when new content is added to their learning plan or a track in which they are interested. | Yes |
| Manager Notifications | User managers and/or learning administrators can be notified when certain activities are completed. | Yes |
| Workflow | System allows for creation of workflow to communicate user status to content and people managers. | Yes |

# HRsmart

## Company Information (provided by HRsmart)

**Company Name:**        HRsmart

**Corporate URL:**        www.hrsmart.com

**Main Phone:**        (972) 783-3000

**Main Email:**        marketing@hrsmart.com

**Headquarters Address:**        2929 North Central Expressway, Suite 110, Richardson, TX 75080

**Type of Business or Areas of Focus:**

Talent Management software; Applicant Tracking System, Employee Performance Management System, Career Development and Succession Planning and Learning Management System modules.

**Number of Employees:**        200

**Year Founded:**        1999

**Stock Symbol:**        N/A

## Company Description and History:

HRsmart was founded as a career board in 1999 and shortly after developed the Applicant Tracking System, the first in a series of HRsmart Talent Management solutions.

Today, HRsmart is a leading global provider of unified Talent Management applications that provides the fully-integrated Talent Management Application Suite, including Applicant Tracking, Performance Management, Career Development and Succession Planning and Learning Management. HRsmart's mission is to provide technology, professional expertise and exceptional support services to companies of all sizes, enabling them to effectively recruit, manage and retain top performers.

HRsmart's Talent Management Application Suite brings together every aspect of the Talent Management process into a single, comprehensive view of each employee and allows greater levels of configurability to enable clients to change processes more quickly as they grow in their Talent Management strategy.

Its current technology application suite is organically grown and part of a unified system that provides users with a single point of access for all applications, as well as cross-functional reporting that delivers a bird's-eye-view of an organization's entire human capital performance.

HRsmart is truly a global Talent Management software company, with operations and application development sites in 11 countries and expanding. HRsmart currently has 200 employees and more than 650 clients, including Dr. Pepper Snapple Group, American Eagle, Turner Construction, The Container Store, Rosewood Hotels, CompuCom and Drexel University.

## Products/Services/Solutions:

### 1. Applicant Tracking System

HRsmart's Applicant Tracking System expedites the recruiting and hiring process, while reducing the costs per hire by as much as 40 percent, through the use of robust technology that can interface with most existing HRIS/HRMS and is configurable to meet the unique needs of the company. The system comes standard with tools to facilitate sourcing, screening, interview scheduling, offer management and onboarding.

### 2. Employee Performance System

HRsmart's Employee Performance Management System can accommodate an organization's current appraisal process while adding new functionality that can only be obtained through an electronic process such as automated scheduling and reminders, continuous appraisal and feedback and complete tracking and documentation of all performance-related activities. This unique system function, based on industry best practices, facilitates the four-phased performance process and goal alignment strategies.

### 3. Career Development and Succession Planning System

HRsmart's Career Development & Succession Planning System enables an organization to track employees' career plans and goals along with skills and abilities, in order to map them to the organization's goals and leadership needs. Company executives have access to key reporting features to uncover talent gaps, view domino reports and identify mission critical positions.

### 4. Learning Management System

HRsmart's Learning Management System is a valuable resource for providing training to internal employees and external business partners or customers. The system facilities delivery of content from internal and external sources and gives an organization the ability to track learning activities and tie them to employee performance assessments.

## Author's HRsmart Functionality Matrix

| Function | Function Description | Response |
|---|---|---|

Talent Acquisition

| Requisition Management & Posting | | |
|---|---|---|
| Multiple requisition forms allowed (Example: hourly, internal transfer, business unit specific, reoccurring, sourcing, college) | More than one requisition form/template can be configured in a client's database to accommodate variance in business units or type of recruiting. (Example: A user from the Manufacturing group can enter a requisition and only see and populate fields that are applicable to Mfg. A different user from the Services group can enter a requisition and only see the fields designated for a Services requisition within the same database. | Yes |

| Function | Function Description | Response |
|---|---|---|
| Data Segregation | Ability to segregate requisitions and candidates by hire type (executive, HR, etc.) or organization. | Yes |
| Requisition approval routing workflow and approval status indicator | Select a list of approvers, route for approval via email. Approvals should be able to be sent in parallel or sequentially. | Yes |
| Approval status tracking | The status of the approval process is tracked and displayed real-time on the requisition in the application as well as in the subsequent emails that go to the second and third approver, etc. | Yes |
| Pre-defined approval routing lists | Lists of approvers can be created, saved, and/or assigned to a user or requisition, or defined by the organizational structure automatically. | Yes |
| Approvals can take place directly from an email | When approving a requisition, the approver can take action directly from the email notification without having to log into the application. | Yes |
| Pre-qualifying questions based on position/job needs, including weighting to filter for top candidates | Questions developed, defined and delivered to a candidate in the online application process tied directly to the job posting/requirements, including weighting to filter for top candidates. | Yes |
| Knock-out questions | Ability to establish certain questions to be disqualifiers, where if the candidate does not answer correctly, the process is ended. | Yes |
| Job posting scheduling | Check a box to select the appropriate career site(s) for the job to appear. Scheduling of start and end dates of posting to any given site to allow for staggered posting. | Yes |

| Function | Function Description | Response |
|---|---|---|
| Advanced job descriptions - Formatting and Spell Checking | Ability to edit and format job descriptions and marketing messages with MS Word, like functions for Bolding, Underlining and Spell Checking. | Yes |
| Electronic job board relationship management (facilitation of job positing to all e-media providers) | Ability to identify and post job opportunities to an unlimited number of electronic job boards and other end destinations. Ability to multi-select boards and push positions out to the market. | Yes |
| **Candidate Experience** | | |
| Unlimited Career Site portals | Ability to establish an unlimited number of integrated career sites for different purposes - such as college recruiting, location-specific kiosks or for a specific job family like Sales or Engineering. Determine if there are additional costs per Career Section. | Yes |
| Online profile form(s) defined by the client | Data collection form(s) that can be pushed to a candidate to gather needed information for relationship management and interested resume submissions. Customers can tailor the form to their specification, adding or removing fields. | Yes |
| User-defined secure login user name and password. | User-created login and password authentication for accessing profile and career management activities. | Yes |
| Candidate login optional | Candidate can submit resume and apply to jobs without establishing a password-protected user account. | No |
| Resume submission via upload of file - Candidate | Candidate can browse the hard drive for formatted resume and upload to candidate resume repository. | Yes |

| Function | Function Description | Response |
|---|---|---|
| Resume submission via upload of file - Recruiter/Manager | Recruiter/Manager can browse the hard drive for formatted resume and upload to candidate resume repository. | Yes |
| Resume builder functionality | Ability for candidates without a formal resume to submit a resume via a "Resume Builder." | Yes |
| Extraction of data from resume to create profile | Extraction engine behind the text or uploaded resume for population of fielded data in the candidate profile. | Yes |
| Candidate-defined Job Agents | Candidates can establish job search parameters and be notified when jobs are posted which meet their preferences. | Yes |
| Candidate status check | Candidates can login to check the status of their resume submissions. | Yes |
| Ability to upload attachments | | Yes |
| Ability for candidate to save a submission as a draft | | No |
| Candidate self-withdrawal | Ability for candidates to remove themselves from consideration for a position. | Yes |
| Conceptual search for the candidate when searching for jobs | Candidates can use "free form" language to search for jobs. | Yes |
| Sourcing/CRM | | |
| Specific job referral and general referrals | Employees can submit a resume as a general referral or to a specific job. | Yes |
| Notifications to the referring employee and the referred candidate | Email notifications are automatically sent to the employee making the referral and to the candidate who was referred. | Yes |

| Function | Function Description | Response |
|---|---|---|
| Referral status check | Employees can review a list of candidates they have referred and check their status. | Yes |
| Tracking steps and status searches | Recruiters can search for candidates based on their tracking steps and status against requisitions | Yes |
| Keyword search against free form text and fielded data | Keyword search against text records from candidate and fielded data in the same search. | Yes |
| Search criteria high-lighted for relevance in record review | Search results with indicators for criteria matching and relevance in the results. | Yes |
| Configurable search results list | The column headers that are displayed in a search results list can be configured with different data elements from the candidate record. (Example: Education, Work History, Phone Number). | Yes |
| Ability to search file attachments | Keyword searching will scan the re-sumes that have been submitted as file attachments as well as text fields. | Yes |
| Ability to create "overnight" searches | | Yes |
| Conceptual search engine to match resumes | Ability to use the requisition's job description or a large text phrase to find matching resumes using a concep-tual search or natural language search engine. Conceptual searches should also be able to be conducted with fielded search. | Yes |
| "More like this" searching | Ability to take a resume and conduct a search to find other resumes that are similar to it (more like it). | Yes |

| Function | Function Description | Response |
|---|---|---|
| Library of candidate correspondence/ communication templates | Ability for clients to create a library of correspondence templates that can be sent to candidates at the user's discretion. | Yes |
| Editable correspondence at the user level | Users can make edits to the correspondence at the time of generation and distribution. | Yes |
| Agency Portal | Functionality designed for the management of third party staffing agencies. Includes the ability to push requisitions to one or more suppliers and receive agency resume submissions. | Yes |
| Contingent Labor Management | Functionality designed specifically for the requisition and management of contract labor including the distribution of job requirements to multiple vendors, submission and review of resumes, tracking of assignment, time reporting and billing. | Yes |
| Candidate Pool Generation (Leads/ Prospective Candidates) | Able to enter limited candidate information (less required fields than regular candidate profile without comprising the configuration of the candidate profile) and develop target candidate pool for key skills. | Yes/No |
| Marketing Campaigns (Leads/Prospective Candidates) | Includes proactive candidate pool in messaging, advertising campaigns or special event invitations. This should include the ability to send emails to thousands of candidates (as necessary). | Yes |
| Sending resumes to a manager | Ability to send a "Formatted Resume" to a Hiring Manager. | Yes |

| Function | Function Description | Response |
|---|---|---|
| **Assessment and Interview Management** | | |
| Customer-defined workflow steps and status | Customer can set up steps and status for tracking a candidate through the recruiting process, with ability to tailor it for required and desired steps. | Yes |
| Customer can define multiple process workflows (Example: employee referral, internal transfers, etc.) | Ability to create multiple applicant workflows (set of tracking steps & status) to be selected at the requisition level. | Yes |
| Workflow triggered alerts | Alerts can be set up in the system to drive the next step in the process or to function as reminders. | Yes |
| Ability to create a "tree-structure" workflow (i.e. step A can be followed by step B, C, D or E) | | Yes |
| Volume hiring updates | The ability to change the status for a group of candidates to hired in a single step (e.g. mass hiring in one step). | Yes/No |
| Integrated Assessments | Ability to store and/or integrate validated assessment tools into the recruiting workflow for certain jobs. | Yes |
| Assessment Triggers | Ability for Assessment to automatically be presented to candidates based on their responses to pre-screening questions or other data in their profile. | Yes |
| Assessment on demand | Ability to push an online assessment to a candidate on demand via email link. | Yes |
| Interview team member history | Ability to select and record a list of interviewing team members for a requisition. | Yes |

| Function | Function Description | Response |
|---|---|---|
| Interview team notifications | Ability to send an email notification (including a calendar meeting request) to the interview team members when scheduling the interview within the system (including interview packets, resumes, etc. when sending the email request). | Yes |
| Storage of interviewer comments | Ability to configure an online interview feedback form to capture the comments from each interviewer. | Yes |
| Interviewer attachments | Ability to include attachments to the interviewer notifications (e.g. interview guidelines, interview schedule, resume, etc.) | Yes |
| **Offer Management and Onboarding** | | |
| Approval routing and status tracking | Select a list of approvers, route for approval via email. In addition, the status of the approval process is tracked and displayed real-time on the Offer in the application as well as in the subsequent emails that go to the second and third approver, etc. | Yes |
| Pre-defined approval routing lists | Lists of approvers can be created, saved, and/or assigned to a user or requisition. | Yes |
| Approvals can take place directly from an email | When approving an Offer, the approver can take action directly from the email notification without having to log into the application. | Yes |
| Offer letters can be generated by merging fields into letter templates. | Data can be merged from the candidate record, the requisition and the offer terms into offer letter templates. | Yes |

| Function | Function Description | Response |
|---|---|---|
| Offer letters can be edited at the user level | Users can make edits to the offer letter at the time of generation and distribution. | Yes |
| Specific Onboarding Module | Does the product offer a specific On-boarding module, allowing clients to define required notifications at hire and send notifications through the system? (e.g. provisioning, IT for user account setup, new hire, manager checklist, etc.) | Yes |
| Onboarding Documentation Management | Electronically provide new hire paper-work and track completion of key documents (I-9, Non Disclosures, Benefits Paperwork). | Yes |
| **Global Capabilities & Compliance** | | |
| EEO Compliance data collection | Configurable notification and collection of EEO compliance information at variable points in the process. | Yes |
| Global - in country data collection based on regulations | Configurable data requests based on in-country requirements. Example: Germany, martial status, number of children. | Yes |
| Ability to present Career Sections in Multiple Languages | Ability to present Career Sections in Multiple Languages. | Yes |
| Ability to present the Recruiter and Manager Portals in multiple languages | Ability to present the Recruiter and Manager Portals in multiple languages. | Yes |
| Data Segregation by country, region or predefined type | Data Segregation, i.e.preventing users from a particular country or location from seeing candidates who are in another country or location. | No |

| Function | Function Description | Response |
|---|---|---|
| OFCCP Compliance tools to enable search and applicant declaration | Functionality consistent with the new OFCCP definition of Internet Applicant (record keeping for searches, candidate submissions, etc.) | Yes |
| Privacy Policy acknowledgements | Ability to require that candidates agree with the privacy policy before they submit. | Yes |
| Compliance with Data Privacy | Ability for customers to remove a candidate's data at that candidate's request. | Yes |
| Tax Credit Screening & Processing | Provides automatic Tax ID and SSN validation. Automatically transmits request to conduct tax credit screening for WOTC, WTW and more through to screening partners. Display those results within the Candidate profile for review and processing upon hire. | No |
| **Reporting & Integration** | | |
| Standard reports are delivered with the system | System is delivered with a minimum of 10 standard reports | Yes |
| Ad-hoc reporting capability | System is delivered with an ad-hoc report-writing tool so that clients can create their own reports as needed. | Yes |
| Reporting Security | Ability to enable field-level security and access to report creation, output and distribution. | Yes for ad hoc; No for standard |
| Reporting Distribution | Ability to generate scheduled reports and distribute through email. | Yes for ad hoc; No for standard |
| Real-Time Reporting | Ability to report on data in the application in real time (not based on a refresh of data in a reporting environment). | No for ad hoc; Yes for standard |

| Function | Function Description | Response |
|---|---|---|
| HRIS Integration | Ability to create bi-directional integrations from an HRIS to the ATS. | Yes |
| Integration - Client Self-Service Tools | Ability for clients to create their own integration touch points as needed (and make them operational). | Yes/No |
| Integration - API capability | Ability to allow clients to create integrations through APIs. | Yes |

## Performance Management

| Performance Dashboard | | |
|---|---|---|
| Dashboard configuration | Ability to configure dashboard based on user preference. | Yes |
| Create and display reports | Display reports that can be generated (i.e. review completion progress, goal progress). | Yes |
| Create and display charts and graphs | Display charts and graphs that are available to display planning actions. | Yes |
| Display help and reference tools | Display and view help and reference tools that can be selected by link or mouse hover. | Yes |
| **Employee Information Review (Data Import from HRIS/LMS)** | | |
| Import and display employee information | Display name, address, phone, email, location, photo, education (typically pulled from HRIS). | Yes |
| Import and display employee position information | Display current job title, job summary, job family, job level/grade, job code, FLSA, shift, status (FT/PT) (typically pulled through HRIS). | Yes |
| Create and display work history | Display created previous work history (i.e. name of company, job title, responsibilities/duties, employment dates). | Yes |

| Function | Function Description | Response |
|---|---|---|
| Create and display years in management | Display created years of management experience (manually entered or via integration). | No |
| Create and display years in industry | Display created years of experience in industry (primarily entered manually). | No |
| Import, create and display employee language(s) | Display employee languages (i.e. read, written, fluent). Primarily entered manually. | Yes |
| Import, create and display employee affiliations | Display employee affiliation memberships. | Yes |
| Import, create and display employee certifications | Display employee certifications and dates. | Yes |
| Import, create and display employee licenses | Display employee licenses and dates (usually a text box) - important to include expiration dates (could be for transportation, professional licenses, healthcare licenses, etc.) | Yes |
| Import and display organizational information | Display company name, company division, company department (typically imported from HRIS). | Yes |
| Import and display management hierarchy information | Display multiple levels of management names and information (i.e. Executive Management, Division Head, Department Head, Direct Manager, Employee). | No |
| Import and display direct reports | Display name and information of employee direct reports. | Yes |
| Import and display matrix manager hierarchy information | Display multiple levels of matrix management names and information (i.e. Employee has dotted line reporting relationships). | No |

| Function | Function Description | Response |
|---|---|---|
| Import and display multiple manager hierarchy information | Display multiple levels of numerous management names and information (i.e. Employee reports to more than one manager directly). | No |
| Organizational Chart View | Organizational information can be displayed in an Org Chart view (note how this is displayed visually). | Yes |
| Organizational Change Requests | Due to potential errors within HRMS, manager has the ability to request an employee change in hierarchy (i.e. manager name, organization, location, job role); changes can be configured to require approval. | Yes |
| Import and display employee current and past compensation | Display employee's past and current base salary, bonus, equity, commission, etc. | No |
| Import and display employee's most recent performance measures | Display employee's current competencies, goals, skills, projects, performance rating, development plan, personal improvement plan. | Yes |
| Import and display employee previous performance measures | Display employee's previous competencies, goals, skills, projects, performance rating, development plan, personal improvement plan. | Yes |
| Complete and display employee training | Display employee's completed and assigned training (i.e. mandatory/development) - Note if there is any integration with LMS. | Yes |
| External Identifier | Ability to have an external identifier field to bring in content on goals from a third-party application (i.e. description, start date, critical, public goal) - can be configured to be read-only for imports. | Yes |

| Function | Function Description | Response |
|----------|---------------------|----------|
| UDFs | Available user-defined fields for employee profile. | Yes |
| **Career Planning / Personal Development (Employee)** | | |
| Create and display future career plan scenarios | Display multiple future career plans (vertical, horizontal, both). Where does the employee want to go next? (lateral, promotion, etc.) | Yes |
| Select and display positions, job families and organizations/divisions of interest | Display selected positions and organizations of interest from import of job list and organization list (mentorships and cross-training) - gives the employee the opportunity to identify a position, job-family or organization of interest. | Yes |
| Create and display training requests | Display developmental training requests (entered by an employee or manager) - this could be an integration point to the LMS. | Yes |
| Create and display executive/professional requests | Display various executive/professional requests (i.e. executive coaching, cross training, job shadowing, speaking engagements, writing submittals, managing people, presentations, mentoring, apprenticeships). | Yes |
| Create and display organization affiliations and/or conferences/seminars | Display employee organization/affiliation or conference/seminar requests to join or attend. | Yes |
| Select and display competency development | Display selected desired competencies (entered by employee). | Yes |
| Create self-asses job readiness | Display selected self-readiness from list of options (i.e. Now, 0-3 months, 3-6 months, 6-9 months, 9-12 months, 12 months +). | No |

| Function | Function Description | Response |
|----------|---------------------|----------|
| Display position Gap % | Display gap % of employee readiness to ideal position as well as required training, license(s), education, certification(s) - this could be automatically calculated by the system (key differentiator). This is a gap analysis on the underlying competencies (most recent performance rating vs. competencies required for next position). | Yes |
| Select and display willingness to relocate | Display selected willingness to relocate (i.e. Yes, no, maybe, comments). | Yes |
| Display career prerequisites | Display required training, education, certification(s), license(s) for position of interest. | Yes |
| Submit development requests for approval | Submit development self -assessments to direct manager for review, feedback and approval (areas where the development needs to occur, as well as specific courses and conferences to help meet these development areas). Could be an integration point with LMS. | Yes |
| **Career Development (Manager)** | | |
| Create or select and display employee training goals | Display created or selected employee completed training, assigned training (mandatory/development), scheduled training and employee training requests. This is the manager identifying training goals for an employee. | Yes |
| Competency Development | Display assigned professional/leadership competencies. | Yes |

| Function | Function Description | Response |
|----------|--------------------|----------|
| Create and display executive/professional assignments | Display various executive/professional recommendations (i.e. executive coaching, cross training, job shadowing, speaking engagements, writing submittals, managing people, presentations, mentoring, apprenticeships). | Yes |
| Create and display organization affiliations and/or conferences/seminars | Display employee organization/affiliation or conference/seminar recommendations. | Yes |
| **Individual Goal / Self-Assessment (Employee)** | | |
| Select, create and display individual development goals | Display selected or created completed training, improvement competencies, executive coaching, promotion, cross-training. | Yes |
| Select competency development | Display selected development competencies - this is where the employees select competencies they want to develop for their career on the annual review. | Yes |
| Submit goal/competency assessment for approval | Submit manual or automatic goal/competency assessment to direct manager. | Yes |
| Solicit and display feedback | Select employees (i.e. managers, matrix managers, peers) to solicit performance feedback (i.e. 360, peer review, business review) and display results. | Yes |
| Create and display self-performance notes | Display created performance notes (i.e. kudos) throughout the review cycle (manually entered by employee or can solicit feedback throughout project). | Yes |
| Create and display self-goal assessment progress | Display created self-goal progress (i.e. quantitative % of completion, qualitative to include customer satisfaction, timeline to include start/completion date). | Yes |

| Function | Function Description | Response |
|---|---|---|
| Submit goal/competency review for approval | Submit manual or automatic goal/competency assessment to direct manager and higher levels. | Yes |
| UDFs | Available user-defined fields for employee goals. | No |
| **Review Process (Employee and Manager)** | | |
| Select and display competencies | Display selected professional or leadership competencies. | Yes |
| Select and display goals/objectives | Display selected goals/objectives (i.e. quantitative and/or qualitative). | Yes |
| Select and display goal alignment | Display selected goal alignment to company, organization, department and/or manager goals (cascading goals). | Yes |
| Select or create and display projects | Display selected or created projects. | Yes |
| Select and display project alignment to goals | Display selected project alignment to company, organization, department and/or manager goals. | Yes |
| Select or create and display skills | Display selected or created company, organization, department, employee skills. | Yes |
| Create and display employee performance notes | Display created performance notes (positive or negative) throughout the review cycle. These are notes created by the manager. | Yes |
| Solicit and display feedback | Select employees (i.e. managers, matrix managers, peers) to solicit performance feedback (i.e. 360, peer review, business review) and display. Pay particular attention to how this feedback is gathered and entered into the system. | Yes |

| Function | Function Description | Response |
|----------|---------------------|----------|
| Create and display employee goal assessment review | Display created employee goal progress (i.e. quantitative % of completion, qualitative to include customer satisfaction, timeline to include start/completion date) - this is the manager entering the assessment. | Yes |
| Performance review filtering | Manager can filter performance review information based on approval status, assigned to, author/owner, manager, employee, organization, location, job field, job role, review cycle, review group, review group owner, overall rating; filtering can be cumulative. | |
| Batch activities | Manager can take group actions on multiple employees simultaneously. | No |
| UDFs | Available user-defined fields for employee competencies. | No |
| **Workflow** | | |
| Review cycles | Ability to configure multiple review cycles and tied to various reviews. | Yes |
| Review groups | Ability to define review recipients based on dates, job function, organization, job code, etc. | Yes |
| Workflow Order | Ability to configure order of workflow (i.e. self-assessments can be configured to be completed first). | Yes |
| Notifications | Ability to push reviews to employees and managers. | Yes |
| Reminders | Ability to send reminders to employees and managers via email (manual and automatic). | Yes |

| Function | Function Description | Response |
|---|---|---|
| Acknowledgements | Ability to send auto-acknowledgements triggered by event/activity. | Yes |
| Next Level Approval | Ability to auto/manually route to multiple levels of approval. | Yes |
| Configurable work-flow | Ability to configure various steps of the review process, to make review steps mandatory, to have manager override and to display/hide visual graphic work-flow diagram. | Yes |
| Auto/Manual Progression | Ability to automatically or manually progress through the review process. | Yes |
| Review form | Exportable and printable review form. | Yes |
| **System Admin** | | |
| Review sections | Ability to configure multiple review sections, including goals, competencies, comments, rating models, etc. | Yes |
| Configurable rating models | Does it configure and display alpha and numeric values? Can values be rounded (up/down/both), value ranges, number of decimals (1-5)? | Yes |
| Comments | Displayed and available in individual review sections and overall review. Can they be configured to be mandatory and ability to override by management? | Yes |
| Goals | Ability to link organizational, divisional, departmental, individual goals into sections and ability to display goal progress. | Yes |
| Competencies | Ability to link competencies into sections. | Yes |
| Weightings | Ability to weigh employee performance based on goals and competencies. | Yes |

| Function | Function Description | Response |
|----------|---------------------|----------|
| **Search Functionality** | | |
| Basic Employee Search | Basic search by employee name (i.e. first or last name or a combination of both). | Yes |
| Job/Position Basic Search | Basic search by job role or position title, etc. | Yes |
| Competency Basic Search | Basic search by competency name. | Yes |
| Advanced Search | More detailed search capabilities that combine various search criteria or fields - may include optional weighting to determine which employees are retrieved in a search as well as each person's rank in the search results. | Yes |
| Succession Planning Search | Search functionality that dynamically generates the criteria used to match employees who would make good succession candidates with a specific position profile (could have various levels of "fit"). | Yes |
| **Employee View / Navigation / Help / Other** | | |
| List View | Display employee goals, business goals or projects; the list mode is a list of items with information on key dates and progress. | Yes |
| Card View | Display employee goals, business goals or projects using the card mode; the card mode provides details on one item at a time and offers the possibility of editing progress. This can also include employee photos as well. | Yes |
| Timeline / Gantt | Display employee goals, business goals or projects using the timeline mode; the timeline mode provides a timeline view of an item's start and due dates. | No |

| Function | Function Description | Response |
|---|---|---|
| Org Chart | Managers can access and manage information on their direct reports for all functionalities activated; the organizational chart will provide key data (i.e. risk of loss or most recent performance rating) for each of the manager's direct reports. | Yes |
| Mini-Org Chart | Displays a single analytic data point at a time; the manager can drill down into all layers of his organization and can view key metrics (i.e. performance reviews, goals, succession). | Yes |
| Graphs | Graphical display of various information (i.e. Gap Analysis, goal progress, review completion progress). | Yes |
| Help Links | Online help, FAQs, customer support, product version. | Yes |
| Attach Documents | Ability to attach reference documents to various sections within the system. | Yes |
| Browser capabilities | Supported by general Internet access (works with standard browsers: IE, Safari, Mozilla, Opera). | Yes |
| Mouse-Over Hover | Additional tooltips or descriptions that display when user hovers mouse pointer over various graphics or words within the system. | Yes |
| Web 2.0 | Ability to utilize Web 2.0 functionality, i.e. social networking. | Yes |
| **Security** | | |
| Logging In | Various login options (i.e. manual, SSO, LDAP). | Yes |

| Function | Function Description | Response |
|---|---|---|
| File Transfer | Various file transfer protocol (i.e. FTP, sFTP, vendor-specific transfer import/export tool). | Yes |
| Encryption | Various data encryption ability (i.e. PGP). | Yes |
| Roles / Permissions | Configurable list of permission-based roles with detailed access rights to various organizations, levels, etc. Typically employees only view within their own organization hierarchy. | Yes |
| Integration | Ability to integrate organizational data i.e. HRIS/ATS/LMS and employee data, including competencies, training, development plans, etc. | Yes |
| **Reporting** | | |
| Standard reports are delivered with the system | System is delivered with a set number of standard reports. | Yes |
| Ad-hoc reporting capability | System is delivered with an ad-hoc report-writing tool so that clients can create own reports as needed. | Yes |
| Advanced Value metrics | Data analysis of employee review process status, goal progress by hierarchy. | Yes |
| Reporting Security | Ability to enable field-level security and access to report creation, output and distribution. | Yes |
| Reporting UDFs | Ability to report user-defined fields. | Yes |
| Exporting reports | Reports can easily be exported to other applications (i.e. .xls, .pdf, .txt). | Yes |

| Function | Function Description | Response |
|---|---|---|

## Succession Planning

| Succession Planning (Manager - Planning of Individual Talent Matched to Critical Roles) | | |
|---|---|---|
| Create and display critical roles for today | Display critical job roles (i.e. title, level, location, division, organization). | Yes |
| Create and display critical roles for future | Display critical job roles (i.e. title, level, location, division, organization) for future (workforce planning-like tools). | No |
| Calculate and display performance rating | Performance rating is automatically averaged from various sections of the performance review and displayed (current and past). | Yes |
| Calculate and display performance ranking | High potential employees will be automatically ranked according to order of fit with critical role (i.e. 9-box grid, numeric ranking, high performer, high potential) - can be ranked by position, organization, etc. | Yes |
| Multi-dimensional matrix | Matrix that can be configured up to various # of cells (i.e. 9-box, 12-box, 16-box, 25-box); text within grid is configurable. | Yes |
| Various dimensions of matrix | Matrix displays employee performance, potential, number of succession plans an employee is on, years in management, years in industry. | Yes |
| Navigation from multi-dimensional matrix | Manager can select an employee within the matrix and navigate to employee information (i.e. Performance review, talent profile, employee goals, career plan). | Yes |

| Function | Function Description | Response |
|----------|---------------------|----------|
| Display employee comparisons | Display comparison of multiple high-potential employees according to fit to critical role (i.e. # of employees to compare, comparable data, fit gap analysis, ranking analysis, bench strength). | Yes |
| Create and display role readiness | Manager can create and display high potential employee role readiness (i.e. now, 0-3 months, 3-6 months, 6-9 months, 9-12 months, 12+ months). | Yes |
| Create and display retention risk | Manager can create and display high potential employee retention/loss/flight risk (i.e. high, medium, low, comments). | Yes |
| Create and display role willingness | Manager can create and display high potential employee role willingness (i.e. Yes, no, comments). | Yes |
| Create and display willingness to relocate | Manager can create and display high potential employee willingness to relocate (i.e. Yes, no, maybe, comments). | Yes |
| Create and display willingness to travel | Manager can create and display high potential employee willingness to travel (i.e. none, 25-50%, 50-75%, 75-100%). | Yes |
| Create and display interest in international assignment | Manager can create and display high potential employee interest in international assignment (i.e. Yes, no, maybe). | No |
| Create and display interim replacement for critical role | Manager can create and display high potential interim replacement for critical roles. | No |
| Display of gap analysis | Automatically calculate and display high potential employees' fit gap analysis to their next position and ranking analysis of employee to that next position. | Yes |
| UDFs | Available user-defined fields for succession planning. | No |

| Function | Function Description | Response |
|----------|--------------------|----------|
| **Succession Pooling (Manager - Planning of a Talent Pool for Critical Roles)** ||| 
| Display high potential pool | Display nominated and/or approved high potential pool (i.e. employee information, designated nominators, designated approvers, approvals, rejections, role readiness, rejection comments). | Yes |
| Calculate and display performance rating | Performance rating is automatically averaged from various sections of the performance review and displayed (current and past). | Yes |
| Calculate and display performance ranking | Pool of high potential employees will be automatically ranked according to order of fit with critical role (i.e. 9-box grid, numeric ranking, high performer, high potential). | Yes |
| Display employee comparisons | Display comparison of multiple high potential employees according to fit to critical role (i.e. # of employees to compare, comparable data, fit gap analysis, ranking analysis, bench strength). | Yes |
| Create and display role readiness | Manager can create and display high potential employee role readiness (i.e. now, 0-3 months, 3-6 months, 6-9 months, 9-12 months, 12+ months). | Yes |
| Create and display retention risk | Manager can create and display high potential employee retention/loss/flight risk (i.e. high, medium, low, comments). | Yes |
| Create and display role willingness | Manager can create and display high potential employee role willingness (i.e. Yes, no, comments). | Yes |
| Create and display willingness to relocate | Manager can create and display high potential employee willingness to relocate (i.e. Yes, no, maybe, comments). | Yes |

| Function | Function Description | Response |
|---|---|---|
| Create and display willingness to travel | Manager can create and display high potential employee willingness to travel (i.e. none, 25-50%, 50-75%, 75-100%). | Yes |
| Create and display interest in international assignment | Manager can create and display high potential employee interest in international assignment (i.e. Yes, no, maybe). | Yes |
| Create and display interim replacement for critical role | Manager can create and display high potential interim replacement for critical roles. | Yes |
| Display of gap analysis | Automatically calculate and display high potential employees' fit gap analysis to position and ranking analysis to position. | Yes |
| UDFs | Available user-defined fields for succession pooling | No |
| **Workflow** | | |
| Succession approval workflow | Ability to define or edit approvers, add/remove users and roles, ability to change the approval order, ability to reject with comments. | No |
| Nominations for succession pool | Ability to nominate, reject and enter comments on nominated HiPo employees. | Yes |
| **Reporting** | | |
| Standard reports are delivered with the system | System is delivered with a set number of standard reports. | Yes |
| Ad-hoc reporting capability | System is delivered with an ad-hoc report-writing tool so that clients can create their own reports as needed. | Yes |
| Advanced Value metrics | Data analysis of high performers / high potential employees, identified gaps, critical roles. | Yes |

| Function | Function Description | Response |
|---|---|---|
| Reporting Security | Ability to enable field-level security and access to report creation, output and distribution. | Yes |
| Reporting UDFs | Ability to report user-defined fields. | Yes |
| Exporting reports | Reports can easily be exported to other applications (i.e. .xls, .pdf, .txt). | Yes |

## Learning Management

| Content Management and Delivery | | |
|---|---|---|
| Application Simulation | Client content owners can create application simulations for use in training (i.e. "Show Me"/"Try Me" Flash-type simulations). | No |
| Assign learning content-based employee data | Learning content can be assigned to employees based on their job function or organizational data (not specific to position, but job family or organization). | Yes |
| Catalogs | Employees can search through and browse course catalogs to identify courses in which they are interested. | Yes |
| Competency Management - Third-Party Defined | Courses and learning plans can be built around competencies, driven by integration with a third-party vendor. | Yes |
| Competency Management – Customer Defined | Courses and learning plans can be built around competencies as determined by the customer. | Yes |
| Offline Capabilities | Learning content can be downloaded for completion even if the user is not connected to the Internet/network. Can also upload results. | No |

| Function | Function Description | Response |
|---|---|---|
| Employee Profile Management | System can house employee profiles that can be used for learning plan assignment, development plan creation and management (could be integration point). | Yes |
| External Content Integration | Employees can access, review, and register for courses in systems and online portals that are integrated with the LMS. | Yes |
| Internal Content Authoring | WYSIWYG (what you see is what you get) editor is built into the system for creation of learning materials within the system by client content owners. | No |
| Learning Plans | Customer can create learning plans for employees. Employees can manage their progress, review schedules, register for courses and access online courses from plans. Collaboration with employees and managers to create this learning plan (and appropriate workflow). Could be an integration point from PM tool. | Yes |
| Multiple Languages | System supports multiple languages for global implementations. | Yes |
| PowerPoint Conversion | System allows for uploading of PowerPoint files as learning content. | Yes |
| Repository | Digital repository for management of draft and active content is available in the system. Content managers would use this functionality (and allows for collaboration). | No |
| Scheduling | Users can book resources, locations and structures from within the system. This is an integration point as well. | Yes |
| Single Sign-On | Standard SSO capability for integration with client Intranet. | Yes |

| Function | Function Description | Response |
|---|---|---|
| Version Control | Content owners have the ability to manage content versioning. | No |
| Virtual Classrooms | System provides virtual classroom functionality for live, remote learning sessions. | No |
| **Testing and Tracking** | | |
| General Assessments | System allows for creation of assessments that aren't tied to particular training content. Could be tied to competencies. | Yes |
| Content Test Completion | Users can complete tests online as assigned. Could be offline as well. | Yes |
| Content Test Creation | System allows for creation of tests for learning content. | Yes |
| Polling | Polling can be conducted through one or more channels (e.g. Content, User Home Page Interface, etc.). | No |
| Test Completion Tracking | User test completion status and rates can be tracked. | Yes |
| Test Score Tracking | User test scores can be stored and tracked. | Yes |
| **Reporting** | | |
| Ad-hoc reporting capability | System is delivered with an ad-hoc report-writing tool so that clients can create their own reports as needed. | Yes |
| Data analysis | System provides functionality for advanced data analysis and dashboarding. | Yes |
| Reporting Security | Ability to enable field-level security and access to report creation, output and distribution. | Yes |

| Function | Function Description | Response |
|---|---|---|
| Standard reports are delivered with the system | System is delivered with a minimum of 10 standard reports. | Yes |
| **Integration** | | |
| Employee Profile Integration | System allows for employee profile integration with other talent management solutions (e.g. Performance, Succession, Compensation, Recruitment, etc.). | Yes |
| Integration | Ability to allow clients to create integrations through APIs, XML, flat files, etc. | Yes |
| **Web 2.0 Features** | | |
| Blogs | System allows for creation of blogs for content delivery. | No |
| Forums | System allows for creation and maintenance of forums to capture user-generated content and enable collaborative learning activities. | No |
| Other Collaborative Learning Tools | Additional collaborative learning tools are available. | Yes |
| Podcasting | System allows for creation of podcasts for content delivery. | No |
| RSS Feeds | System allows users to identify content "tracks" that they wish to monitor on a regular basis and displays updates in an RSS-like format. | No |
| Wikis | System allows for creation and maintenance of wikis to capture user-generated content and enable collaborative learning activities. | No |

| Function | Function Description | Response |
|---|---|---|
| **User Communication** | | |
| Completion Date Reminders | Users can be notified when they are approaching a target content completion date. | Yes |
| Completion Reminders | Users can be reminded to complete content that has been saved in progress. | No |
| Content Notifications | Users can be notified when new content is added to their learning plan or a track in which they are interested. | Yes |
| Manager Notifications | User managers and/or learning administrators can be notified when certain activities are completed. | Yes |
| Workflow | System allows for creation of workflow to communicate user status to content and people managers. | No |

# Kenexa

## Company Information (provided by Kenexa)

**Company Name:**         Kenexa®

**Corporate URL:**        www.kenexa.com

**Main Phone:**           (877) 971-9171

**Headquarters Address:**    650 East Swedesford Road, 2$^{nd}$ Floor, Wayne, PA 19087

**Type of Business or Areas of Focus:**

Integrated Talent Management, including delivery of science, business process optimization consulting, technology/services for recruiting (both software and RPO), assessments, onboarding, goals management, performance management, career development, succession planning, pay-for-performance compensation planning, engagement and employee lifecycle surveys and employment branding.

**Number of Employees:**    1600+

**Year Founded:**         1987

**Stock Symbol:**         KNXA

## Company Description and History:

Kenexa is a leader in building the world's greatest workforces. Using the unique combination of software, science and business process optimization, Kenexa helps organizations hire and retain a more productive workforce. We take great pride in being the only company in the world to offer these combined services, which ultimately link human resource processes to business outcomes.

We believe that no matter who they are, or what part of the world in which they live, people define themselves by the work they do. When people are in jobs they love, and are in environments that maximize their potential, they are not only more productive employees, they are better parents, friends, partners and neighbors. It's the core of our mission, our passion and our purpose—globally serving humanity, everyday. Kenexa has more than 4,000 customers, with employees located in more than 200 countries/ territories, speaking more than 80 languages, including 60 percent of the Fortune 100, 40 percent of the Fortune 500 and 42 percent of the Global 100. Kenexa is a market leader in R&D, spending $35 million in 2007 and more than $40 million in 2008. Kenexa's global footprint includes more than 30 offices in 18 countries.

## Products/Services/Solutions:

### 1. Assessment Solutions

Kenexa's flexible, customizable assessment solutions (more than 1,200 assessments) help companies select top performers for employment, identify areas for development and determine successors in an organization, including:
- Skills testing
- Structured interviews
- Engagement prediction tools
- Simulation exercises
- Competency modeling
- Assessment centers
- Culture fit assessment
- Behavioral/personality assessments

### 2. Recruitment Process Outsourcing

Kenexa's customizable recruitment process outsourcing offerings improve new hire quality, increase speed of hiring and reduce the cost of recruitment, including:
- Workforce transformation
- Vendor management
- College/campus recruiting
- Employment branding

- 24x7 global delivery centers
- Employee referral programs
- Diversity recruiting
- Gated recruitment
- Recruitment process support
- Change management

3. **Talent Management Applications**

Kenexa's configurable solutions automate hiring, retention, learning and succession planning processes to give organizations usable hiring and retention data, including:

- Large enterprise applicant tracking (Kenexa Recruiter® Brassring)
- Mid-market applicant tracking (Kenexa Recruiter® [formerly WebHire])
- Onboarding
- Competency management (Kenexa CareerTracker® [KCT])
- Goals management (included in KCT)
- Performance management (included in KCT)
- Succession planning (included in KCT)
- Career development (included in KCT)
- Compensation planning (included in KCT)
- Learning management
- Career center optimization / employment branding
- Workforce intelligence

4. **Survey**

Kenexa's customized survey solutions are a key diagnostic tool that helps organizations understand and act on the drivers of engagement and high performance in their culture to improve overall business results and drive organizational change, including:

- Employee engagement/satisfaction
- 360 multi-rater feedback
- SOX compliance surveys
- Exit interviews
- Brand proximity surveys
- New hire surveys
- Action planning
- Normative data
- Linkage research

# Author's Kenexa Functionality Matrix

| Function | Function Description | Response |
|---|---|---|
| **Talent Acquisition** | | |
| **Requisition Management & Posting** | | |
| Multiple requisition forms allowed (Example: hourly, internal transfer, business unit specific, reoccurring, sourcing, college) | More than one requisition form/template can be configured in a client's database to accommodate variance in business units or type of recruiting. (Example: A user from the Manufacturing group can enter a requisition and only see and populate fields that are applicable to Mfg. A different user from the Services group can enter a requisition and only see the fields designated for a Services requisition within the same database. | Yes |
| Data Segregation | Ability to segregate requisitions and candidates by hire type (executive, HR, etc.) or organization. | Yes |
| Requisition approval routing workflow and approval status indicator | Select a list of approvers, route for approval via email. Approvals should be able to be sent in parallel or sequentially. | Yes – Parallel Only |
| Approval status tracking | The status of the approval process is tracked and displayed real-time on the requisition in the application as well as in the subsequent emails that go to the second and third approver, etc. | Yes |
| Pre-defined approval routing lists | Lists of approvers can be created, saved, and/or assigned to a user or requisition, or defined by the organizational structure automatically. | Yes |

| Function | Function Description | Response |
|---|---|---|
| Approvals can take place directly from an email | When approving a requisition, the approver can take action directly from the email notification without having to log into the application. | Yes |
| Pre-qualifying questions based on position/job needs, including weighting to filter for top candidates | Questions developed, defined and delivered to a candidate in the online application process tied directly to the job posting/requirements, including weighting to filter for top candidates. | Yes |
| Knock-out questions | Ability to establish certain questions to be disqualifiers, where if the candidate does not answer correctly, the process is ended. | Yes |
| Job posting scheduling | Check a box to select the appropriate career site(s) for the job to appear. Scheduling of start and end dates of posting to any given site to allow for staggered posting. | Yes |
| Advanced job descriptions - Formatting and Spell Checking | Ability to edit and format job descriptions and marketing messages with MS Word, like functions for Bolding, Underlining and Spell Checking. | Yes |
| Electronic job board relationship management (facilitation of job positing to all e-media providers) | Ability to identify and post job opportunities to an unlimited number of electronic job boards and other end destinations. Ability to multi-select boards and push positions out to the market. | Yes |

| Function | Function Description | Response |
|---|---|---|
| **Candidate Experience** | | |
| Unlimited Career Site portals | Ability to establish an unlimited number of integrated career sites for different purposes - such as college recruiting, location-specific kiosks, or for a specific job family like Sales or Engineering. Determine if there are additional costs per Career Section. | Yes |
| Online profile form(s) defined by the client | Data collection form(s) that can be pushed to a candidate to gather needed information for relationship management and interested resume submissions. Customers can tailor the form to their specification, adding or removing fields. | Yes |
| User-defined secure login user name and password | User-created login and password authentication for accessing profile and career management activities. | Yes |
| Candidate login optional | Candidate can submit resume and apply to jobs without establishing a password protected user account. | Yes |
| Resume submission via upload of file - Candidate | Candidates can browse hard drives for their formatted resume and upload to candidate resume repository. | Yes |
| Resume submission via upload of file - Recruiter/Manager | Recruiter/Manager can browse the hard drive for the formatted resume and up-load to candidate resume repository. | Yes |
| Resume builder functionality | Ability for candidates without a formal resume to submit a resume via a "Resume Builder." | Yes |
| Extraction of data from resume to create profile | Extraction engine behind the text or up-loaded resume for population of fielded data in the candidate profile. | Yes |

| Function | Function Description | Response |
|---|---|---|
| Candidate-defined Job Agents | Candidate can establish job search parameters and be notified when jobs are posted which meet their preferences. | Yes |
| Candidate status check | Candidates can login to check the status of their resume submissions. | Yes |
| Ability to upload attachments | | Yes |
| Ability for candidate to save a submission as a draft | | Yes |
| Candidate self-withdrawal | Ability for candidates to remove themselves from consideration for a position. | Yes |
| Conceptual search for the candidate when searching for jobs | Candidates can use "free form" language to search for jobs. | Yes |
| **Sourcing/CRM** | | |
| Specific job referral and general referrals | Employees can submit a resume as a general referral or to a specific job. | Yes |
| Notifications to the referring employee and the referred candidate | Email notifications are automatically sent to the employee making the referral and to the candidate who was referred. | Yes |
| Referral status check | Employees can review a list of candidates they have referred and check their status. | Yes |
| Tracking steps and status searches | Recruiters can search for candidates based on their tracking steps and status against requisitions. | Yes |

| Function | Function Description | Response |
|---|---|---|
| Keyword search against free-form text and fielded data | Keyword search against text records from candidate and fielded data in the same search. | Yes |
| Search criteria high-lighted for relevance in record review | Search results with indicators for criteria matching and relevance in the results. | Yes |
| Configurable search results list | The column headers that are displayed in a search results list can be configured with different data elements from the candidate record. (Example: Education, Work History, Phone Number). | Yes |
| Ability to search file attachments | Keyword searching will scan the resumes that have been submitted as file attachments as well as text fields. | No (Attached resumes are parsed for searching) |
| Ability to create "overnight" searches | | Yes |
| Conceptual search engine to match resumes | Ability to use the requisition's job description or a large text phrase to find matching resumes using a conceptual search or natural language search engine. Conceptual searches should also be able to be conducted with fielded search. | Yes |
| "More like this" searching | Ability to take a resume and conduct a search to find other resumes that are similar to it (more like it). | Yes |
| Library of candidate correspondence/ communication templates | Ability for clients to create a library of correspondence templates that can be sent to candidates at the user's discretion. | Yes |

| Function | Function Description | Response |
|---|---|---|
| Editable correspondence at the user level | Users can make edits to the correspondence at the time of generation and distribution. | Yes |
| Agency Portal | Functionality designed for the management of third-party staffing agencies. Includes the ability to push requisitions to one or more suppliers and receive agency resume submissions. | Yes |
| Contingent Labor Management | Functionality designed specifically for the requisition and management of contract labor including the distribution of job requirements to multiple vendors, submission and review of resumes, tracking of assignment, time reporting and billing. | No |
| Candidate Pool Generation (Leads/Prospective Candidates) | Able to enter limited candidate information (less required fields than regular candidate profile without comprising the configuration of the candidate profile) and develop target candidate pool for key skills. | Yes |
| Marketing Campaigns (Leads/Prospective Candidates) | Include proactive candidate pool in messaging, advertising campaigns or special event invitations. This should include the ability to send emails to thousands of candidates (as necessary). | Yes |
| Sending resumes to a manager | Ability to send a "Formatted Resume" to a Hiring Manager. | Yes |
| **Assessment and Interview Management** | | |
| Customer-defined workflow steps and status | Customer can set up steps and status for tracking a candidate through the recruiting process, with ability to tailor it for required and desired steps. | Yes |

| Function | Function Description | Response |
|---|---|---|
| Customer can define multiple process workflows (Example: employee referral, internal transfers, etc.) | Ability to create multiple applicant work-flows (set of tracking steps and status) to be selected at the requisition level. | Yes |
| Workflow triggered alerts | Alerts can be set up in the system to drive the next step in the process or to function as reminders. | Yes |
| Ability to create a "tree-structure" workflow (i.e. step A can be followed by step B, C, D or E) | | Yes |
| Volume hiring updates | The ability to change the status for a group of candidates to hired in a single step (e.g. mass hiring in one step). | Yes |
| Integrated Assess-ments | Ability to store and/or integrate validated assessment tools into the recruiting workflow for certain jobs. | Yes |
| Assessment Triggers | Ability for Assessment to automatically be presented to a candidate based on his/her responses to pre-screening ques-tions or other data in his/her profile. | Yes |
| Assessment on demand | Ability to push an online assessment to a candidate on demand via email link. | Yes |
| Interview team member history | Ability to select and record a list of inter-viewing team members for a requisition. | Yes |
| Interview team notifi-cations | Ability to send an email notification (including a calendar meeting request) to the interview team members when scheduling the interview within the system (including interview packets, resumes, etc. when sending the email request). | Yes |

| Function | Function Description | Response |
|---|---|---|
| Storage of interviewer comments | Ability to configure an online interview feedback form to capture the comments from each interviewer. | Yes |
| Interviewer attachments | Ability to include attachments to the interviewer notifications (e.g. interview guidelines, interview schedule, resume, etc.) | Yes |
| **Offer Management and Onboarding** | | |
| Approval routing and status tracking | Select a list of approvers, route for approval via email. In addition, the status of the approval process is tracked and displayed real-time on the offer in the application as well as in the subsequent emails that go to the second and third approver, etc. | Yes |
| Pre-defined approval routing lists | Lists of approvers can be created, saved, and/or assigned to a user or requisition. | Yes |
| Approvals can take place directly from an email | When approving an offer, the approver can take action directly from the email notification without having to log into the application. | Yes |
| Offer letters can be generated by merging fields into letter templates | Data can be merged from the candidate record, the requisition and the offer terms into offer letter templates. | Yes |
| Offer letters can be edited at the user level | Users can make edits to the offer letter at the time of generation and distribution. | Yes |
| Specific Onboarding Module | Does the product offer a specific Onboarding module, allowing clients to define required notifications at hire and send notifications through the system? (e.g. provisioning, IT for user account setup, new hire, manager checklist, etc.) | Yes |

| Function | Function Description | Response |
|----------|---------------------|----------|
| Onboarding Documentation Management | Electronically provides new hire paperwork and tracks completion of key documents (I-9, Non Disclosures, Benefits Paperwork). | Yes |
| **Global Capabilities & Compliance** | | |
| EEO Compliance data collection | Configurable notification and collection of EEO compliance information at variable points in the process. | Yes |
| Global in-country data collection based on regulations | Configurable data requests based on in-country requirements. Example: Germany, martial status, number of children. | Yes |
| Ability to present Career Sections in Multiple Languages | Ability to present Career Sections in Multiple Languages. | Yes |
| Ability to present the Recruiter and Manager Portals in multiple languages | Ability to present the Recruiter and Manager Portals in multiple languages. | Yes |
| Data Segregation by country, region or predefined type | Data Segregation, i.e. preventing users from a particular country or location from seeing candidates who are in another country or location. | Yes |
| OFCCP Compliance tools to enable search and applicant declaration | Functionality consistent with the new OFCCP definition of Internet Applicant (record keeping for searches, candidate submissions, etc.) | Yes |
| Privacy Policy acknowledgements | Ability to require that candidates agree with the privacy policy before they submit. | Yes |
| Compliance with Data Privacy | Ability for customers to remove a candidate's data at that candidate's request. | Yes |

| Function | Function Description | Response |
|---|---|---|
| Tax Credit Screening & Processing | Provides automatic Tax ID and SSN validation. Automatically transmits request to conduct tax credit screening for WOTC, WTW and more through to screening partners and display those results within the Candidate profile for review and processing upon hire. | Yes |
| **Reporting & Integration** | | |
| Standard reports are delivered with the system | System is delivered with a minimum of 10 standard reports. | Yes |
| Ad-hoc reporting capability | System is delivered with an ad-hoc report-writing tool so that clients can create their own reports as needed. | Yes |
| Reporting Security | Ability to enable field-level security and access to report creation, output and distribution. | Yes |
| Reporting Distribution | Ability to generate scheduled reports and distribute through email | Yes |
| Real-Time Reporting | Ability to report on data in the application in real time (not based on a refresh of data in a reporting environment). | No |
| HRIS Integration | Ability to create bi-directional integrations from an HRIS to the ATS. | Yes |
| Integration - Client Self-Service Tools | Ability for clients to create their own integration touch points as needed (and make them operational). | Yes |
| Integration - API capability | Ability to allow clients to create integrations through APIs. | No – Planned Q3 2009 |

| Function | Function Description | Response |
|---|---|---|

## Performance Management

| Performance Dashboard | | |
|---|---|---|
| Dashboard configuration | Ability to configure dashboard based on user preference. | No – Planned Q3 2009 |
| Create and display reports | Display reports that can be generated (i.e. review completion progress, goal progress). | Yes |
| Create and display charts and graphs | Display available charts and graphs to show planning actions. | Yes |
| Display help and reference tools | Display and view help and reference tools that can be selected by link or mouse hover. | Yes |
| Employee Information Review (Data Import from HRIS/LMS) | | |
| Import and display employee information | Display name, address, phone, email, location, photo, education (typically pulled from HRIS). | Yes |
| Import and display employee position information | Display current job title, job summary, job family, job level/grade, job code, FLSA, shift, status (FT/PT) - typically pulled through HRIS. | Yes |
| Create and display work history | Display created previous work history (i.e. name of company, job title, responsibilities/duties, employment dates). | Yes |
| Create and display years in management | Display created years of management experience (manually entered or via integration). | Yes |
| Create and display years in industry | Display created years of experience in industry (primarily entered manually). | Yes |

| Function | Function Description | Response |
|---|---|---|
| Import, create and display employee language(s) | Display employee languages (i.e. read, written, fluent) (primarily entered manually). | Yes |
| Import, create and display employee affiliations | Display employee affiliation memberships. | Yes |
| Import, create and display employee certifications | Display employee certifications and dates. | Yes |
| Import, create and display employee licenses | Display employee licenses and dates (usually a text box) - important to include expiration dates (could be for transportation, professional licenses, healthcare licenses, etc.) | Yes |
| Import and display organizational information | Display company name, company division, company department (typically imported from HRIS). | Yes |
| Import and display management hierarchy information | Display multiple levels of management names and information (i.e. Executive Management, Division Head, Department Head, Direct Manager, Employee). | Yes |
| Import and display direct reports | Display name and information of employee direct reports. | Yes |
| Import and display matrix manager hierarchy information | Display multiple levels of matrix management names and information (i.e. Employee has dotted line reporting relationships). | Yes |
| Import and display multiple manager hierarchy information | Display multiple levels of multiple management names and information (i.e. Employee reports to more than one manager directly). | Yes |

| Function | Function Description | Response |
|---|---|---|
| Organizational Chart View | Organizational information can be displayed in an Org Chart view (note how this is displayed visually). | Yes |
| Organizational Change Requests | Due to potential errors within HRMS, manager has the ability to request an employee change in hierarchy (i.e. manager name, organization, location, job role); changes can be configured to require approval. | Yes |
| Import and display employee current and past compensation | Display employee's past and current base salary, bonus, equity, commission, etc. | Yes |
| Import and display employee's most recent performance measures | Display employee's current competencies, goals, skills, projects, performance rating, development plan, personal improvement plan. | Yes |
| Import and display employee previous performance measures | Display employee's previous competencies, goals, skills, projects, performance rating, development plan, personal improvement plan. | Yes |
| Complete and display employee's training | Display employee's completed and assigned training (i.e. mandatory/development) - Note if there is any integration with LMS. | Yes |
| External Identifier | Ability to have an external identifier field to bring in content on goals from a third-party application (i.e. description, start date, critical, public goal) - can be configured to be read-only for imports. | Yes |
| UDFs | Available user-defined fields for employee profile. | Yes |

| Function | Function Description | Response |
|---|---|---|
| **Career Planning / Personal Development (Employee)** | | |
| Create and display future career plan scenarios | Display multiple future career plans (vertical, horizontal, both) - where does the employee want to go next? (lateral, promotion, etc.) | Yes |
| Select and display positions, job families and organizations/divisions of interest | Display selected positions and organizations of interest from import of job list and organization list (mentorships and cross-training) - gives the employee the opportunity to identify a position, job-family or organization of interest. | Yes |
| Create and display training requests | Display developmental training requests (entered by an employee or manager) - this could be an integration point to the LMS. | Yes |
| Create and display executive/professional requests | Display various executive/professional requests (i.e. executive coaching, cross-training, job shadowing, speaking engagements, writing submittals, managing people, presentations, mentoring, apprenticeships). | Yes |
| Create and display organization affiliations and/or conferences/seminars | Display employee organization/affiliation or conference/seminar requests to join or attend. | Yes |
| Select and display competency development | Display selected desired competencies (entered by employee). | Yes |
| Create self-asses job readiness | Display selected self-readiness from list of options (i.e. Now, 0-3 months, 3-6 months, 6-9 months, 9-12 months, 12 months +). | Yes |

| Function | Function Description | Response |
|---|---|---|
| Display position Gap % | Display gap % of employee readiness to ideal position as well as required training, license(s), education, certification(s) - this could be automatically calculated by the system (key differentiator). This is a gap analysis on the underlying competencies (most recent performance rating vs. competencies required for next position). | Yes |
| Select and display willingness to relocate | Display selected willingness to relocate (i.e. Yes, no, maybe, comments). | Yes |
| Display career prerequisites | Display required training, education, certification(s), license(s) for position of interest. | Yes |
| Submit development requests for approval | Submit development self-assessments to direct manager for review, feedback and approval (areas where the development needs to occur, as well as specific courses, conferences to help meet these development areas). Could be an integration point with LMS. | Yes |
| **Career Development (Manager)** | | |
| Create or select and display employee training goals | Display created or selected employee completed training, assigned training (mandatory/development), scheduled training and employee training requests. This is the manager identifying training goals for an employee. | Yes |
| Competency Development | Display assigned professional/leadership competencies. | Yes |

| Function | Function Description | Response |
|----------|---------------------|----------|
| Create and display executive/professional assignments | Display various executive/professional recommendations (i.e. executive coaching, cross-training, job shadowing, speaking engagements, writing submittals, managing people, presentations, mentoring, apprenticeships). | Yes |
| Create and display organization affiliations and/or conferences/seminars | Display employee organization/affiliation or conference/seminar recommendations. | Yes |
| **Individual Goal / Self Assessment (Employee)** | | |
| Select, create and display individual development goals | Display selected or created completed training, improvement competencies, executive coaching, promotion, cross-training. | Yes |
| Select competency development | Display selected development competencies - this is where the employee selects competencies to develop for his/her career on the annual review. | Yes |
| Submit goal/competency assessment for approval | Submit manual or automatic goal/competency assessment to direct manager. | Yes |
| Solicit and display feedback | Select employees (i.e. managers, matrix managers, peers) to solicit performance feedback (i.e. 360, peer review, business review) and display results. | Yes |
| Create and display self-performance notes | Display created performance notes (i.e. kudos) throughout the review cycle (manually entered by employee or can solicit feedback throughout project). | Yes |
| Create and display self-goal assessment progress | Display created self-goal progress (i.e. quantitative % of completion, qualitative to include customer satisfaction, timeline to include start/completion date). | Yes |

| Function | Function Description | Response |
|---|---|---|
| Submit goal/competency review for approval | Submit manual or automatic goal/competency assessment to direct manager and higher levels. | Yes |
| UDFs | Available user-defined fields for employee goals. | Yes |
| **Review Process (Employee and Manager)** | | |
| Select and display competencies | Display selected professional or leadership competencies. | Yes |
| Select and display goals/objectives | Display selected goals/objectives (i.e. quantitative and/or qualitative). | Yes |
| Select and display goal alignment | Display selected goal alignment to company, organization, department and/or manager goals (cascading goals). | Yes |
| Select or create and display projects | Display selected or created projects. | Yes |
| Select and display project alignment to goals | Display selected project alignment to company, organization, department and/or manager goals. | Yes |
| Select or create and display skills | Display selected or created company, organization, department, employee skills. | Yes |
| Create and display employee performance notes | Display created performance notes (positive or negative) throughout the review cycle. These are notes created by the manager. | Yes |
| Solicit and display feedback | Select employees (i.e. managers, matrix managers, peers) to solicit performance feedback (i.e. 360, peer review, business review) and display. Pay particular attention to how this feedback is gathered and entered into the system. | Yes |

| Function | Function Description | Response |
|---|---|---|
| Create and display employee goal assessment review | Display created employee goal progress (i.e. quantitative % of completion, qualitative to include customer satisfaction, timeline to include start/completion date) - this is the manager entering the assessment. | Yes |
| Performance review filtering | Manager can filter performance review information based on approval status, assigned to, author/owner, manager, employee, organization, location, job field, job role, review cycle, review group, review group owner, overall rating; filtering can be cumulative. | Yes |
| Batch activities | Manager can take group actions on multiple employees simultaneously. | Yes |
| UDFs | Available user-defined fields for employee competencies. | Yes |
| **Workflow** | | |
| Review cycles | Ability to configure multiple review cycles and tied to various reviews. | Yes |
| Review groups | Ability to define review recipients based on dates, job function, organization, job code, etc. | Yes |
| Workflow Order | Ability to configure order of workflow (i.e. self-assessments can be configured to be completed first). | Yes |
| Notifications | Ability to push reviews to employees and managers. | Yes |
| Reminders | Ability to send reminders to employees and managers via email (manual and automatic). | Yes |

| Function | Function Description | Response |
|----------|---------------------|----------|
| Acknowledgements | Ability to send auto-acknowledgements triggered by event/activity. | Yes |
| Next Level Approval | Ability to auto/manually route to multiple levels of approval. | Yes |
| Configurable work-flow | Ability to configure various steps of the review process, to make review steps mandatory, to have manager override ability, to display/hide visual graphic workflow diagram. | Yes |
| Auto/Manual Pro-gression | Ability to automatically or manually progress through the review process. | Yes |
| Review form | Exportable and printable review form. | Yes |
| **System Admin** | | |
| Review sections | Ability to configure multiple review sections, including goals, competencies, comments, rating models, etc. | Yes |
| Configurable rating models | Does it configure and display alpha and numeric values. Can values be rounded (up/down/both), value ranges, number of decimals (1-5)? | Yes |
| Comments | Displayed and available in individual review sections and overall review. Can they be configured to be mandatory with ability to override by management? | Yes |
| Goals | Ability to link organizational, divisional, departmental, individual goals into sections and to display goal progress. | Yes |
| Competencies | Ability to link competencies into sections. | Yes |
| Weightings | Ability to weigh employee performance based on goals and competencies. | Yes |

| Function | Function Description | Response |
|---|---|---|
| **Search Functionality** | | |
| Basic Employee Search | Basic search by employee name (i.e. first or last name or a combination of both). | Yes |
| Job/Position Basic Search | Basic search by job role or position title, etc. | Yes |
| Competency Basic Search | Basic search by competency name. | Yes |
| Advanced Search | More detailed search capabilities that combine various search criteria or fields - may include optional weighting to determine which employees are retrieved in a search as well as each person's rank in the search results. | Yes |
| Succession Planning Search | Search functionality that dynamically generates the criteria used to match employees who would make good succession candidates with a specific position profile (could have various levels of "fit"). | Yes |
| **Employee View / Navigation / Help / Other** | | |
| List View | Display employee goals, business goals or projects; the list mode is a list of items with information on key dates and progress. | Yes |
| Card View | Display employee goals, business goals or projects using the card mode; the card mode provides details on one item at a time and offers the possibility of editing progress. This can also include employee photos as well. | Yes |
| Timeline / Gantt | Display employee goals, business goals or projects using the timeline mode; the timeline mode provides a timeline view of an item's start and due dates. | Yes |

| Function | Function Description | Response |
|---|---|---|
| Org Chart | Managers can access and manage information on their direct reports for all functionalities activated; the organizational chart will provide key data (i.e. risk of loss or most recent performance rating) for each of the manager's direct reports. | Yes |
| Mini-Org Chart | Displays a single analytic data point at a time; the manager can drill down into all layers of his organization and can view key metrics (i.e. performance reviews, goals, succession). | Yes |
| Graphs | Graphical display of various information (i.e. Gap Analysis, goal progress, review completion progress). | Yes |
| Help Links | Online help, FAQs, customer support, product version. | Yes |
| Attach Documents | Ability to attach reference documents to various sections within the system. | Yes |
| Browser capabilities | Supported by general Internet access (works with standard browsers: IE, Safari, Mozilla, Opera). | Yes |
| Mouse-Over Hover | Additional tooltips or descriptions that display when user hovers mouse pointer over various graphics or words within the system. | Yes |
| Web 2.0 | Ability to utilize Web 2.0 functionality, i.e. social networking. | No – Planned Q3 09 |
| **Security** | | |
| Logging In | Various login options (i.e. manual, SSO, LDAP). | Yes |

| Function | Function Description | Response |
|---|---|---|
| File Transfer | Various file transfer protocol (i.e. FTP, sFTP, vendor-specific transfer import/export tool). | Yes |
| Encryption | Various data encryption ability (i.e. PGP). | Yes |
| Roles / Permissions | Configurable list of permission-based roles with detailed access rights to various organizations, levels, etc. Typically employees only view within their own organization hierarchy. | Yes |
| Integration | Ability to integrate organizational data i.e. HRIS/ATS/ LMS and employee data including competencies, training, development plans, etc. | Yes |
| **Reporting** | | |
| Standard reports are delivered with the system | System is delivered with a set number standard reports. | Yes |
| Ad-hoc reporting capability | System is delivered with an ad-hoc report-writing tool so that clients can create their own reports as needed. | Yes |
| Advanced Value metrics | Data analysis of employee review process status, goal progress by hierarchy. | No – Planned Q3 2009 |
| Reporting Security | Ability to enable field-level security and access to report creation, output and distribution. | Yes |
| Reporting UDFs | Ability to report user-defined fields. | Yes |
| Exporting reports | Reports can easily be exported to other applications (i.e. .xls, .pdf, .txt). | Yes |

| Function | Function Description | Response |
|---|---|---|

## Succession Planning

| Succession Planning (Manager - Planning of Individual Talent Matched to Critical Roles) | | |
|---|---|---|
| Create and display critical roles for today | Display critical job roles (i.e. title, level, location, division, organization). | Yes |
| Create and display critical roles for future | Display critical job roles (i.e. title, level, location, division, organization) for future (workforce planning-like tools). | Yes |
| Calculate and display performance rating | Performance rating is automatically averaged from various sections of the performance review and displayed (current and past). | Yes |
| Calculate and display performance ranking | High potential employees will be automatically ranked according to order of fit with critical role (i.e. 9-box grid, numeric ranking, high performer, high potential) - can be ranked by position, organization, etc. | Yes |
| Multi-dimensional matrix | Matrix that can be configured up to various # of cells (i.e. 9-box, 12-box, 16-box, 25-box); text within grid is configurable. | Yes |
| Various dimensions of matrix | Matrix displays employee performance, potential, number of succession plans an employee is on, years in management, years in industry. | Yes |
| Navigation from multi-dimensional matrix | Manager can select an employee within the matrix and navigate to employee information (i.e. Performance review, talent profile, employee goals, career plan). | Yes |

| Function | Function Description | Response |
|---|---|---|
| Display employee comparisons | Display comparison of multiple high potential employees according to fit to critical role (i.e. # of employees to compare, comparable data, fit gap analysis, ranking analysis, bench strength). | Yes |
| Create and display role readiness | Manager can create and display high potential employee role readiness (i.e. now, 0-3 months, 3-6 months, 6-9 months, 9-12 months, 12+ months). | Yes |
| Create and display retention risk | Manager can create and display high potential employee retention/loss/flight risk (i.e. high, medium, low, comments). | Yes |
| Create and display role willingness | Manager can create and display high potential employee role willingness (i.e. yes, no, comments). | Yes |
| Create and display willingness to relocate | Manager can create and display high potential employee willingness to relocate (i.e. yes, no, maybe, comments). | Yes |
| Create and display willingness to travel | Manager can create and display high potential employee willingness to travel (i.e. none, 25-50%, 50-75%, 75-100%). | Yes |
| Create and display interest in international assignment | Manager can create and display high potential employee interest in international assignment (i.e. yes, no, maybe). | Yes |
| Create and display interim replacement for critical role | Manager can create and display high potential interim replacement for critical roles. | Yes |
| Display of gap analysis | Automatically calculate and display high potential employee fit gap analysis of employee to next position and ranking analysis of employee to that next position. | Yes |

| Function | Function Description | Response |
|---|---|---|
| UDFs | Available user-defined fields for succession planning. | Yes |
| **Succession Pooling (Manager - Planning of a Talent Pool for Critical Roles)** | | |
| Display high potential pool | Display nominated and/or approved high potential pool (i.e. employee information, designated nominators, designated approvers, approvals, rejections, role readiness, rejection comments). | Yes |
| Calculate and display performance rating | Performance rating is automatically averaged from various sections of the performance review and displayed (current and past). | Yes |
| Calculate and display performance ranking | Pool of high potential employees will be automatically ranked according to order of fit with critical role (i.e. 9-box grid, numeric ranking, high performer, high potential). | Yes |
| Display employee comparisons | Display comparison of multiple high potential employees according to fit to critical role (i.e. # of employees to compare, comparable data, fit gap analysis, ranking analysis, bench strength). | Yes |
| Create and display role readiness | Manager can create and display high potential employee role readiness (i.e. now, 0-3 months, 3-6 months, 6-9 months, 9-12 months, 12+ months). | Yes |
| Create and display retention risk | Manager can create and display high potential employee retention/loss/flight risk (i.e. high, medium, low, comments). | Yes |
| Create and display role willingness | Manager can create and display high potential employee role willingness (i.e. yes, no, comments). | Yes |

| Function | Function Description | Response |
|---|---|---|
| Create and display willingness to relocate | Manager can create and display high potential employee willingness to relocate (i.e. yes, no, maybe, comments). | Yes |
| Create and display willingness to travel | Manager can create and display high potential employee willingness to travel (i.e. none, 25-50%, 50-75%, 75-100%). | Yes |
| Create and display interest in international assignment | Manager can create and display high potential employee interest in international assignment (i.e. yes, no, maybe). | Yes |
| Create and display interim replacement for critical role | Manager can create and display high potential interim replacement for critical roles. | Yes |
| Display of gap analysis | Automatically calculate and display high potential employee fit gap analysis to position and ranking analysis of employee to position. | Yes |
| UDFs | Available user-defined fields for succession pooling. | Yes |
| **Workflow** | | |
| Succession approval workflow | Ability to define or edit approvers, add/remove users and roles, change the approval order and reject with comments. | Yes |
| Nominations for succession pool | Ability to nominate, reject and enter comments on nominated HiPo employees. | Yes |
| **Reporting** | | |
| Standard reports are delivered with the system | System is delivered with a set number of standard reports. | Yes |
| Ad-hoc reporting capability | System is delivered with an ad-hoc report-writing tool so that clients can create their own reports as needed. | Yes |

| Function | Function Description | Response |
|---|---|---|
| Advanced Value metrics | Data analysis of high performers / high potential employees, identified gaps, critical roles. | Yes |
| Reporting Security | Ability to enable field-level security and access to report creation, output and distribution. | Yes |
| Reporting UDFs | Ability to report user-defined fields. | Yes |
| Exporting reports | Reports can easily be exported to other applications (i.e. .xls, .pdf, .txt). | Yes |

## Compensation Management

| Compensation Dashboard | | |
|---|---|---|
| Dashboard configuration | Ability to configure dashboard based on user preference. | Yes |
| Create and display a compensation worksheet | Display a compensation worksheet that will provide individual and org planning status and detail. | Yes |
| Create and display reports | Display reports that can be generated, i.e. budget usage by merit, bonus, equity, adjustment and percent of planning completed | Yes |
| Create and display charts and graphs | Display charts and graphs that are available to show planning actions. | Yes |
| Import and display allocation guidelines | Display compensation allocation guidelines for merit, bonus, equity and adjustments - also refer to the time allocation/ workflow to complete this process. | Yes |
| Import and display eligibility guidelines | Display employee eligibility guidelines for planning, i.e. FT, PT, commission, LOA, new hire, etc. - Guidelines are input by compensation department. | Yes |

| Function | Function Description | Response |
|---|---|---|
| Display help and reference tools | Display and view help and reference tools that can be selected by link or mouse hover. | Yes |
| **Compensation Budget** | | |
| Import and display multiple aggregate planning budget by org | Display multiple approved allocated budgets by diverse business groups on all pages (usually imported from financial system). | Yes |
| Import and display aggregate merit budget by org | Display approved allocated merit budgets by diverse business groups on all pages. | Yes |
| Import and display aggregate bonus budget by org | Display approved allocated bonuses by diverse business groups on all pages. | Yes |
| Import and display aggregate equity budget by org | Display approved allocated equity budgets by diverse business groups on all pages. | Yes |
| Import and display aggregate adjust-ment budget by org | Display approved allocated adjustment budgets by diverse business groups on all pages. | Yes |
| **Employee Information Review** | | |
| Import and display employee Informa-tion | Display name, location, photo, org, direct manager (typically imported from PM tool). | Yes |
| Import and display employee position | Display current job title, job code, level/grade. | Yes |
| Import and display employee prior compensation plan-ning period data | Display current hourly rate, annual rate, bonus percent, bonus amount, equity allocation, total compensation. | Yes |

| Function | Function Description | Response |
|---|---|---|
| Import and display employee prior performance rating | Display prior performance rating. | Yes |
| Import and display new employee performance rating | Display new performance rating. | Yes |
| Import and display employee's position salary range | Display employee's salary range. | Yes |
| Import and display salary penetration % based on position salary range | Display % of penetration that employee's salary falls within the range. | Yes |
| **Promotion** | | |
| Display position information | Ability to select and display job titles, job codes, job level/grades. | Yes |
| Import and display corporate promotion guidelines | Ability to display promotion guidelines per position, including salary range and percent increase guidelines. | Yes |
| Promotion amount | Ability to enter promotion percent or amount. | Yes |
| Auto-calculate promotion amount | System to auto-populate promotion amount based on percent increase. | Yes |
| Ability to calculate hourly rate | System to auto-populate new hourly rate based on promotion increase. | Yes |
| Ability to auto-calculate annual rate | System to auto-populate new annual rate based on promotion increase. | Yes |
| Promotion approval chain | Promotion approval chain. | Yes |

| Function | Function Description | Response |
|----------|---------------------|----------|
| Develop documentation | Ability to document the promotion justification. | Yes |
| **Adjustment** | | |
| Import and display adjustment guidelines | Ability to display adjustment allocation guidelines, including salary range and percent increase guidelines. | Yes |
| Adjustment allocation | Ability to enter and submit an adjustment percent or amount. | Yes |
| Auto-calculate hourly amount | System to auto-populate new hourly rate based on adjustment percent increase. | Yes |
| Auto-calculate adjustment amount | System to auto-populate new annual rate based on adjustment percent increase. | Yes |
| Adjustment approvals | | Yes |
| Develop documentation | Ability to document the adjustment justification. | Yes |
| **Merit** | | |
| Import and display promotion guidelines | Ability to display merit allocation guidelines, including salary range and percent increase guidelines. | Yes |
| Performance-based recommendations | Merit allocation can be based on performance rating. | Yes |
| Merit allocation | Ability to enter and submit a merit percent or amount. | Yes |
| Import and display proration of merit based on hire date | System to auto-calculate merit increase based on hire date, i.e. less than one year would be calculated by months employed. | Yes |

| Function | Function Description | Response |
|---|---|---|
| Auto-calculate hourly amount | System to auto-populate new hourly rate based on merit percent increase. | Yes |
| Auto-calculate adjustment amount | System to auto-populate new annual rate based on merit percent increase. | Yes |
| Merit approvals | | Yes |
| Develop documentation | Ability to document the merit justification. | Yes |
| **Bonus** | | |
| Import and display bonus allocation guidelines | Ability to display bonus allocation guidelines. | Yes |
| Performance-based recommendations | Bonus allocation can be based on performance rating. | Yes |
| Bonus allocation | Ability to enter and submit a bonus percent or amount. | Yes |
| Bonus adjustment | Auto-Proration of bonus based on hired or leave, i.e. severance date. | Yes |
| Bonus approvals | Ability to obtain appropriate approvals (workflow to select appropriate approvers). | Yes |
| Develop documentation | Ability to document the merit justification. | Yes |
| **Equity** | | |
| Import and display equity allocation guidelines | Ability to display equity allocation guidelines. | Yes |
| Performance-based recommendations | Equity allocation can be based on performance rating. | Yes |

| Function | Function Description | Response |
|---|---|---|
| Equity allocation | Ability to enter and submit equity percent or amount. | Yes |
| Equity allocation adjustment | Auto-Proration of equity allocation based on hire date. | Yes |
| Equity approvals | | Yes |
| Develop documentation | Ability to document the merit justification. | Yes |
| **Other** | | |
| Ability to assign a delegate | Ability to assign a delegate to complete compensation planning, i.e. Admin. | Yes |
| Employee Filter | Ability to sort by employee name or data, i.e. first name, last name, employee ID, etc. | Yes |
| Employee Search | Ability to search throughout the tool by employee name or data, i.e. first name, last name, employee ID, etc. | Yes |
| Revert or change functionality | Ability for planning administrators to revert or change submitted data. | Yes |
| Collaborative work-flow | Ability for managers, compensation and HR Partners to collaborate on various compensation workflows. | Yes |
| Display out-of-guideline entries | Ability to display out-of-guideline entries made within adjustments, merit, bonus, equity. | Yes |
| **Reporting** | | |
| Standard reports are delivered with the system | System is delivered with a set number of standard reports. | Yes |

| Function | Function Description | Response |
|---|---|---|
| Ad-hoc reporting capability | System is delivered with an ad-hoc report-writing tool so that clients can create their own reports as needed. | Yes |
| Advanced Value metrics | Data analysis of comp gaps based on roles, hierarchy. | Yes |
| Reporting Security | Ability to enable field-level security and access to report creation, output and distribution. | Yes |
| **Security** | | |
| Logging In | Various login options (i.e. manual, SSO, LDAP). | Yes |
| File Transfer | Various file transfer protocol (i.e. FTP, sFTP, vendor-specific transfer import/export tool). | Yes |
| Encryption | Various data encryption ability (i.e. PGP). | Yes |
| Roles / Permissions | Configurable list of permission-based roles with detailed access rights to various organizations, levels, etc. Typically employees only view within their own organization hierarchy. | Yes |
| Integration | Ability to integrate organizational data with appropriate org system, i.e. HRIS/Payroll, employee data including employee salaries, levels, performance rating, etc. | Yes |
| Reporting UDFs | Ability to report user-defined fields. | Yes |
| Exporting reports | Reports can easily be exported to other applications (i.e. .xls, .pdf, .txt). | Yes |

| Function | Function Description | Response |
|---|---|---|

## Learning Management

| Content Management and Delivery | | |
|---|---|---|
| Application Simulation | Client content owners can create application simulations for use in training (i.e. "Show Me"/"Try Me" Flash-type simulations). | No |
| Assign learning content-based employee data | Learning content can be assigned to employees based on their job function or organizational data (not specific to position, but job family or organization). | Yes |
| Catalogs | Employees can search through and browse course catalogs to identify courses in which they are interested. | Yes |
| Competency Management - Third-Party Defined | Courses and learning plans can be built around competencies, driven by integration with a third-party vendor. | Yes |
| Competency Management – Customer-Defined | Courses and learning plans can be built around competencies as determined by the customer. | Yes |
| Offline Capabilities | Learning content can be downloaded for completion even if the user is not connected to the Internet/network. Can also upload results. | No |
| Employee Profile Management | System can house employee profiles that can be used for learning plan assignment, development plan creation and management (could be integration point). | Yes |
| External Content Integration | Employees can access, review, and register for courses in systems and online portals that are integrated with the LMS. | Yes |

| Function | Function Description | Response |
|----------|--------------------|----------|
| Internal Content Authoring | WYSIWYG (what you see is what you get) editor is built into the system for creation of learning materials within the system by client content owners. | Yes |
| Learning Plans | Customer can create learning plans for employees. Employees can manage their progress, review schedules, register for courses and access online courses from plans. Collaboration with employees and managers to create this learning plan (and appropriate workflow). Could be an integration point from PM tool. | Yes |
| Multiple Languages | System supports multiple languages for global implementations. | Yes |
| PowerPoint Conversion | System allows for uploading of PowerPoint files as learning content. | Yes |
| Repository | Digital repository for management of draft and active content is available in the system. Content managers would use this functionality (and allows for collaboration). | Yes |
| Scheduling | Users can book resources, locations and structures from within the system. This is an integration point as well. | Yes |
| Single Sign-On | Standard SSO capability for integration with client Intranet. | Yes |
| Version Control | Content owners have the ability to manage content versioning. | No |
| Virtual Classrooms | System provides virtual classroom functionality for live, remote learning sessions. | Yes |

| Function | Function Description | Response |
|---|---|---|
| **Testing and Tracking** | | |
| General Assessments | System allows for creation of assessments that aren't tied to particular training content. Could be tied to competencies. | Yes |
| Content Test Completion | Users can complete tests online as assigned. Could be offline as well. | Yes |
| Content Test Creation | System allows for creation of tests for learning content. | Yes |
| Polling | Polling can be conducted through one or more channels (e.g. Content, User Home Page Interface, etc.) | No |
| Test Completion Tracking | User test completion status and rates can be tracked. | Yes |
| Test Score Tracking | User test scores can be stored and tracked. | Yes |
| **Reporting** | | |
| Ad-hoc reporting capability | System is delivered with an ad-hoc report-writing tool so that clients can create their own reports as needed. | Yes |
| Data analysis | System provides functionality for advanced data analysis and dashboarding. | Yes |
| Reporting Security | Ability to enable field-level security and access to report creation, output and distribution. | Yes |
| Standard reports are delivered with the system | System is delivered with a minimum of 10 standard reports. | Yes |

| Function | Function Description | Response |
|---|---|---|
| **Integration** | | |
| Employee Profile Integration | System allows for employee profile integration with other talent management solutions (e.g. Performance, Succession, Compensation, Recruitment, etc.) | Yes |
| Integration | Ability to allow clients to create integrations through APIs, XML, flat files, etc. | No – Planned Q3 09 |
| **Web 2.0 Features** | | |
| Blogs | System allows for creation of blogs for content delivery. | Yes |
| Forums | System allows for creation and maintenance of forums to capture user-generated content and enable collaborative learning activities. | Yes |
| Other Collaborative Learning Tools | Additional collaborative learning tools are available. | Yes |
| Podcasting | System allows for creation of podcasts for content delivery. | Yes |
| RSS Feeds | System allows users to identify content "tracks" that they wish to monitor on a regular basis and displays updates in an RSS-like format. | No – Planned Q3 09 |
| Wikis | System allows for creation and maintenance of wikis to capture user-generated content and enable collaborative learning activities. | No – Planned Q3 09 |

| Function | Function Description | Response |
|---|---|---|
| **User Communication** | | |
| Completion Date Reminders | Users can be notified when they are approaching a target content completion date. | Yes |
| Completion Reminders | Users can be reminded to complete content that has been saved in progress. | Yes |
| Content Notifications | Users can be notified when new content is added to their learning plan or a track in which they are interested. | Yes |
| Manager Notifications | User managers and/or learning administrators can be notified when certain activities are completed. | Yes |
| Workflow | System allows for creation of workflow to communicate user status to content and people managers. | Yes |

# Peopleclick

## Company Information (provided by Peopleclick)

Company Name:            Peopleclick, Inc.

Corporate URL:           www.peopleclick.com

Main Phone:              (919) 645-2800

Main Email:              http://www.peopleclick.com/about/
                         contact_form.asp

Headquarters Address:    Two Hannover Square, 7th Floor,
                         Raleigh, NC 27601

**Type of Business or Areas of Focus:**
Talent Acquisition.

Number of Employees:     335

Year Founded:            1997

Stock Symbol:            N/A

## Company Description and History:

Peopleclick provides software and services that empower companies around the world to find, attract and hire quality people—in less time, with less risk. We offer the best technology, consulting expertise, support that give companies the vision to see and the flexibility to manage their entire staff, whether it be salaried, hourly, or contingent. Focused exclusively on the unique needs of the talent acquisition industry, Peopleclick has the extensive experience and proven technology necessary to help companies successfully manage this business-critical process. A privately-held company, Peopleclick serves 1,800 current clients in 192 countries, including 54 of the Fortune 100.

## Products/Services/Solutions:

### 1. Peopleclick® Recruitment Management System (RMS)

Peopleclick® RMS is an enterprise-wide recruitment management system that streamlines the work of recruiters and hiring managers. Delivered as software-as-a-service, the solution simplifies, automates and tracks the entire hiring process. Clients use RMS to reduce time-to-hire while increasing hiring quality through candidate identification, prescreening, selection and results measurement.

### 2. Peopleclick® RMS High Volume Solution

Peopleclick High Volume, a recruitment solution for high-volume and hourly recruiting, empowers hiring managers and the occasional user to quickly select qualified candidates from their Talent Inventory™ when a position becomes available. The solution has an intuitive interface designed to increase user adoption and also provides unique functionality to optimize candidate opportunities.

### 3. Peopleclick® Vendor Management System (VMS)

Peopleclick® VMS is an enterprise-wide, vendor management system that helps reduce the cost and increase the quality of contingent labor. Delivered on a software-as-a-service business model, the solution automates, tracks and reports on processes for engaging contractors and working with staffing firms. Clients use VMS to leverage preferred vendor relationships, negotiate lower rates, eliminate maverick spend and manage headcount to budget.

### 4. Peopleclick® Business Intelligence Platform

The Peopleclick Business Intelligence Platform provides an enterprise-wide picture of the entire staffing and recruiting process across all types of labor and all Peopleclick products. With the ability to schedule reports and display key information through dashboards, organizations can ensure all decision makers are provided with actionable data.

### 5. Peopleclick® Onboarding

Peopleclick Onboarding is a full-featured product that integrates seamlessly into the current Peopleclick RMS™ workflow to not only automate forms and task management but to extend the corporate culture into the employee's home through the extensive socialization features available in the New Hire Portal.

### 6. Peopleclick® Interview Scheduling

Peopleclick Interview Scheduling automates high-volume interview management. Through a self-service interface, interviewers and candidates can schedule interviews quickly and efficiently, saving time and significantly reducing costs.

### 7. Peopleclick Contact Management™

Peopleclick Contact Management is a revolutionary solution designed specifically for the HR industry to enable organizations to build a talent bank of contacts and convert them into potential candidates. It facilitates proactive, personal communication and supports image-awareness campaigns to build brand recognition with potential candidates.

### 8. Peopleclick® Affirmative Action Solutions

Peopleclick Affirmative Action Solutions offers the gold standard in affirmative action planning and OFCCP audit consulting services. Whether the organization prefers to run software and manage plans internally or outsource plan preparation to experts, Peopleclick solutions simplify affirmative action planning and analysis by giving clients the tools and consultants to generate 100 percent technically-compliant plans.

# Author's Peopleclick Functionality Matrix

| Function | Function Description | Response |
|---|---|---|

## Talent Acquisition

| Requisition Management & Posting | | |
|---|---|---|
| Multiple requisition forms allowed (Example: hourly, internal transfer, business unit specific, reoccurring, sourcing, college) | More than one requisition form/template can be configured in a client's database to accommodate variance in business units or type of recruiting. (Example: A user from the Manufacturing group can enter a requisition and only see and populate fields that are applicable to Mfg. A different user from the Services group can enter a requisition and only see the fields designated for a Services requisition within the same database. | Yes |
| Data Segregation | Ability to segregate requisitions and candidates by hire type (executive, HR, etc.) or organization. | Yes |
| Requisition approval routing workflow and approval status indicator | Select a list of approvers, route for approval via email. Approvals should be able to be sent in parallel or sequentially. | Yes |
| Approval status tracking | The status of the approval process is tracked and displayed real-time on the requisition in the application as well as in the subsequent emails that go to the second and third approver, etc. | Yes |
| Pre-defined approval routing lists | Lists of approvers can be created, saved and/or assigned to a user or requisition, or defined by the organizational structure automatically. | Yes |

| Function | Function Description | Response |
|---|---|---|
| Approvals can take place directly from an email | When approving a requisition, the approver can take action directly from the email notification without having to log into the application. | Yes |
| Pre-qualifying questions based on position/job needs, including weighting to filter for top candidates | Questions developed, defined and delivered to a candidate in the online application process tied directly to the job posting/requirements, including weighting to filter for top candidates. | Yes |
| Knock-out questions | Ability to establish certain questions to be disqualifiers, where if the candidate does not answer correctly, the process is ended. | Yes |
| Job posting scheduling | Check a box to select the appropriate career site(s) for the job to appear. Scheduling of start and end dates of posting to any given site to allow for staggered posting. | Yes |
| Advanced job descriptions - Formatting and Spell Checking | Ability to edit and format job descriptions and marketing messages with MS Word, like functions for Bolding, Underlining and Spell Checking. | Yes |
| Electronic job board relationship management (facilitation of job positing to all e-media providers) | Ability to identify and post job opportunities to an unlimited number of electronic job boards and other end destinations. Ability to multi-select boards, and push positions out to the market. | Yes |
| **Candidate Experience** | | |
| Unlimited Career Site Portals | Ability to establish an unlimited number of integrated career sites for different purposes - such as college recruiting, location-specific kiosks, or for a specific job family-like Sales or Engineering. Determine if there are additional costs per Career Section. | Yes |

| Function | Function Description | Response |
|---|---|---|
| Online profile form(s) defined by the client | Data collection form(s) that can be pushed to a candidate to gather needed information for relationship management and interested resume submissions. Customer can tailor the form to his/her specification, adding or removing fields. | Yes |
| User-defined secure login user name and password. | User created login and password authentication for accessing profile and career management activities. | Yes |
| Candidate login optional | Candidate can submit resume and apply to jobs without establishing a password-protected user account. | Yes |
| Resume submission via upload of file - Candidate | Candidate can browse hard drive for formatted resume and upload to candidate resume repository. | Yes |
| Resume submission via upload of file - Recruiter/Manager | Recruiter/Manager can browse hard drive for formatted resume and upload to candidate resume repository. | Yes |
| Resume builder functionality | Ability for candidates without a formal resume to submit a resume via a "Resume Builder." | Yes |
| Extraction of data from resume to create profile | Extraction engine behind the text or uploaded resume for population of fielded data in the candidate profile. | Yes |
| Candidate-defined Job Agents | Candidates can establish job search parameters and be notified when jobs that meet their preferences are posted. | Yes |
| Candidate status check | Candidates can login to check the status of their resume submissions. | Yes |
| Ability to upload attachments | | Yes |

| Function | Function Description | Response |
|---|---|---|
| Ability for candidate to save a submission as a draft | | Yes |
| Candidate self-withdrawal | Ability for candidates to remove themselves from consideration for a position. | Yes |
| Conceptual search for the candidate when searching for jobs | Candidates can use "free form" language to search for jobs. | Yes |
| **Sourcing/CRM** | | |
| Specific job referral and general referrals | Employees can submit a resume as a general referral or to a specific job. | Yes |
| Notifications to the referring employee and the referred candidate | Email notifications are automatically sent to referring employee and to the candidate who was referred. | Yes |
| Referral status check | Employees can review a list of candidates they have referred and check their status. | Yes |
| Tracking steps and status searches | Recruiters can search for candidates based on their tracking steps and status against requisitions. | Yes |
| Keyword search against free form text and fielded data | Keyword search against text records from candidate and fielded data in the same search. | Yes |
| Search criteria highlighted for relevance in record review | Search results with indicators for criteria matching and relevance in the results. | Yes |
| Configurable search results list | Column headers displayed in a search results list can be configured with different data elements from the candidate record. (Example: Education, Work History, Phone Number.) | Yes |

| Function | Function Description | Response |
|---|---|---|
| Ability to search file attachments | Keyword searching will scan resumes that have been submitted as file attachments as well as text fields. | Yes |
| Ability to create "overnight" searches | | Yes |
| Conceptual search engine to match resumes | Ability to use the requisition's job description or a large text phrase to find matching resumes using a conceptual search or natural language search engine. Conceptual searches should also be able to be conducted with fielded search. | Yes |
| "More like this" searching | Ability to take a resume and conduct a search to find other resumes that are similar to it (more like it). | Yes |
| Library of candidate correspondence/ communication templates | Ability for clients to create a library of correspondence templates that can be sent to candidates at the user's discretion. | Yes |
| Editable correspondence at the user level | Users can make edits to the correspondence at the time of generation and distribution. | Yes |
| Agency Portal | Functionality designed for the management of third-party staffing agencies. Includes the ability to push requisitions to one or more suppliers and receive agency resume submissions. | Yes |
| Contingent Labor Management | Functionality designed specifically for the requisition and management of contract labor including distribution of job requirements to multiple vendors, submission and review of resumes, tracking of assignment, time reporting and billing. | Yes |

| Function | Function Description | Response |
|---|---|---|
| Candidate Pool Generation (Leads/ Prospective Candidates) | Able to enter limited candidate information (less required fields than regular candidate profile without comprising the configuration of the candidate profile) and develop target candidate pool for key skills. | Yes |
| Marketing Campaigns (Leads/Prospective Candidates) | Includes proactive candidate pool in messaging. Advertising campaigns or special event invitations. This should include the ability to send emails to thousands of candidates (as necessary). | Yes |
| Sending resumes to a manager | Ability to send a "Formatted Resume" to a Hiring Manager. | Yes |
| **Assessment and Interview Management** | | |
| Customer-defined workflow steps and status | Customer can set up steps and status for tracking candidates through the recruiting process, with ability to tailor it for required and desired steps. | Yes |
| Customer can define multiple process workflows (Example: employee referral, internal transfers, etc.) | Ability to create multiple applicant workflows (set of tracking steps & status) to be selected at the requisition level. | Yes |
| Workflow triggered alerts | Alerts can be set up in the system to drive the next step in the process or to function as reminders. | Yes |
| Ability to create a "tree-structure" workflow (i.e. step A can be followed by step B, C, D or E) | | Yes |

| Function | Function Description | Response |
|----------|---------------------|----------|
| Volume hiring updates | The ability to change the status for a group of candidates to hired in a single step (e.g. mass hiring in one step). | Yes |
| Integrated Assessments | Ability to store and/or integrate validated assessment tools into the recruiting workflow for certain jobs. | Yes |
| Assessment Triggers | Ability for Assessment to automatically be presented to candidates based on responses to pre-screening questions or other data in their profile. | Yes |
| Assessment on demand | Ability to push an online assessment to a candidate on demand via email link. | Yes |
| Interview team member history | Ability to select and record a list of inter-viewing team members for a requisition. | Yes |
| Interview team notifications | Ability to send an email notification (including a calendar meeting request) to the interview team members when scheduling the interview within the system (including interview packets, resumes, etc. when sending the email request). | Yes |
| Storage of interview-er comments | Ability to configure an online interview feedback form to capture the comments from each interviewer. | Yes |
| Interviewer attach-ments | Ability to include attachments to the interviewer notifications (e.g. interview guidelines, interview schedule, resume, etc.) | Yes |

| Function | Function Description | Response |
|---|---|---|
| **Offer Management and Onboarding** | | |
| Approval routing and status tracking | Select a list of approvers, route for approval via email. In addition, the status of the approval process is tracked and displayed real-time on the offer in the application as well as in the subsequent emails that go to the second and third approver, etc. | Yes |
| Pre-defined approval routing lists | Lists of approvers can be created, saved, and/or assigned to a user or requisition. | Yes |
| Approvals can take place directly from an email | When approving an offer, the approver can take action directly from the email notification without having to log into the application. | Yes |
| Offer letters can be generated by merging fields into letter templates | Data can be merged from the candidate record, the requisition and the offer terms into offer letter templates. | Yes |
| Offer letters can be edited at the user level | Users can make edits to the offer letter at the time of generation and distribution. | Yes |
| Specific Onboarding Module | Does the product offer a specific Onboarding module, allowing clients to define required notifications at hire and send notifications through the system? (e.g. provisioning, IT for user account setup, new hire, manager checklist, etc.) | Yes |
| Onboarding Documentation Management | Electronically provide new hire paperwork and track completion of key documents (I-9, Non Disclosures, Benefits Paperwork). | Yes |

| Function | Function Description | Response |
|---|---|---|
| **Global Capabilities & Compliance** | | |
| EEO Compliance data collection | Configurable notification and collection of EEO compliance information at variable points in the process. | Yes |
| Global – in-country data collection based on regulations | Configurable data requests based on in-country requirements. Example: Germany, martial status, number of children. | Yes |
| Ability to present Career Sections in Multiple Languages | Ability to present Career Sections in Multiple Languages. | Yes |
| Ability to present the Recruiter and Manager Portals in multiple languages | Ability to present the Recruiter and Manager Portals in multiple languages. | Yes |
| Data Segregation by country, region or predefined type | Data Segregation, .i.e. preventing users from a particular country or location from seeing candidates who are in another country or location. | Yes |
| OFCCP Compliance tools to enable search and applicant declaration | Functionality consistent with the new OFCCP definition of Internet Applicant (record keeping for searches, candidate submissions, etc.) | Yes |
| Privacy Policy acknowledgements | Ability to require that candidates agree with the privacy policy before they submit. | Yes |
| Compliance with Data Privacy | Ability for customers to remove a candidate's data at that candidate's request. | Yes |
| Tax Credit Screening & Processing | Provides automatic Tax ID and SSN validation. Automatically transmits request to conduct tax credit screening for WOTC, WTW and more through to screening partners and displays those results within the Candidate profile for review and processing upon hire. | Yes |

| Function | Function Description | Response |
|---|---|---|
| **Reporting & Integration** | | |
| Standard reports are delivered with the system | System is delivered with a minimum of 10 standard reports. | Yes |
| Ad-hoc reporting capability | System is delivered with an ad-hoc report-writing tool so that clients can create their own reports as needed. | Yes |
| Reporting Security | Ability to enable field-level security and access to report creation, output and distribution. | Yes |
| Reporting Distribution | Ability to generate scheduled reports and distribute through email. | Yes |
| Real-Time Reporting | Ability to report on data in the application in real time (not based on a refresh of data in a reporting environment). | Yes |
| HRIS Integration | Ability to create bi-directional integrations from an HRIS to the ATS. | Yes |
| Integration - Client Self-Service Tools | Ability for clients to create their own integration touch points as needed (and make them operational). | No |
| Integration - API capability | Ability to allow clients to create integrations through APIs. | No |

# Saba

## Company Information (provided by Saba)

**Company Name:** Saba

**Corporate URL:** www.saba.com

**Main Phone:** (650) 581-2500

**Main Email:** info@saba.com

**Headquarters Address:** 2400 Bridge Pkwy., Redwood Shores, CA 94065

**Type of Business or Areas of Focus:**
Human Capital Management Software and Services.

**Number of Employees:** 560

**Year Founded:** 1997

**Stock Symbol (If Applicable):** Nasdaq SABA

## Company Description and History:

Saba provides unified solutions for people management and productivity across learning, collaboration, performance, compensation and talent management, enabling customers to align, develop, manage and reward their people by using various sets of formal and informal processes. In people management, Saba has the most global capability; the most successful implementations at large global enterprises and the most flexible range of deployment options in the business. This is based on over 10 years of focus on people management, full ownership of IP and over $200 million of R&D invested in our solutions.

In 1997, Saba delivered the first enterprise learning management system, enabling customers to significantly increase training efficiency and effectiveness through the Internet. In 2003, Saba introduced the first unified learning and performance management solution to align learning objectives to organizational goals. In 2005, Saba delivered the first fully-unified HCM solution to align learning plans, performance plans and talent pools to competency requirements and goals and objectives of the organization. In 2006, Saba acquired Centra Software and created the first enterprise people management solution with real-time collaboration. In 2008, Saba took advantage of the rich person profile, competency-driven expertise and real-time collaboration available in its people management platform to introduce the most powerful enterprise social networking platform to connect people to expertise—Saba Social.

## Products/Services/Solutions:

### 1. Saba Learning Suite

Saba Learning Suite provides comprehensive management systems for formal and informal learning, so that organizations can identify, manage, develop and measure the capabilities and knowledge of people throughout an enterprise and the supply chain. It empowers employees to connect and contribute their expertise and knowledge. These management systems maximize people's contributions to the organization's goals and performance and drives productivity through a connected corporate community.

- Differentiators
  - Provides best-in-class capabilities for catalog and curriculum management; compliance, continuing education and competency management; for-profit training; content development and management; virtual learning; informal learning and collaboration.
  - Offers the broadest approach to blended learning—real-time or self-paced, formal or informal.
  - Features strong governance capabilities for delegation and control within multi-business unit enterprises.
  - Contains unification with other components of people management lifecycle including performance management, succession planning and compensation management.

## 2. Saba Centra Suite

Saba Centra Suite facilitates real-time knowledge sharing between people across a connected, corporate community of employees, customers, partners, suppliers and prospects to accelerate mission-critical initiatives, improve learning and productivity and reduce costs. It deploys learning through virtual classes and recorded sessions that extend the reach of the LMS.

- Differentiators
  - Has unique ability to extend the value of the virtual class. No other Web conferencing tool offers as powerful virtual labs or recording and playback features, enabling organizations to build a high level of interactivity into both live and recorded sessions to enable greater learning effectiveness.
  - Features tight integration to Saba Learning Suite providing the easiest administration and best ownership experience.
  - Provides excellent support for mixed bandwidth environments to extend accessibility.

## 3. Saba Performance Suite

Saba Performance Suite enables organizations to continuously align individual's activities with key organizational goals and establish a relevant performance review process that clarifies expectations, measures results, increases accountability and identifies actionable improvements.

- Differentiators
  - Delivers a more strategic approach that focuses on communicating a complete "Success Plan" to engage and align the workforce. Automatically loads pre-set objectives, goals and competencies directly into a configurable performance review.
  - Enables a more informed, relevant performance review process, while providing HR administrators with all the tools they need to track and analyze performance measures.
  - Offers unique collaborative capabilities, including the ability to cascade and share goals along people-centric, organizational or cross-functional lines, and identify and connect with expertise.
  - Is completely configurable, so that user experience, people policies and even depth of functionality can be changed per business unit.

### 4. Saba Talent Suite

Saba Talent Suite enables organizations to reduce risk through proactive workforce and succession planning that includes identifying, developing, tracking and measuring current individual capabilities, organizational capabilities, as well as the capabilities of future leaders.

- Differentiators
  - — Enables a pervasive, proactive approach to talent by empowering every manager, not just HR, with the dynamic decision support tools needed to mine the organization for needed talent, proactively develop individuals for success, model different organizational scenarios, identify risk and take action.
  - — Features robust profiles that include experience, education, learning history, competency proficiency, career interests, flight risk, potential and much more. It gives the broadest, most comprehensive view of talent across the organization and the supply chain.
  - — Contains a workforce modeling solution that takes rich people profiles and detailed job requirements into account, not just positions and budgets.
  - — Provides rich organizational charting and workforce analytics capabilities to enable quick decision-making.

## Author's Saba Functionality Matrix

| Function | Function Description | Response |
|---|---|---|

Performance Management

| Performance Dashboard | | |
|---|---|---|
| Dashboard configuration | Ability to configure dashboard based on user preference. | Yes |
| Create and display reports | Display reports that can be generated (i.e. review completion progress, goal progress). | Yes |

| Function | Function Description | Response |
|---|---|---|
| Create and display charts and graphs | Display charts and graphs that are available to illustrate planning actions. | Yes |
| Display help and reference tools | Display and view help and reference tools that can be selected by link or mouse hover. | Yes |
| **Employee Information Review (Data Import from HRIS/LMS)** | | |
| Import and display employee information | Display name, address, phone, email, location, photo, education (typically pulled from HRIS). | Yes |
| Import and display employee position information | Display current job title, Job summary, job family, job level/grade, job code, FLSA, shift, status (FT/PT) (typically pulled through HRIS). | Yes |
| Create and display work history | Display created previous work history (i.e. name of company, job title, responsibilities/duties, employment dates). | Yes |
| Create and display years in management | Display created years of management experience (manually entered or via integration). | Yes |
| Create and display years in industry | Display created years of experience in industry (primarily entered manually). | Yes |
| Import, create and display employee language(s) | Display employee languages (i.e. read, written, fluent) (primarily entered manually). | Yes |
| Import, create and display employee affiliations | Display employee affiliation memberships. | Yes |
| Import, create and display employee certifications | Display employee certifications and dates. | Yes |

| Function | Function Description | Response |
|---|---|---|
| Import, create and display employee licenses | Display employee licenses and dates (usually a text box) to include expiration dates (transportation, professional licenses, healthcare licenses, etc.) | Yes |
| Import and display organizational information | Display company name, company division, company department (typically imported from HRIS). | Yes |
| Import and display management hierarchy information | Display multiple levels of management names and information (i.e. Executive Management, Division Head, Department Head, Direct Manager, Employee). | Yes |
| Import and display direct reports | Display name and information of employee direct reports. | Yes |
| Import and display matrix manager hierarchy information | Display multiple levels of matrix management names and information (i.e. Employee has dotted line reporting relationships). | Yes |
| Import and display multiple manager hierarchy information | Display multiple levels of numerous management names and information (i.e. Employee reports to more than one manager directly). | Yes |
| Organizational Chart View | Organizational information can be displayed in an Org Chart View (note how this is displayed visually). | Yes |
| Organizational Change Requests | Due to potential errors within HRMS, manager has the ability to request an employee change in hierarchy (i.e. manager name, organization, location, job role); changes can be configured to require approval. | Yes |
| Import and display employee current and past compensation | Display employee's past and current base salary, bonus, equity, commission, etc. | Yes |

| Function | Function Description | Response |
|---|---|---|
| Import and display employee's most recent performance measures | Display employee's current competencies, goals, skills, projects, performance rating, development plan and personal improvement plan. | Yes |
| Import and display employee's previous performance measures | Display employee's previous competencies, goals, skills, projects, performance rating, development plan, personal improvement plan. | Yes |
| Complete and display employee training | Display employee's completed and assigned training (i.e. mandatory/development) - Note if there is any integration with LMS. | Yes |
| External Identifier | Ability to have external identifier field to bring in content on goals from a third-party application (i.e. description, start date, critical, public goal); can be configured to be read-only for imports. | Yes |
| UDFs | Available user-defined fields for employee profile. | Yes |
| **Career Planning / Personal Development (Employee)** | | |
| Create and display future career plan scenarios | Display multiple future career plans (vertical, horizontal, both). Where does employee want to go next? (lateral, promotion, etc.) | Yes |
| Select and display positions, job families and organizations/ divisions of interest | Display selected positions and organizations of interest from import of job list and organization list (mentorships and cross-training) - gives the employee the opportunity to identify a position, job-family or organization of interest. | Yes |
| Create and display training requests | Display developmental training requests (entered by an employee or manager). This could be an integration point to the LMS. | Yes |

| Function | Function Description | Response |
|---|---|---|
| Create and display executive/professional requests | Display various executive/professional requests (i.e. executive coaching, cross training, job shadowing, speaking engagements, writing submittals, managing people, presentations, mentoring, apprenticeships). | Yes |
| Create and display organization affiliations and/or conferences/seminars | Display employee organization/affiliation or conference/seminar requests to join or attend. | Yes |
| Select and display competency development | Display selected desired competencies (entered by employee). | Yes |
| Create self-asses job readiness | Display selected self-readiness from list of options (i.e. Now, 0-3 months, 3-6 months, 6-9 months, 9-12 months, 12 months +). | Yes |
| Display position Gap % | Display gap % of employee readiness to ideal position as well as required training, license(s), education, certification(s). This could be automatically calculated by system (key differentiator). This is a gap analysis on underlying competencies (most recent performance rating vs. competencies required for next position). | Yes |
| Select and display willingness to relocate | Display selected willingness to relocate (i.e. yes, no, maybe, comments). | Yes |
| Display career prerequisites | Display required training, education, certification(s), license(s) for position of interest. | Yes |

| Function | Function Description | Response |
|---|---|---|
| Submit development requests for approval | Submit development self-assessments to direct manager for review, feedback and approval (areas where the development needs to occur, as well as specific courses, conferences to help meet these development areas). Could be an integration point with LMS. | Yes |
| **Career Development (Manager)** | | |
| Create or select and display employee training goals | Display created or selected employee completed training, assigned training (mandatory/development), scheduled training and employee training requests. This is the manager identifying training goals for an employee. | Yes |
| Competency Development | Display assigned professional/leadership competencies. | Yes |
| Create and display executive/professional assignments | Display various executive/professional recommendations (i.e. executive coaching, cross-training, job shadowing, speaking engagements, writing submittals, managing people, presentations, mentoring, apprenticeships). | Yes |
| Create and display organization affiliations and/or conferences/seminars | Display employee organization/affiliation or conference/seminar recommendations. | Yes |
| **Individual Goal / Self-Assessment (Employee)** | | |
| Select, create and display individual development goals | Display selected or created completed training, improvement competencies, executive coaching, promotion, cross-training. | Yes |

| Function | Function Description | Response |
|----------|---------------------|----------|
| Select competency development | Display selected development competencies. Employees select competencies they want to develop for their career in the annual review. | Yes |
| Submit goal/competency assessment for approval | Submit manual or automatic goal/competency assessment to direct manager. | Yes |
| Solicit and display feedback | Select employees (i.e. managers, matrix managers, peers) to solicit performance feedback (i.e. 360, peer review, business review) and display results. | Yes |
| Create and display self- performance notes | Display created performance notes (i.e. kudos) throughout the review cycle (manually entered by employee or can solicit feedback throughout project). | Yes |
| Create and display self-goal assessment progress | Display created self-goal progress (i.e. quantitative % of completion, qualitative to include customer satisfaction, timeline to include start/completion date). | Yes |
| Submit goal/competency review for approval | Submit manual or automatic goal/competency assessment to direct manager and higher levels. | Yes |
| UDFs | Available user-defined fields for employee goals. | Yes |
| **Review Process (Employee and Manager)** | | |
| Select and display competencies | Display selected professional or leadership competencies. | Yes |
| Select and display goals/objectives | Display selected goals/objectives (i.e. quantitative and/or qualitative). | Yes |
| Select and display goal alignment | Display selected goal alignment to company, organization, department and/or manager goals (cascading goals). | Yes |

| Function | Function Description | Response |
|---|---|---|
| Select or create and display projects | Display selected or created projects. | Yes |
| Select and display project alignment to goals | Display selected project alignment to company, organization, department and/or manager goals. | Yes |
| Select or create and display skills | Display selected or created company, organization, department, employee skills. | Yes |
| Create and display employee performance notes | Display created performance notes (positive or negative) throughout the review cycle. These are notes created by the manager. | Yes |
| Solicit and display feedback | Select employees (i.e. managers, matrix managers, peers) to solicit performance feedback (i.e. 360, peer review, business review) and display. Pay particular attention to how this is gathered and entered into the system. | Yes |
| Create and display employee goal assessment review | Display created employee goal progress (i.e. quantitative % of completion, qualitative to include customer satisfaction, timeline to include start/completion date). This is the manager entering the assessment. | Yes |
| Performance review filtering | Manager can filter performance review information based on approval status, assigned to, author/owner, manager, employee, organization, location, job field, job role, review cycle, review group, review group owner, overall rating; filtering can be cumulative. | Yes |
| Batch activities | Manager can take group actions on multiple employees simultaneously. | Yes |
| UDFs | Available user-defined fields for employee competencies. | Yes |

| Function | Function Description | Response |
|---|---|---|
| **Workflow** | | |
| Review cycles | Ability to configure multiple review cycles and tie to various reviews. | Yes |
| Review groups | Ability to define review recipients based on dates, job function, organization, job code, etc. | Yes |
| Workflow Order | Ability to configure order of workflow (i.e. self-assessments can be configured to be completed first). | Yes |
| Notifications | Ability to push reviews to employees and managers | Yes |
| Reminders | Ability to send reminders to employees and managers via email (manual and automatic). | Yes |
| Acknowledgements | Ability to send auto-acknowledgements triggered by event/activity. | Yes |
| Next Level Approval | Ability to auto/manually route to multiple levels of approval. | Yes |
| Configurable work-flow | Ability to configure various steps of the review process, to make review steps mandatory, to have manager override capability, to display/hide visual graphic workflow diagram. | Yes |
| Auto/Manual Pro-gression | Ability to automatically or manually prog-ress through the review process. | Yes |
| Review form | Exportable and printable review form. | Yes |
| **System Admin** | | |
| Review sections | Ability to configure multiple review sec-tions, including goals, competencies, comments, rating models, etc. | Yes |

| Function | Function Description | Response |
|----------|---------------------|----------|
| Configurable rating models | Does it configure and display alpha and numeric values? Can values be rounded (up/down/both), value ranges, number of decimals (1-5)? | Yes |
| Comments | Display comments that are available in individual review sections and overall review. Can they be configured to be mandatory with ability to be overridden by management? | Yes |
| Goals | Ability to link organizational, divisional, departmental, individual goals into sections and to display goal progress. | Yes |
| Competencies | Ability to link competencies into sections. | Yes |
| Weightings | Ability to weigh employee performance based on goals and competencies. | Yes |
| **Search Functionality** | | |
| Basic Employee Search | Basic search by employee name (i.e. first or last name or a combination of both). | Yes |
| Job/Position Basic Search | Basic search by job role or position title, etc. | Yes |
| Competency Basic Search | Basic search by competency name. | Yes |
| Advanced Search | More detailed search capabilities that combine various search criteria or fields; may include optional weighting to determine which employees are retrieved in a search as well as each person's rank in the search results. | Yes |

| Function | Function Description | Response |
|---|---|---|
| Succession Planning Search | Search functionality that dynamically generates the criteria used to match employees who would make good succession candidates with a specific position profile (could have various levels of "fit"). | Yes |
| **Employee View / Navigation / Help / Other** | | |
| List View | Display employee goals, business goals or projects; the list mode is a list of items with information on key dates and progress. | Yes |
| Card View | Display employee goals, business goals or projects using the card mode; the card mode provides details on one item at a time and offers the possibility of editing progress. This can also include employee photos as well. | Yes |
| Timeline / Gantt | Display employee goals, business goals or projects using the timeline mode; the timeline mode provides a timeline view of an item's start and due dates. | Yes |
| Org Chart | Managers can access and manage information on their direct reports for all functionalities activated; the organizational chart will provide key data (i.e. risk of loss or most recent performance rating) for each of the manager's direct reports. | Yes |
| Mini-Org Chart | Displays a single analytic data point at a time; the manager can drill down into all layers of his organization and can view key metrics (i.e. performance reviews, goals, succession). | Yes |
| Graphs | Graphical display of various information (i.e. Gap Analysis, goal progress, review completion progress). | Yes |

| Function | Function Description | Response |
|---|---|---|
| Help Links | Online help, FAQs, customer support, product version. | Yes |
| Attach Documents | Ability to attach reference documents to various sections within the system. | Yes |
| Browser capabilities | Supported by general Internet access (works with standard browsers: IE, Safari, Mozilla, Opera). | Yes |
| Mouse-Over Hover | Additional tooltips or descriptions that display when users hover mouse pointer over various graphics or words within the system. | Yes |
| Web 2.0 | Ability to utilize Web 2.0 functionality, i.e. social networking. | Yes |
| **Security** | | |
| Logging In | Various login options (i.e. manual, SSO, LDAP). | Yes |
| File Transfer | Various file transfer protocol (i.e. FTP, sFTP, vendor-specific transfer import/export tool). | Yes |
| Encryption | Various data encryption ability (i.e. PGP). | Yes |
| Roles / Permissions | Configurable list of permission-based roles with detailed access rights to various organizations, levels, etc. Typically employees only view within their own organization hierarchy. | Yes |
| Integration | Ability to integrate organizational data i.e. HRIS/ATS/ LMS and employee data including competencies, training, development plans, etc. | Yes |

| Function | Function Description | Response |
|---|---|---|
| **Reporting** | | |
| Standard reports are delivered with the system | System is delivered with a set number of standard reports | Yes |
| Ad-hoc reporting capability | System is delivered with an ad-hoc report-writing tool so that clients can create reports as needed. | No |
| Advanced Value metrics | Data analysis of employee review process status, goal progress by hierarchy. | Yes |
| Reporting Security | Ability to enable field-level security and access to report creation, output and distribution. | Yes |
| Reporting UDFs | Ability to report user-defined fields. | Yes |
| Exporting reports | Reports can easily be exported to other applications (i.e. .xls, .pdf, .txt). | Yes |

## Succession Planning

| Succession Planning (Manager - Planning of Individual Talent Matched to Critical Roles) | | |
|---|---|---|
| Create and display critical roles for today | Display critical job roles (i.e. title, level, location, division, organization). | Yes |
| Create and display critical roles for future | Display critical job roles (i.e. title, level, location, division, organization) for future (workforce planning-like tools). | Yes |
| Calculate and display performance rating | Performance rating is automatically averaged from various sections of the performance review and displayed (current and past). | Yes |

| Function | Function Description | Response |
|---|---|---|
| Calculate and display performance ranking | High potential employees will be automatically ranked according to order of fit with critical role (i.e. 9-box grid, numeric ranking, high performer, high potential); can be ranked by position, organization, etc. | Yes |
| Multi-dimensional matrix | Matrix that can be configured up to various # of cells (i.e. 9-box, 12-box, 16-box, 25-box); text within grid is configurable. | Yes |
| Various dimensions of matrix | Matrix displays employee performance, potential, number of succession plans an employee is on, years in management, years in industry. | Yes |
| Navigation from multi-dimensional matrix | Manager can select an employee within the matrix and navigate to employee information (i.e. Performance review, talent profile, employee goals, career plan). | Yes |
| Display employee comparisons | Display comparison of multiple high potential employees according to fit to critical role (i.e. # of employees to compare, comparable data, fit gap analysis, ranking analysis, bench strength). | Yes |
| Create and display role readiness | Manager can create and display high potential employee role readiness (i.e. now, 0-3 months, 3-6 months, 6-9 months, 9-12 months, 12+ months). | Yes |
| Create and display retention risk | Manager can create and display high potential employee retention/loss/flight risk (i.e. high, medium, low, comments). | Yes |
| Create and display role willingness | Manager can create and display high potential employee role willingness (i.e. yes, no, comments). | Yes |
| Create and display willingness to relocate | Manager can create and display high potential employee willingness to relocate (i.e. yes, no, maybe, comments). | Yes |

| Function | Function Description | Response |
|----------|---------------------|----------|
| Create and display willingness to travel | Manager can create and display high potential employee willingness to travel (i.e. none, 25-50%, 50-75%, 75-100%). | Yes |
| Create and display interest in international assignment | Manager can create and display high potential employee interest in international assignment (i.e. yes, no, maybe). | Yes |
| Create and display interim replacement for critical role | Manager can create and display high potential interim replacement for critical roles. | Yes |
| Display of gap analysis | Automatically calculate and display high potential employees' fit gap analysis to their next position and ranking. | Yes |
| UDFs | Available user-defined fields for succession planning. | Yes |
| **Succession Pooling (Manager - Planning of a Talent Pool for Critical Roles)** | | |
| Display high potential pool | Display nominated and/or approved high potential pool (i.e. employee information, designated nominators, designated approvers, approvals, rejections, role readiness, rejection comments). | Yes |
| Calculate and display performance rating | Performance rating is automatically averaged from various sections of the performance review and displayed (current and past). | Yes |
| Calculate and display performance ranking | Pool of high potential employees will be automatically ranked according to order of fit with critical role (i.e. 9-box grid, numeric ranking, high performer, high potential). | Yes |

| Function | Function Description | Response |
|----------|---------------------|----------|
| Display employee comparisons | Display comparison of multiple high potential employees according to fit to critical role (i.e. # of employees to compare, comparable data, fit gap analysis, ranking analysis, bench strength). | Yes |
| Create and display role readiness | Manager can create and display high potential employee role readiness (i.e. now, 0-3 months, 3-6 months, 6-9 months, 9-12 months, 12+ months). | Yes |
| Create and display retention risk | Manager can create and display high potential employee retention/loss/flight risk (i.e. high, medium, low, comments). | Yes |
| Create and display role willingness | Manager can create and display high potential employee role willingness (i.e. yes, no, comments). | Yes |
| Create and display willingness to relocate | Manager can create and display high potential employee willingness to relocate (i.e. yes, no, maybe, comments). | Yes |
| Create and display willingness to travel | Manager can create and display high potential employee willingness to travel (i.e. none, 25-50%, 50-75%, 75-100%). | Yes |
| Create and display interest in international assignment | Manager can create and display high potential employee interest in international assignment (i.e. yes, no, maybe). | Yes |
| Create and display interim replacement for critical role | Manager can create and display high potential interim replacement for critical roles. | Yes |
| Display of gap analysis | Automatically calculate and display high potential employees' fit gap analysis to position and ranking analysis of employees to position. | Yes |
| UDFs | Available user-defined fields for succession pooling. | Yes |

| Function | Function Description | Response |
|---|---|---|
| **Workflow** | | |
| Succession approval workflow | Ability to define or edit approvers, add/remove users and roles; ability to change the approval order; ability to reject with comments. | Yes |
| Nominations for succession pool | Ability to nominate, reject and enter comments on nominated HiPo employees. | Yes |
| **Reporting** | | |
| Standard reports are delivered with the system | System is delivered with a set number of standard reports. | Yes |
| Ad-hoc reporting capability | System is delivered with an ad-hoc report-writing tool so that clients can create their own reports as needed. | No |
| Advanced Value metrics | Data analysis of high performers / high potential employees, identified gaps, critical roles. | Yes |
| Reporting Security | Ability to enable field- level security and access to report creation, output and distribution. | Yes |
| Reporting UDFs | Ability to report user-defined fields. | Yes |
| Exporting reports | Reports can easily be exported to other applications (i.e. .xls, .pdf, .txt). | Yes |

## Learning Management

| Content Management and Delivery | | |
|---|---|---|
| Application Simulation | Client content owners can create application simulations for use in training (i.e. "Show Me"/"Try Me" Flash-type simulations). | Yes |

| Function | Function Description | Response |
|----------|---------------------|----------|
| Assign learning content-based employee data | Learning content can be assigned to employees based on their job function or organizational data (not specific to position, but job family or organization). | Yes |
| Catalogs | Employees can search through and browse course catalogs to identify courses in which they are interested. | Yes |
| Competency Management - Third-Party Defined | Courses and learning plans can be built around competencies, driven by integration with a third-party vendor. | Yes |
| Competency Management - Customer-Defined | Courses and learning plans can be built around competencies as determined by the customer. | Yes |
| Offline Capabilities | Learning content can be downloaded for completion even if the user is not connected to the Internet/network. Can also upload results. | Yes |
| Employee Profile Management | System can house employee profiles that can be used for learning plan assignment, development plan creation and management (could be integration point). | Yes |
| External Content Integration | Employees can access, review and register for courses in systems and online portals that are integrated with the LMS. | Yes |
| Internal Content Authoring | WYSIWYG (what you see is what you get) editor is built into the system for creation of learning materials within the system by client content owners. | Yes |

| Function | Function Description | Response |
|---|---|---|
| Learning Plans | Customer can create learning plans for employees. Employees can manage their progress, review schedules, register for courses and access online courses from plans. Collaboration with employees and managers to create this learning plan (and appropriate workflow). Could be an integration point from PM tool. | Yes |
| Multiple Languages | System supports multiple languages for global implementations. | Yes |
| PowerPoint Conversion | System allows for uploading of PowerPoint files as learning content. | Yes |
| Repository | Digital repository for management of draft and active content is available in the system. Content managers would use this functionality (allows for collaboration). | Yes |
| Scheduling | Users can book resources, locations, and structures from within the system. This is an integration point as well. | Yes |
| Single Sign-On | Standard SSO capability for integration with client Intranet. | Yes |
| Version Control | Content owners have the ability to manage content versioning. | Yes |
| Virtual Classrooms | System provides virtual classroom functionality for live, remote learning sessions. | Yes |
| **Testing and Tracking** | | |
| General Assessments | System allows for creation of assessments that aren't tied to particular training content. Could be tied to competencies. | Yes |

| Function | Function Description | Response |
|---|---|---|
| Content Test Completion | Users can complete tests online as assigned. Could be offline as well. | Yes |
| Content Test Creation | System allows for creation of tests for learning content. | Yes |
| Polling | Polling can be conducted through one or more channels (e.g. Content, User Home Page Interface, etc.) | Yes |
| Test Completion Tracking | User test completion status and rates can be tracked. | Yes |
| Test Score Tracking | User test scores can be stored and tracked. | Yes |
| **Reporting** | | |
| Ad-hoc reporting capability | System is delivered with ad-hoc report-writing tool so clients can create their own reports as needed. | No |
| Data analysis | System provides functionality for advanced data analysis and dash-boarding. | Yes |
| Reporting Security | Ability to enable field-level security and access to report creation, output and distribution. | Yes |
| Standard reports are delivered with the system | System is delivered with a minimum of 10 standard reports. | Yes |
| **Integration** | | |
| Employee Profile Integration | System allows for employee profile integration with other talent management solutions (e.g. Performance, Succession, Compensation, Recruitment, etc.). | Yes |
| Integration | Ability to allow clients to create integrations through APIs, XML, flat files, etc. | Yes |

| Function | Function Description | Response |
|---|---|---|
| **Web 2.0 Features** | | |
| Blogs | System allows for creation of blogs for content delivery. | No – In Beta, for release Q2 09 |
| Forums | System allows for creation and mainte-nance of forums to capture user-gener-ated content and enable collaborative learning activities. | Yes |
| Other Collaborative Learning Tools | Additional collaborative learning tools are available. | Yes |
| Podcasting | System allows for creation of podcasts for content delivery. | Yes |
| RSS Feeds | System allows users to identify content "tracks" that they wish to monitor on a regular basis and displays updates in an RSS-like format. | Yes |
| Wikis | System allows for creation and mainte-nance of wikis to capture user-generated content and enable collaborative learn-ing activities. | Yes |
| **User Communication** | | |
| Completion Date Reminders | Users can be notified when they are approaching a target content completion date. | Yes |
| Completion Remind-ers | Users can be reminded to complete con-tent that has been saved in progress. | Yes |
| Content Notifica-tions | Users can be notified when new content is added to their learning plan or a track in which they are interested. | Yes |

| Function | Function Description | Response |
|---|---|---|
| Manager Notifications | User managers and/or learning administrators can be notified when certain activities are completed. | Yes |
| Workflow | System allows for creation of workflow to communicate user status to content and people managers. | Yes |

# SilkRoad

## Company Information (provided by SilkRoad)

**Company Name:** SilkRoad Technology, Inc.

**Corporate URL:** www.silkroad.com

**Main Phone:** (336) 201-5100

**Main Email:** info@silkroad.com

**Headquarters Address:** 102 W. Third Street, Suite 250, Winston-Salem, NC 27101

**Type of Business or Areas of Focus:**
Recruiting management/applicant tracking system, onboarding & life events, performance management, learning management and employee intranet.

**Number of Employees:** 240

**Year Founded:** 2003

**Stock Symbol:** N/A

## Company Description and History:

SilkRoad Technology, Inc. was started in 2003 by current Chairman and CEO, Andrew J. "Flip" Filipowski and the current executive management team. SilkRoad provides software-as-a-service (SaaS) solutions that significantly improve the talent within its more than 800 customers across the globe. The SilkRoad Life Suite solution set includes OpenHire for recruiting management, RedCarpet for employee onboarding and life events, Wingspan for flexible employee performance management, GreenLight™ for compensation management and Eprise for employee intranets and content management.

SilkRoad technology is well-funded and is growing at an exceptional rate with over 240 employees in the following locations: Winston-Salem, NC (headquarters); Bedford, MA; Chicago, IL; West Long Branch, NJ; Hamburg, Germany; Sydney, Australia and Singapore.

## Products/Services/Solutions:

### 1. OpenHire (recruiting management)

OpenHire's is a fully automated recruiting management and applicant tracking solution that allows recruiters, hiring managers and human resources personnel to find and attract top talent as quickly and cost-effectively as possible. Features such as sourcing options, qualification screening and resume management make it one of the most effective tools on the market. OpenHire is also the only recruitment management tool that integrates with hundreds of job boards. Intelligent searching gives recruiters tools such as robust searching, hot match capabilities and job agents. OpenHire also provides career microsite capabilities and allows organizations to stay in compliance with EEO and OFCCP regulations.

### 2. RedCarpet (onboarding and life events)

RedCarpet, SilkRoad's onboarding and life events solution, manages transitions such as onboarding, offboarding, crossboarding, promotions, transfers and leaves of absence effectively. Robust task management in RedCarpet eases the administrative process by allowing a full view of an employee's internal tasks and development; and electronic forms allows new hires to complete any necessary paperwork prior to their first day! RedCarpet also provides a seamless interface with the Department of Homeland Security's E-Verify system, allowing companies to verify employment eligibility without ever leaving RedCarpet.

RedCarpet also offers powerful socialization tools for new and transitioning employees. Any content that a company wishes to deliver to an employee can be provided in a completely customizable portal.

### 3. WingSpan (performance management)

SilkRoad technology's WingSpan™ is a powerful employee performance management solution that enables companies to maximize their employee talent. WingSpan is a full featured and fully integrated solution with multi-rater assessments, competency and skill management, development planning, goal-setting and performance planning, performance and appraisal reviews and career development with succession planning.

### 4. GreenLight (learning management)

GreenLight™, SilkRoad's online learning environment, allows organizations to centrally manage the entire process of creating, delivering and tracking online and offline training programs for a global workforce. GreenLight enables clients to create, capture, assemble, publish, deliver and store content, as well as share learning objects and manage learner performance data. Including the basic management of classroom and standards-based eLearning training interventions, the GreenLight solution will manage and track student marks and progress for SCORM—or AICC—compliant Web-based training, instructor-led courses (training events) and on-the-job training (assignments).

## Author's SilkRoad Functionality Matrix

| Function | Function Description | Response |
|---|---|---|

### Talent Acquisition

| Requisition Management & Posting | | |
|---|---|---|
| Multiple requisition forms allowed (Example: hourly, internal transfer, business unit specific, reoccurring, sourcing, college) | More than one requisition form/template can be configured in a client's database to accommodate variance in business units or type of recruiting. (Example: A user from the Manufacturing group can enter a requisition and only see and populate fields that are applicable to Mfg. A different user from the Services group can enter a requisition and only see the fields designated for a Services requisition within the same database. | Yes |

| Function | Function Description | Response |
|---|---|---|
| Data Segregation | Ability to segregate requisitions and candidates by hire type (executive, HR, etc.) or organization. | No |
| Requisition approval routing workflow and approval status indicator | Select a list of approvers, route for approval via email. Approvals should be able to be sent in parallel or sequentially. | Yes |
| Approval status tracking | The status of the approval process is tracked and displayed real-time on the requisition in the application as well as in the subsequent emails that go to the second and third approver, etc. | Yes |
| Pre-defined approval routing lists | Lists of approvers can be created, saved, and/or assigned to a user or requisition, or defined by the organizational structure automatically. | No |
| Approvals can take place directly from an email | When approving a requisition, the approver can take action directly from the email notification without having to log into the application. | Yes |
| Pre-qualifying questions based on position/job needs, including weighting to filter for top candidates | Questions developed, defined and delivered to a candidate in the online application process tied directly to the job posting/requirements, including weighting to filter for top candidates. | Yes |
| Knock-out questions | Ability to establish certain questions to be disqualifiers, where if the candidate does not answer correctly, the process is ended. | Yes |
| Job posting scheduling | Check a box to select the appropriate career site(s) for the job to appear. Scheduling of start and end dates of posting to any given site to allow for staggered posting. | No |

| Function | Function Description | Response |
|---|---|---|
| Advanced job descriptions - Formatting and Spell Checking | Ability to edit and format job descriptions and marketing messages with MS Word, like functions for Bolding, Underlining, and Spell Checking. | Yes |
| Electronic job board relationship management (facilitation of job positing to all e-media providers) | Ability to identify and post job opportunities to an unlimited number of electronic job boards and other end destinations. Ability to multi-select boards and push positions out to the market. | Yes |
| **Candidate Experience** | | |
| Unlimited Career Site portals | Ability to establish an unlimited number of integrated career sites for different purposes, such as college recruiting, location-specific kiosks or for a specific job family like Sales or Engineering. Determine if there are additional costs per Career Section. | Yes |
| Online profile form(s) defined by the client | Data collection form(s) that can be pushed to a candidate to gather needed information for relationship management and interested resume submissions. Customers can tailor the form to their specification, adding or removing fields. | Yes |
| User-defined secure login user name and password | User-created login and password authentication for accessing profile and career management activities. | Yes |
| Candidate login optional | Candidate can submit resume and apply to jobs without establishing a password-protected user account. | Yes |
| Resume submission via upload of file - Candidate | Candidate can browse the hard drive for formatted resume and upload to candidate resume repository. | Yes |

| Function | Function Description | Response |
|---|---|---|
| Resume submission via upload of file - Recruiter/Manager | Recruiter/Manager can browse the hard drive for formatted resume and upload to candidate resume repository. | Yes |
| Resume builder functionality | Ability for candidates without a formal resume to submit a resume via a "Resume Builder." | Yes |
| Extraction of data from resume to create profile | Extraction engine behind the text or uploaded resume for population of fielded data in the candidate profile. | Yes |
| Candidate-defined Job Agents | Candidates can establish job search parameters and be notified when jobs are posted which meet their preferences. | Yes |
| Candidate status check | Candidates can login to check the status of their resume submissions. | Yes |
| Ability to upload attachments | | Yes |
| Ability for candidate to save a submission as a draft | | No |
| Candidate self-withdrawal | Ability for candidates to remove themselves from consideration for a position. | Yes |
| Conceptual search for the candidate when searching for jobs | Candidates can use "free form" language to search for jobs. | Yes |
| Sourcing/CRM | | |
| Specific job referral and general referrals | Employees can submit a resume as a general referral or to a specific job. | Yes |
| Notifications to the referring employee and the referred candidate | Email notifications are automatically sent to the employee making the referral and to the candidate who was referred. | Yes |

| Function | Function Description | Response |
|---|---|---|
| Referral status check | Employees can review a list of candidates they have referred and check their status. | No |
| Tracking steps and status searches | Recruiters can search for candidates based on their tracking steps and status against requisitions. | Yes |
| Keyword search against free-form text and fielded data | Keyword search against text records from candidate and fielded data in the same search. | Yes |
| Search criteria highlighted for relevance in record review | Search results with indicators for criteria matching and relevance in the results. | Yes |
| Configurable search results list | The column headers that are displayed in a search results list can be configured with different data elements from the candidate record. (Example: education, work history, phone number.) | No |
| Ability to search file attachments | Keyword searching will search the resumes that have been submitted as file attachments as well as text fields. | No |
| Ability to create "overnight" searches | | Yes |
| Conceptual search engine to match resumes | Ability to use the requisition's job description or a large text phrase to find matching resumes using a conceptual search or natural language search engine. Conceptual searches should also be able to be conducted with fielded search. | Yes |
| "More like this" searching | Ability to take a resume and conduct a search to find other resumes that are similar to it (more like it). | Yes |

| Function | Function Description | Response |
|----------|---------------------|----------|
| Library of candidate correspondence/ communication templates | Ability for clients to create a library of correspondence templates that can be sent to candidates at the user's discretion. | Yes |
| Editable correspondence at the user level | Users can make edits to the correspondence at the time of generation and distribution. | Yes |
| Agency Portal | Functionality designed for the management of third-party staffing agencies. Includes the ability to push requisitions to one or more suppliers and receive agency resume submissions. | Yes |
| Contingent Labor Management | Functionality designed specifically for the requisition and management of contract labor including the distribution of job requirements to multiple vendors; submission and review of resumes; tracking of assignment, time reporting and billing. | No |
| Candidate Pool Generation (Leads/ Prospective Candidates) | Able to enter limited candidate information (less required fields than regular candidate profile without comprising the configuration of the candidate profile) and develop target candidate pool for key skills. | Yes |
| Marketing Campaigns (Leads/Prospective Candidates) | Includes proactive candidate pool in messaging, advertising campaigns or special event invitations. This should include the ability to send emails to thousands of candidates (as necessary). | Yes |
| Sending resumes to a manager | Ability to send a "Formatted Resume" to a Hiring Manager. | Yes |

| Function | Function Description | Response |
|---|---|---|
| **Assessment and Interview Management** | | |
| Customer-defined workflow steps and status | Customer can set up steps and status for tracking candidates through their recruiting process, with ability to tailor them for required and desired steps. | Yes |
| Customer can define multiple process workflows (Example: employee referral, internal transfers, etc.) | Ability to create multiple applicant workflows (set of tracking steps & status) to be selected at the requisition level. | Yes |
| Workflow triggered alerts | Alerts can be set up in the system to drive the next step in the process or to function as reminders. | Yes |
| Ability to create a "tree-structure" workflow (i.e. step A can be followed by step B, C, D or E) | | Yes |
| Volume hiring updates | The ability to change the status for a group of candidates to hired in a single step (e.g. mass hiring in one step). | Yes |
| Integrated Assessments | Ability to store and/or integrate validated assessment tools into the recruiting workflow for certain jobs. | Yes |
| Assessment Triggers | Ability for Assessment to automatically be presented to candidates based on responses to pre-screening questions or other data in their profiles. | Yes |
| Assessment on demand | Ability to push an online assessment to a candidate on demand via email link. | No |
| Interview team member history | Ability to select and record a list of interviewing team members for a requisition. | Yes |

| Function | Function Description | Response |
|---|---|---|
| Interview team notifications | Ability to send an email notification (including a calendar meeting request) to the interview team members when scheduling the interview within the system (including interview packets, resumes, etc., when sending the email request). | Yes |
| Storage of interviewer comments | Ability to configure an online interview feedback form to capture the comments from each interviewer. | Yes |
| Interviewer attachments | Ability to include attachments to the interviewer notifications (e.g. interview guidelines, interview schedule, resume, etc.) | Yes |
| **Offer Management and Onboarding** | | |
| Approval routing and status tracking | Select a list of approvers, route for approval via email. In addition, the status of the approval process is tracked and displayed real-time on the offer in the application as well as in the subsequent emails that go to the second and third approvers, etc. | Yes |
| Pre-defined approval routing lists | Lists of approvers can be created, saved, and/or assigned to a user or requisition. | Yes |
| Approvals can take place directly from an email | When approving an offer, the approver can take action directly from the email notification without having to log into the application. | Yes |
| Offer letters can be generated by merging fields into letter templates. | Data can be merged from the candidate record, the requisition and the offer terms into offer letter templates. | Yes |
| Offer letters can be edited at the user level | Users can make edits to the offer letter at the time of generation and distribution. | Yes |

| Function | Function Description | Response |
|---|---|---|
| Specific Onboarding Module | Does the product offer a specific Onboarding module, allowing clients to define required notifications at hire and send notifications through the system? (e.g. provisioning, IT for user account setup, newhire, manager checklist, etc.) | Yes |
| Onboarding Documentation Management | Electronically provide new hire paperwork and track completion of key documents (I-9, Non Disclosures, Benefits Paperwork). | Yes |
| **Global Capabilities & Compliance** | | |
| EEO Compliance data collection | Configurable notification and collection of EEO compliance information at variable points in the process. | Yes |
| Global – in-country data collection based on regulations | Configurable data requests based on in-country requirements. Example: Germany, martial status, number of children. | Yes |
| Ability to present Career Sections in Multiple Languages | Ability to present Career Sections in Multiple Languages. | Yes |
| Ability to present the Recruiter and Manager Portals in multiple languages | Ability to present the Recruiter and Manager Portals in multiple languages. | No |
| Data Segregation by country, region or predefined type | Data Segregation, i.e. preventing users from a particular country or location from seeing candidates who are in another country or location. | Yes |
| OFCCP Compliance tools to enable search and applicant declaration | Functionality consistent with the new OFCCP definition of Internet Applicant (record keeping for searches, candidate submissions, etc.) | Yes |

| Function | Function Description | Response |
|---|---|---|
| Privacy Policy acknowledgements | Ability to require that candidates agree with the privacy policy before they submit. | Yes |
| Compliance with Data Privacy | Ability for customers to remove a candidate's data at that candidate's request. | Yes |
| Tax Credit Screening & Processing | Provides automatic Tax ID and SSN validation. Automatically transmits request to conduct tax credit screening for WOTC, WTW and more through to screening partners and displays those results within the Candidate profile for review and processing upon hire. | No |
| **Reporting & Integration** | | |
| Standard reports are delivered with the system | System is delivered with a minimum of 10 standard reports. | Yes |
| Ad-hoc reporting capability | System is delivered with an ad-hoc report-writing tool so that clients can create their own reports as needed. | Yes |
| Reporting Security | Ability to enable field-level security and access to report creation, output and distribution. | No |
| Reporting Distribution | Ability to generate scheduled reports and distribute through email. | Yes |
| Real -Time Reporting | Ability to report on data in the application in real time (not based on a refresh of data in a reporting environment). | Yes |
| HRIS Integration | Ability to create bi-directional integrations from an HRIS to the ATS. | Yes |
| Integration - Client Self-Service Tools | Ability for clients to create their own integration touchpoints as needed (and make them operational). | No |

| Function | Function Description | Response |
|---|---|---|
| Integration - API capability | Ability to allow clients to create integrations through APIs. | Yes |

## Performance Management

| Performance Dashboard | | |
|---|---|---|
| Dashboard configuration | Ability to configure dashboard based on user preference. | No |
| Create and display reports | Display reports that can be generated (i.e. review completion progress, goal progress). | Yes |
| Create and display charts and graphs | Display charts and graphs that are available to show planning actions. | No |
| Display help and reference tools | Display and view help and reference tools that can be selected by link or mouse hover. | No |
| **Employee Information Review (Data Import from HRIS/LMS)** | | |
| Import and display employee information | Display name, address, phone, email, location, photo, education (typically pulled from HRIS). | Yes |
| Import and display employee position information | Display current job title, job summary, job family, job level/grade, job code, FLSA, shift, status (FT/PT) (typically pulled through HRIS). | Yes |
| Create and display work history | Display created previous work history (i.e. name of company, job title, responsibilities/duties, employment dates). | Yes |
| Create and display years in management | Display created years of management experience (manually entered or via integration). | No |
| Create and display years in industry | Display created years of experience in industry (primarily entered manually). | No |

| Function | Function Description | Response |
|---|---|---|
| Import, create and display employee language(s) | Display employee languages (i.e. read, written, fluent) primarily entered manually. | No |
| Import, create and display employee affiliations | Display employee affiliation memberships. | No |
| Import, create and display employee certifications | Display employee certifications and dates. | No |
| Import, create and display employee licenses | Display employee licenses and dates (usually a text box); important to include expiration dates (could be for transportation, professional licenses, healthcare licenses, etc.) | No |
| Import and display organizational information | Display company name, company division, company department (typically imported from HRIS). | Yes |
| Import and display management hierarchy information | Display multiple levels of management names and information (i.e. Executive Management, Division Head, Department Head, Direct Manager, Employee). | No |
| Import and display direct reports | Display name and information of employee direct reports. | Yes |
| Import and display matrix manager hierarchy information | Display multiple levels of matrix management names and information (i.e. Employee has dotted line reporting relationships). | No |
| Import and display multiple manager hierarchy information | Display multiple levels of numerous management names and information (i.e. Employee reports to more than one manager directly). | No |

| Function | Function Description | Response |
|----------|---------------------|----------|
| Organizational Chart View | Organizational information can be displayed in an Org Chart view (note how this is displayed visually). | No |
| Organizational Change Requests | Due to potential errors within HRMS, manager has the ability to request an employee change in hierarchy (i.e. manager name, organization, location, job role); changes can be configured to require approval. | No |
| Import and display employee current and past compensation | Display employee's past and current base salary, bonus, equity, commission, etc. | Yes |
| Import and display employee most recent performance measures | Display employee's current competencies, goals, skills, projects, performance rating, development plan, personal improvement plan. | Yes |
| Import and display employee previous performance measures | Display employee's previous competencies, goals, skills, projects, performance rating, development plan, personal improvement plan. | Yes |
| Complete and display employee training | Display employee's completed and assigned training (i.e. mandatory/development). Note if there is any integration with LMS. | Yes |
| External Identifier | Ability to have an external identifier field to bring in content on goals from a third-party application (i.e. description, start date, critical, public goal); can be configured to be read-only for imports. | Yes |
| UDFs | Available user-defined fields for employee profile. | No |

| Function | Function Description | Response |
|---|---|---|
| **Career Planning / Personal Development (Employee)** | | |
| Create and display future career plan scenarios | Display multiple future career plans (vertical, horizontal, both). Where does the employee want to go next? (lateral, promotion, etc.) | Yes |
| Select and display positions, job families and organizations/divisions of interest | Display selected positions and organizations of interest from import of job list and organization list (mentorships and cross-training) - gives the employee the opportunity to identify a position, job-family or organization of interest. | No |
| Create and display training requests | Display developmental training requests (entered by an employee or manager); this could be an integration point to the LMS. | Yes |
| Create and display executive/professional requests | Display various executive/professional requests (i.e. executive coaching, cross-training, job shadowing, speaking engagements, writing submittals, managing people, presentations, mentoring, apprenticeships). | No |
| Create and display organization affiliations and/or conferences/seminars | Display employee organization/affiliation or conference/seminar requests to join or attend. | No |
| Select and display competency development | Display selected desired competencies (entered by employee). | No |
| Create self-asses job readiness | Display selected self-readiness from list of options (i.e. Now, 0-3 months, 3-6 months, 6-9 months, 9-12 months, 12 months +). | Yes |

| Function | Function Description | Response |
|----------|---------------------|----------|
| Display position Gap % | Display gap percentage of employee readiness to ideal position as well as required training, license(s), education, certification(s). This could be automatically calculated by the system (key differentiator). This is a gap analysis on the underlying competencies (most recent performance rating vs. competencies required for next position). | No |
| Select and display willingness to relocate | Display selected willingness to relocate (i.e. yes, no, maybe, comments). | No |
| Display career prerequisites | Display required training, education, certification(s), license(s) for position of interest. | No |
| Submit development requests for approval | Submit development self-assessments to direct manager for review, feedback and approval (areas where the development needs to occur, as well as specific courses, conferences to help meet these development areas). Could be an integration point with LMS. | Yes |
| **Career Development (Manager)** | | |
| Create or select and display employee training goals | Display created or selected employee completed training, assigned training (mandatory/development), scheduled training and employee training requests. This is the manager identifying training goals for an employee. | No |
| Competency Development | Display assigned professional/leadership competencies. | Yes |

| Function | Function Description | Response |
|---|---|---|
| Create and display executive/professional assignments | Display various executive/professional recommendations (i.e. executive coaching, cross-training, job shadowing, speaking engagements, writing submittals, managing people, presentations, mentoring, apprenticeships). | Yes |
| Create and display organization affiliations and/or conferences/seminars | Display employee organization/affiliation or conference/seminar recommendations. | No |
| **Individual Goal / Self-Assessment (Employee)** | | |
| Select, create and display individual development goals | Display selected or created completed training, improvement competencies, executive coaching, promotion, cross-training. | Yes |
| Select competency development | Display selected development competencies. This is where the employee selects competencies wanted to develop career on the annual review. | Yes |
| Submit goal/competency assessment for approval | Submit manual or automatic goal/competency assessment to direct manager. | Yes |
| Solicit and display feedback | Select employees (i.e. managers, matrix managers, peers) to solicit performance feedback (i.e. 360, peer review, business review) and display results. | Yes |
| Create and display self-performance notes | Display created performance notes (i.e. kudos) throughout the review cycle (manually entered by employee or can solicit feedback throughout project). | Yes |

| Function | Function Description | Response |
|---|---|---|
| Create and display self-goal assessment progress | Display created self-goal progress (i.e. quantitative percentage of completion; qualitative to include customer satisfaction; timeline to include start/completion date). | Yes |
| Submit goal/competency review for approval | Submit manual or automatic goal/competency assessment to direct manager and higher levels. | Yes |
| UDFs | Available user-defined fields for employee goals. | Yes |
| **Review Process (Employee and Manager)** | | |
| Select and display competencies | Display selected professional or leadership competencies. | Yes |
| Select and display goals/objectives | Display selected goals/objectives (i.e. quantitative and/or qualitative). | Yes |
| Select and display goal alignment | Display selected goal alignment to company, organization, department and/or manager goals (cascading goals). | Yes |
| Select or create and display projects | Display selected or created projects. | No |
| Select and display project alignment to goals | Display selected project alignment to company, organization, department and/or manager goals. | No |
| Select or create and display skills | Display selected or created company, organization, department, employee skills. | No |
| Create and display employee performance notes | Display created performance notes (positive or negative) throughout the review cycle. These are notes created by the manager. | No |

| Function | Function Description | Response |
|---|---|---|
| Solicit and display feedback | Select employees (i.e. managers, matrix managers, peers) to solicit performance feedback (i.e. 360, peer review, business review) and display. Pay particular attention to how this feedback is gathered and entered into the system. | Yes |
| Create and display employee goal assessment review | Display created employee goal progress (i.e. quantitative % of completion; qualitative to include customer satisfaction; timeline to include start/completion date). This is the manager entering the assessment. | Yes |
| Performance review filtering | Manager can filter performance review information based on approval status, assigned to, author/owner, manager, employee, organization, location, job field, job role, review cycle, review group, review group owner, overall rating; filtering can be cumulative. | No |
| Batch activities | Manager can take group actions on multiple employees simultaneously. | No |
| UDFs | Available user-defined fields for employee competencies. | No |
| **Workflow** | | |
| Review cycles | Ability to configure multiple review cycles and tie to various reviews. | Yes |
| Review groups | Ability to define review recipients based on dates, job function, organization, job code, etc. | Yes |
| Workflow Order | Ability to configure order of workflow (i.e. self-assessments can be configured to be completed first). | Yes |

| Function | Function Description | Response |
|---|---|---|
| Notifications | Ability to push reviews to employees and managers. | Yes |
| Reminders | Ability to send reminders to employees and managers via email (manual and automatic). | Yes |
| Acknowledgements | Ability to send auto acknowledgements triggered by event/activity. | Yes |
| Next Level Approval | Ability to auto/manually route to multiple levels of approval. | Yes |
| Configurable work-flow | Ability to configure various steps of the review process, to make review steps mandatory, to have manager override ability, to display/hide visual graphic workflow diagram. | Yes |
| Auto/Manual Progression | Ability to automatically or manually progress through the review process. | Yes |
| Review form | Exportable and printable review form. | Yes |
| **System Admin** | | |
| Review sections | Ability to configure multiple review sections, including goals, competencies, comments, rating models, etc. | Yes |
| Configurable rating models | Does it configure and display alpha and numeric values? Can values be rounded (up/down/both), value ranges, number of decimals (1-5)? | No |
| Comments | Displayed and available in individual review sections and overall review. They can be configured to be mandatory and ability to be overridden by management. | Yes |

| Function | Function Description | Response |
|---|---|---|
| Goals | Ability to link organizational, divisional, departmental, individual goals into sections and ability to display goal progress. | Yes |
| Competencies | Ability to link competencies into sections. | Yes |
| Weightings | Ability to weigh employee performance based on goals and competencies. | Yes |
| **Search Functionality** | | |
| Basic Employee Search | Basic search by employee name (i.e. first or last name or a combination of both). | Yes |
| Job/Position Basic Search | Basic search by job role or position title, etc. | Yes |
| Competency Basic Search | Basic search by competency name. | No |
| Advanced Search | More detailed search capabilities that combine various search criteria or fields - may include optional weighting to determine which employees are retrieved in a search as well as each person's rank in the search results. | Yes |
| Succession Planning Search | Search functionality that dynamically generates the criteria used to match employees who would make good succession candidates with a specific position profile (could have various levels of "fit"). | No |
| **Employee View / Navigation / Help / Other** | | |
| List View | Display employee goals, business goals or projects; the list mode is a list of items with information on key dates and progress. | Yes |

| Function | Function Description | Response |
|---|---|---|
| Card View | Display employee goals, business goals or projects using the card mode; the card mode provides details on one item at a time and offers the possibility of editing progress. This can also include employee photos as well. | No |
| Timeline / Gantt | Display employee goals, business goals or projects using the timeline mode; the timeline mode provides a timeline view of an item's start and due dates. | No |
| Org Chart | Managers can access and manage information on their direct reports for all functionalities activated; the organizational chart will provide key data (i.e. risk of loss or most recent performance rating) for each of the manager's direct reports. | No |
| Mini-Org Chart | Displays a single analytic data point at a time; the manager can drill down into all layers of his organization and can view key metrics (i.e. performance reviews, goals, succession). | No |
| Graphs | Graphical display of various information (i.e. Gap Analysis, goal progress, review completion progress). | No |
| Help Links | Online help, FAQs, customer support, product version. | No |
| Attach Documents | Ability to attach reference documents to various sections within the system. | No |
| Browser capabilities | Supported by general Internet access (works with standard browsers: IE, Safari, Mozilla, Opera). | No |

| Function | Function Description | Response |
|---|---|---|
| Mouse-Over Hover | Additional tooltips or descriptions that display when user hovers the mouse pointer over various graphics or words within the system. | Yes |
| Web 2.0 | Ability to utilize Web 2.0 functionality, i.e. social networking. | No |
| **Security** | | |
| Logging In | Various login options (i.e. manual, SSO, LDAP). | Yes |
| File Transfer | Various file transfer protocol (i.e. FTP, sFTP, vendor-specific transfer import/export tool). | Yes |
| Encryption | Various data encryption ability (i.e. PGP). | Yes |
| Roles / Permissions | Configurable list of permission-based roles with detailed access rights to various organizations, levels, etc. Typically employees only view within their own organization hierarchy. | Yes |
| Integration | Ability to integrate organizational data i.e. HRIS/ATS/ LMS and employee data including competencies, training, development plans, etc. | Yes |
| **Reporting** | | |
| Standard reports are delivered with the system | System is delivered with a set number of standard reports. | Yes |
| Ad-hoc reporting capability | System is delivered with an ad-hoc report-writing tool so that clients can create their own reports as needed. | No |
| Advanced Value metrics | Data analysis of employee review process status, goal progress by hierarchy. | Yes |

| Function | Function Description | Response |
|----------|--------------------|----------|
| Reporting Security | Ability to enable field-level security and access to report creation, output and distribution. | No |
| Reporting UDFs | Ability to report user-defined fields. | No |
| Exporting reports | Reports can easily be exported to other applications (i.e. .xls, .pdf, .txt). | Yes |

## Succession Planning

| Succession Planning (Manager - Planning of Individual Talent Matched to Critical Roles) | | |
|----------|--------------------|----------|
| Create and display critical roles for today | Display critical job roles (i.e. title, level, location, division, organization). | Yes |
| Create and display critical roles for future | Display critical job roles (i.e. title, level, location, division, organization) for future (workforce planning-like tools). | Yes |
| Calculate and display performance rating | Performance rating is automatically averaged from various sections of the performance review and displayed (current and past). | Yes |
| Calculate and display performance ranking | High potential employees will be automatically ranked according to order of fit with critical role (i.e. 9-box grid, numeric ranking, high performer, high potential); Can be ranked by position, organization, etc. | Yes |
| Multi-dimensional matrix | Matrix that can be configured up to various # of cells (i.e. 9-box, 12-box, 16-box, 25-box); text within grid is configurable. | Yes |
| Various dimensions of matrix | Matrix displays employee performance, potential, number of succession plans an employee is on, years in management, years in industry. | Yes |

| Function | Function Description | Response |
|----------|---------------------|----------|
| Navigation from multi-dimensional matrix | Manager can select an employee within the matrix and navigate to employee information (i.e. Performance review, talent profile, employee goals, career plan). | Yes |
| Display employee comparisons | Display comparison of multiple high potential employees according to fit to critical role (i.e. # of employees to compare, comparable data, fit gap analysis, ranking analysis, bench strength). | Yes |
| Create and display role readiness | Manager can create and display high potential employee role readiness (i.e. now, 0-3 months, 3-6 months, 6-9 months, 9-12 months, 12+ months). | Yes |
| Create and display retention risk | Manager can create and display high potential employee retention/loss/flight risk (i.e. high, medium, low, comments). | Yes |
| Create and display role willingness | Manager can create and display high potential employee role willingness (i.e. yes, no, comments). | Yes |
| Create and display willingness to relocate | Manager can create and display high potential employee willingness to relocate (i.e. yes, no, maybe, comments). | Yes |
| Create and display willingness to travel | Manager can create and display high potential employee willingness to travel (i.e. none, 25-50%, 50-75%, 75-100%). | Yes |
| Create and display interest in international assignment | Manager can create and display high potential employee interest in international assignment (i.e. yes, no, maybe). | Yes |
| Create and display interim replacement for critical role | Manager can create and display high potential interim replacement for critical roles. | Yes |

| Function | Function Description | Response |
|---|---|---|
| Display of gap analysis | Automatically calculate and display high potential employees' fit gap analysis to their next position and ranking analysis of employee to that next position. | Yes |
| UDFs | Available user-defined fields for succession planning. | Yes |
| **Succession Pooling (Manager - Planning of a Talent Pool for Critical Roles)** | | |
| Display high potential pool | Display nominated and/or approved high potential pool (i.e. employee information, designated nominators, designated approvers, approvals, rejections, role readiness, rejection comments). | Yes |
| Calculate and display performance rating | Performance rating is automatically averaged from various sections of the performance review and displayed (current and past). | Yes |
| Calculate and display performance ranking | Pool of high potential employees will be automatically ranked according to order of fit with critical role (i.e. 9-box grid, numeric ranking, high performer, high potential). | Yes |
| Display employee comparisons | Display comparison of multiple high potential employees according to fit to critical role (i.e. # of employees to compare, comparable data, fit gap analysis, ranking analysis, bench strength). | Yes |
| Create and display role readiness | Manager can create and display high potential employee role readiness (i.e. now, 0-3 months, 3-6 months, 6-9 months, 9-12 months, 12+ months). | Yes |
| Create and display retention risk | Manager can create and display high potential employee retention/loss/flight risk (i.e. high, medium, low, comments). | Yes |

| Function | Function Description | Response |
|----------|--------------------|----------|
| Create and display role willingness | Manager can create and display high potential employee role willingness (i.e. yes, no, comments). | Yes |
| Create and display willingness to relocate | Manager can create and display high potential employee willingness to relocate (i.e. yes, no, maybe, comments). | Yes |
| Create and display willingness to travel | Manager can create and display high potential employee willingness to travel (i.e. none, 25-50%, 50-75%, 75-100%). | Yes |
| Create and display interest in international assignment | Manager can create and display high potential employee interest in international assignment (i.e. yes, no, maybe). | Yes |
| Create and display interim replacement for critical role | Manager can create and display high potential interim replacement for critical roles. | Yes |
| Display of gap analysis | Automatically calculate and display high potential employees' fit gap analysis to position and ranking analysis of employee to position. | Yes |
| UDFs | Available user-defined fields for succession pooling. | Yes |
| **Workflow** | | |
| Succession approval workflow | Ability to define or edit approvers, add/remove users and roles, ability to change the approval order, ability to reject with comments. | No |
| Nominations for succession pool | Ability to nominate, reject and enter comments on nominated HiPo employees. | Yes |

| Function | Function Description | Response |
|---|---|---|
| **Reporting** | | |
| Standard reports are delivered with the system | System is delivered with a set number of standard reports. | Yes |
| Ad-hoc reporting capability | System is delivered with an ad-hoc report-writing tool so that clients can create their own reports as needed. | No |
| Advanced Value metrics | Data analysis of high performers / high potential employees, identified gaps, critical roles. | Yes |
| Reporting Security | Ability to enable field-level security and access to report creation, output and distribution. | No |
| Reporting UDFs | Ability to report user-defined fields. | Yes |
| Exporting reports | Reports can easily be exported to other applications (i.e. .xls, .pdf, .txt). | Yes |

## Compensation Management

| Function | Function Description | Response |
|---|---|---|
| **Compensation Dashboard** | | |
| Dashboard configuration | Ability to configure dashboard based on user preference. | No |
| Create and display a compensation worksheet | Display a compensation worksheet that will provide individual and org planning status and detail. | No |
| Create and display reports | Display reports that can be generated, i.e. budget usage by merit, bonus, equity, adjustment and percent of planning completed. | Yes |
| Create and display charts and graphs | Display charts and graphs that are available to show planning actions. | No |

| Function | Function Description | Response |
|---|---|---|
| Import and display allocation guidelines | Display compensation allocation guidelines for merit, bonus, equity and adjustments - also refer to the time allocation/workflow to complete this process. | Yes |
| Import and display eligibility guidelines | Display employee eligibility guidelines for planning, i.e. FT, PT, commission, LOA, new hire, etc. Guidelines are input by compensation department. | Yes |
| Display help and reference tools | Display and view help and reference tools that can be selected by link or mouse hover. | No |
| **Compensation Budget** | | |
| Import and display multiple aggregate planning budget by org | Display multiple approved allocated budget by diverse business groups on all pages (usually imported from financial system). | Yes |
| Import and display aggregate merit budget by org | Display approved allocated merit budget by diverse business groups on all pages. | Yes |
| Import and display aggregate bonus budget by org | Display approved allocated bonus by diverse business groups on all pages. | Yes |
| Import and display aggregate equity budget by org | Display approved allocated equity budget by diverse business groups on all pages. | Yes |
| Import and display aggregate adjustment budget by org | Display approved allocated adjustment budget by diverse business groups on all pages. | Yes |
| **Employee Information Review** | | |
| Import and display employee Information | Display name, location, photo, org, direct manager (typically imported from PM tool). | Yes |

| Function | Function Description | Response |
|---|---|---|
| Import and display employee position | Display current job title, job code, level/grade. | Yes |
| Import and display employee prior compensation planning period data | Display current hourly rate, annual rate, bonus percent, bonus amount, equity allocation, total compensation. | Yes |
| Import and display employee prior performance rating | Display prior performance rating. | Yes |
| Import and display new employee performance rating | Display new performance rating. | Yes |
| Import and display employee's position salary range | Display employee's salary range. | Yes |
| Import and display salary penetration percentage based on position salary range | Display percentage of penetration that employee's salary falls within the range. | Yes |
| **Promotion** | | |
| Display position information | Ability to select and display job titles, job codes, job level/grades. | Yes |
| Import and display corporate promotion guidelines | Ability to display promotion guidelines per position including salary range and percent increase guidelines. | Yes |
| Promotion amount | Ability to enter promotion percent or amount. | Yes |
| Auto-calculate promotion amount | System to auto-populate promotion amount based on percent increase. | Yes |
| Ability to calculate hourly rate | System to auto-populate new hourly rate based on promotion increase. | Yes |

| Function | Function Description | Response |
|---|---|---|
| Ability to auto-calculate annual rate | System to auto-populate new annual rate based on promotion increase. | Yes |
| Promotion approval chain | TBD | Yes |
| Develop documentation | Ability to document the promotion justification. | No |
| **Adjustment** | | |
| Import and display adjustment guidelines | Ability to display adjustment allocation guidelines including salary range and percent increase guidelines. | Yes |
| Adjustment allocation | Ability to enter and submit an adjustment percent or amount. | Yes |
| Auto-calculate hourly amount | System to auto-populate new hourly rate based on adjustment percent increase. | Yes |
| Auto-calculate adjustment amount | System to auto-populate new annual rate based on adjustment percent increase. | Yes |
| Adjustment approvals | | Yes |
| Develop documentation | Ability to document the adjustment justification. | No |
| **Merit** | | |
| Import and display promotion guidelines | Ability to display merit allocation guidelines, including salary range and percent increase guidelines. | Yes |
| Performance-based recommendations | Merit allocation can be based on performance rating. | Yes |
| Merit allocation | Ability to enter and submit a merit percent or amount. | Yes |

| Function | Function Description | Response |
|---|---|---|
| Import and display proration of merit based on hire date | System to auto-calculate merit increase based on hire date, i.e. less than one year would be calculated by months employed. | Yes |
| Auto-calculate hourly amount | System to auto-populate new hourly rate based on merit percent increase. | Yes |
| Auto-calculate adjustment amount | System to auto-populate new annual rate based on merit percent increase. | Yes |
| Merit approvals | | Yes |
| Develop documentation | Ability to document the merit justification. | No |
| **Bonus** | | |
| Import and display bonus allocation guidelines | Ability to display bonus allocation guidelines. | Yes |
| Performance-based recommendations | Bonus allocation can be based on performance rating. | Yes |
| Bonus allocation | Ability to enter and submit a bonus percent or amount. | Yes |
| Bonus adjustment | Auto-Proration of bonus based on hired or leave, i.e. severance date. | Yes |
| Bonus approvals | Ability to obtain appropriate approvals (workflow to select appropriate approvers). | Yes |
| Develop documentation | Ability to document the merit justification. | No |
| **Equity** | | |
| Import and display equity allocation guidelines | Ability to display equity allocation guidelines. | Yes |

| Function | Function Description | Response |
|---|---|---|
| Performance-based recommendations | Equity allocation can be based on performance rating. | Yes |
| Equity allocation | Ability to enter and submit equity percent or amount. | Yes |
| Equity allocation adjustment | Auto-Proration of equity allocation based on hire date. | Yes |
| Equity approvals | | Yes |
| Develop documentation | Ability to document the merit justification | No |
| **Other** | | |
| Ability to assign a delegate | Ability to assign a delegate to complete compensation planning, i.e. Admin. | Yes |
| Employee Filter | Ability to sort by employee name or data, i.e. first name, last name, employee ID, etc. | Yes |
| Employee Search | Ability to search throughout the tool by employee name or data, i.e. first name, last name, employee ID, etc. | Yes |
| Revert or change functionality | Ability for planning administrators to revert or change submitted data. | Yes |
| Collaborative workflow | Ability for managers, compensation and HR Partners to collaborate on various compensation workflows. | Yes |
| Display out-of-guideline entries | Ability to display out-of-guideline entries made within adjustments, merit, bonus, equity. | Yes |
| **Reporting** | | |
| Standard reports are delivered with the system | System is delivered with a set number of standard reports. | Yes |

| Function | Function Description | Response |
|---|---|---|
| Ad-hoc reporting capability | System is delivered with an ad-hoc report-writing tool so that clients can create their own reports as needed. | No |
| Advanced Value metrics | Data analysis of comp gaps based on roles, hierarchy. | No |
| Reporting Security | Ability to enable field-level security and access to report creation, output and distribution. | No |
| **Security** | | |
| Logging In | Various login options (i.e. manual, SSO, LDAP). | Yes |
| File Transfer | Various file transfer protocol (i.e. FTP, sFTP, vendor-specific transfer import/export tool). | Yes |
| Encryption | Various data encryption ability (i.e. PGP). | Yes |
| Roles / Permissions | Configurable list of permission-based roles with detailed access rights to various organizations, levels, etc. Typically employees only view within their own organization hierarchy. | Yes |
| Integration | Ability to Integrate organizational data with appropriate org system, i.e. HRIS/Payroll, employee data including employee salaries, levels, performance rating, etc. | Yes |
| Reporting UDFs | Ability to report user-defined fields. | No |
| Exporting reports | Reports can easily be exported to other applications (i.e. .xls, .pdf, .txt). | Yes |

| Function | Function Description | Response |
|---|---|---|

## Learning Management

| Content Management and Delivery | | |
|---|---|---|
| Application Simulation | Client content owners can create application simulations for use in training (i.e. "Show Me"/"Try Me" Flash-type simulations). | Yes |
| Assign learning content based employee data | Learning content can be assigned to employees based on their job function or organizational data (not specific to position, but job family or organization). | Yes |
| Catalogs | Employees can search through and browse course catalogs to identify courses in which they are interested. | Yes |
| Competency Management – Third-Party Defined | Courses and learning plans can be built around competencies, driven by integration with a third-party vendor. | Yes |
| Competency Management - Customer Defined | Courses and learning plans can be built around competencies as determined by the customer. | Yes |
| Offline Capabilities | Learning content can be downloaded for completion even if the user is not connected to the Internet/network. Can also upload results. | No |
| Employee Profile Management | System can house employee profiles that can be used for learning plan assignment, development plan creation and management (could be integration point). | Yes |
| External Content Integration | Employees can access, review, and register for courses in systems and online portals that are integrated with the LMS. | Yes |

| Function | Function Description | Response |
|---|---|---|
| Internal Content Authoring | WYSIWYG (what you see is what you get) editor is built into the system for creation of learning materials within the system by client content owners. | Yes |
| Learning Plans | Customer can create learning plans for employees. Employees can manage their progress, review schedules, register for courses and access online courses from plans. Collaboration with employees and managers to create this learning plan (and appropriate workflow). Could be an integration point from PM tool. | Yes |
| Multiple Languages | System supports multiple languages for global implementations. | Yes |
| PowerPoint Conversion | System allows for uploading of Power-Point files as learning content. | Yes |
| Repository | Digital repository for management of draft and active content is available in the system. Content managers would use this functionality (and allows for collaboration). | Yes |
| Scheduling | Users can book resources, locations and structures from within the system. This is an integration point as well. | Yes |
| Single Sign-On | Standard SSO capability for integration with client intranet. | Yes |
| Version Control | Content owners have the ability to manage content versioning. | Yes |
| Virtual Classrooms | System provides virtual classroom functionality for live, remote learning sessions. | Yes |

| Function | Function Description | Response |
|---|---|---|
| **Testing and Tracking** | | |
| General Assessments | System allows for creation of assessments that aren't tied to particular training content. Could be tied to competencies. | Yes |
| Content Test Completion | Users can complete tests online as assigned. Could be offline as well. | Yes |
| Content Test Creation | System allows for creation of tests for learning content. | Yes |
| Polling | Polling can be conducted through one or more channels (e.g. Content, User Home Page Interface, etc.) | No |
| Test Completion Tracking | User test completion status and rates can be tracked. | Yes |
| Test Score Tracking | User test scores can be stored and tracked. | Yes |
| **Reporting** | | |
| Ad-hoc reporting capability | System is delivered with an ad-hoc report writing tool so that clients can create their own reports as needed. | Yes |
| Data analysis | System provides functionality for advanced data analysis and dashboarding. | Yes |
| Reporting Security | Ability to enable field-level security and access to report creation, output and distribution. | No |
| Standard reports are delivered with the system | System is delivered with a minimum of 10 standard reports. | Yes |

| Function | Function Description | Response |
|---|---|---|
| **Integration** | | |
| Employee Profile Integration | System allows for employee profile integration with other talent management solutions (e.g. Performance, Succession, Compensation, Recruitment, etc.) | Yes |
| Integration | Ability to allow clients to create integrations through APIs, XML, flat files, etc. | Yes |
| **Web 2.0 Features** | | |
| Blogs | System allows for creation of blogs for content delivery. | Yes |
| Forums | System allows for creation and maintenance of forums to capture user-generated content and enable collaborative learning activities. | Yes |
| Other Collaborative Learning Tools | Additional collaborative learning tools are available. | Yes |
| Podcasting | System allows for creation of podcasts for content delivery. | No |
| RSS Feeds | System allows users to identify content "tracks" that they wish to monitor on a regular basis, and displays updates in an RSS-like format. | No |
| Wikis | System allows for creation and maintenance of wikis to capture user-generated content and enable collaborative learning activities. | No |
| **User Communication** | | |
| Completion Date Reminders | Users can be notified when they are approaching a target content completion date. | Yes |

| Function | Function Description | Response |
|---|---|---|
| Completion Reminders | Users can be reminded to complete content that has been saved in progress. | No |
| Content Notifications | Users can be notified when new content is added to their learning plan or a track in which they are interested. | Yes |
| Manager Notifications | User managers and/or learning administrators can be notified when certain activities are completed. | Yes |
| Workflow | System allows for creation of workflow to communicate user status to content and people managers. | Yes |

# Softscape

## Company Information (provided by Softscape)

**Company Name:**          Softscape

**Corporate URL:**         www.softscape.com

**Main Phone:**            (508) 358-1072

**Main Email:**            softscapeinfo@softscape.com

**Headquarters Address:**  One Softscape Center, 526 Boston
                           Post Road, Wayland, MA USA 01778

**Type of Business or Areas of Focus:**
- Complete People Management Platform
- Workforce Performance
- 360 Feedback
- Learning & Development
- Succession Planning
- Compensation Planning
- Incentive Compensation
- Hiring Management
- HR Management
- Survey Management
- Configuration Management

**Number of Employees:**   200+

**Year Founded:**          1995

**Stock Symbol (If Applicable):**  NA

# Company Description and History:

Softscape is the global leader in integrated human capital management (HCM) software, enabling organizations to drive business performance through more effective people management. Recognized by industry analysts as the most comprehensive strategic HCM solution, Softscape provides complete employee lifecycle management, including a core system of record, in a single, integrated platform. The company offers customers of all sizes and in all industries the most flexibility and choice with multiple purchase, configuration and deployment options. As the pioneer in talent management, Softscape is on the cutting edge of advanced technologies that enable organizations around the world to achieve operational excellence. For over a decade, Softscape has helped millions of workers across 156 countries be more successful at their jobs while contributing to bottom-line results. Softscape's customers represent Fortune 500/Global 500, mid-market and government organizations, including Accenture, Procter & Gamble, Barclays, AstraZeneca, Seagate, GKN, Edcon, LandAmerica and the U.S. Department of Homeland Security. Softscape continues to advance the market with innovative technology to link each component of strategic HCM with unprecedented flexibility and ease-of-use. Moving beyond using technology as a way of automating existing processes, Softscape's people-centric systems are redefining the standard for operational excellence to empower people and drive organizational performance.

# Products/Services/Solutions:

### Softscape Apex® 2008

Softscape Apex is the industry's most comprehensive HCM platform that seamlessly links end-to-end workforce processes, improves reporting and business insight, offers a superior user experience and drives overall business performance. Through a single, integrated platform that is easy-to-use, Softscape Apex connects critical workforce processes into a single, end-to-end system to more effectively plan, hire, align, manage, develop, motivate, retain and analyze an organization's high-performing workforce. Each suite has the capability of achieving organizational objectives when independently implemented. Implemented as a whole, the suites define a first-class, fully integrated HCM solution.

## Additional Notes/Comments:

Key Differentiators:
- Most comprehensive HCM platform including core "talent-based" system of record
- Superior functional depth across all HCM components (performance, succession, compensation, learning, recruiting, planning, analytics)
- Extensive customer-enabled configurability covering complete end-to-end processes
- Fully integrated platform offers more reporting breadth and depth
- More flexible delivery options (SaaS, License, and License Hosted)
- Significant global and multi-national domain expertise
- Profitable operations with consistent year-over-year growth
- Continues to maintain an industry high customer satisfaction and retention rate of 98 percent

# Author's Softscape Functionality Matrix

| Function | Function Description | Response |
|---|---|---|

Talent Acquisition

| Requisition Management & Posting | | |
|---|---|---|
| Multiple requisition forms allowed (Example: hourly, internal transfer, business unit specific, reoccurring, sourcing, college) | More than one requisition form/template can be configured in a client's database to accommodate variance in business units or type of recruiting. (Example: A user from the Manufacturing group can enter a requisition and only see and populate fields that are applicable to Mfg. A different user from the Services group can enter a requisition and only see the fields designated for a Services requisition within the same database. | Yes |

| Function | Function Description | Response |
|---|---|---|
| Data Segregation | Ability to segregate requisitions and candidates by hire type (executive, HR, etc.) or organization. | Yes |
| Requisition approval routing workflow and approval status indicator | Select a list of approvers, route for approval via email. Approvals should be able to be sent in parallel or sequentially. | Yes |
| Approval status tracking | The status of the approval process is tracked and displayed real-time on the requisition in the application as well as in the subsequent emails that go to the second and third approver, etc. | Yes |
| Pre-defined approval routing lists | Lists of approvers can be created, saved, and/or assigned to a user or requisition, or defined by the organizational structure automatically. | Yes |
| Approvals can take place directly from an email | When approving a requisition, the approver can take action directly from the email notification without having to log into the application. | Yes |
| Pre-qualifying questions based on position/job needs, including weighting to filter for top candidates | Questions developed, defined and delivered to a candidate in the online application process tied directly to the job posting/requirements, including weighting to filter for top candidates. | Yes |
| Knock-out questions | Ability to establish certain questions to be disqualifiers, i.e. if the candidate does not answer correctly, the process is ended. | Yes |
| Job posting scheduling | Check a box to select the appropriate career site(s) for the job to appear. Scheduling of start and end dates of posting to any given site allow for staggered posting. | Yes |

| Function | Function Description | Response |
|---|---|---|
| Advanced job descriptions - Formatting and Spell Checking | Ability to edit and format job descriptions and marketing messages with MS Word, like functions for Bolding, Underlining and Spell Checking. | Yes |
| Electronic job board relationship management (facilitation of job positing to all e-media providers) | Ability to identify and post job opportunities to an unlimited number of electronic job boards and other end destinations. Ability to multi-select boards and push positions out to the market. | Yes |
| **Candidate Experience** | | |
| Unlimited Career Site portals | Ability to establish an unlimited number of integrated career sites for different purposes - such as college recruiting, location-specific kiosks or for a specific job family like Sales or Engineering. Determine if there are additional costs per Career Section. | Yes |
| Online profile form(s) defined by the client | Data collection form(s) that can be pushed to a candidate to gather needed information for relationship management and interested resume submissions. Customers can tailor the form to their specification, adding or removing fields. | Yes |
| User-defined secure login user name and password. | User created login and password authentication for accessing profile and career management activities. | Yes |
| Candidate login optional | Candidate can submit resume and apply to jobs without establishing a password-protected user account. | Yes |
| Resume submission via upload of file - Candidate | Candidates can browse hard drives for their formatted resume and upload to candidate resume repository. | Yes |

| Function | Function Description | Response |
|---|---|---|
| Resume submission via upload of file - Recruiter/Manager | Recruiter/Manager can browse hard drive for formatted resume and upload to candidate resume repository. | Yes |
| Resume builder functionality | Ability for candidate without a formal resume to submit a resume via a "Resume Builder." | Yes |
| Extraction of data from resume to create profile | Extraction engine behind the text or uploaded resume for population of fielded data in the candidate profile. | Yes |
| Candidate-defined Job Agents | Candidates can establish job search parameters and be notified when jobs are posted which meet their preferences. | Yes |
| Candidate status check | Candidates can login to check the status of their resume submissions. | Yes |
| Ability to upload attachments | | No |
| Ability for candidate to save a submission as a draft | | Yes |
| Candidate self-withdrawal | Ability for candidates to remove themselves from consideration for a position. | Yes |
| Conceptual search for candidates when searching for jobs | Candidates can use "free form" language to search for jobs. | Yes |
| Sourcing/CRM | | |
| Specific job referral and general referrals | Employee can submit a resume as a general referral or to a specific job. | Yes |
| Notifications to the referring employee and the referred candidate | Email notifications are automatically sent to the referring employee and to the candidate who was referred. | Yes |

| Function | Function Description | Response |
|---|---|---|
| Referral status check | Employees can review a list of candidates they have referred and check their status. | Yes |
| Tracking steps and status searches | Recruiters can search for candidates based on their tracking steps and status against requisitions. | Yes |
| Keyword search against free-form text and fielded data | Keyword search against text records from candidate and fielded data in the same search. | Yes |
| Search criteria highlighted for relevance in record review | Search results with indicators for criteria matching and relevance in the results. | Yes |
| Configurable search results list | The column headers that are displayed in a search results list can be configured with different data elements from the candidate record. (Example: Education, Work History, Phone Number). | Yes |
| Ability to search file attachments | Keyword searching will scan the resumes that have been submitted as file attachments as well as text fields. | No |
| Ability to create "overnight" searches | | Yes |
| Conceptual search engine to match resumes | Ability to use the requisition's job description or a large text phrase to find matching resumes using a conceptual search or natural language search engine. Conceptual searches should also be able to be conducted with fielded search. | Yes |
| "More like this" searching | Ability to take a resume and conduct a search to find others that are similar to it (more like it). | Yes |

| Function | Function Description | Response |
|---|---|---|
| Library of candidate correspondence/ communication templates | Ability for clients to create a library of correspondence templates that can be sent to candidates at users' discretion. | Yes |
| Editable correspondence at the user level | Users can make edits to the correspondence at the time of generation and distribution. | Yes |
| Agency Portal | Functionality designed for the management of third-party staffing agencies. Includes the ability to push requisitions to one or more suppliers and receive agency resume submissions. | Yes |
| Contingent Labor Management | Functionality designed specifically for the requisition and management of contract labor, including the distribution of job requirements to multiple vendors, submission and review of resumes, tracking of assignment, time reporting and billing. | Yes |
| Candidate Pool Generation (Leads/ Prospective Candidates) | Able to enter limited candidate information (less required fields than regular candidate profile without comprising the configuration of the candidate profile) and develop target candidate pool for key skills. | Yes |
| Marketing Campaigns (Leads/Prospective Candidates) | Include proactive candidate pool in messaging, advertising campaigns or special event invitations. This should include the ability to send emails to thousands of candidates (as necessary). | Yes |
| Sending resumes to a manager | Ability to send a "Formatted Resume" to a Hiring Manager. | Yes |

| Function | Function Description | Response |
|---|---|---|
| **Assessment and Interview Management** | | |
| Customer-defined workflow steps and status | Customer can set up steps and status for tracking candidates through the recruiting process, with ability to tailor it for required and desired steps. | Yes |
| Customer can define multiple process workflows (Example: employee referral, internal transfers, etc.) | Ability to create multiple applicant workflows (set of tracking steps & status) to be selected at the requisition level. | Yes |
| Workflow-triggered alerts | Alerts can be set up in the system to drive the next step in the process or to function as reminders. | Yes |
| Ability to create a "tree-structure" workflow (i.e. step A can be followed by step B, C, D or E) | | Yes |
| Volume hiring updates | The ability to change the status for a group of candidates to hired in a single step (e.g. mass hiring in one step). | Yes |
| Integrated Assessments | Ability to store and/or integrate validated assessment tools into the recruiting workflow for certain jobs. | Yes |
| Assessment Triggers | Ability for Assessment to automatically be presented to candidates based on their responses to pre-screening questions or other data in their profiles. | Yes |
| Assessment on demand | Ability to push an online assessment to a candidate on demand via email link. | Yes |
| Interview team member history | Ability to select and record a list of interviewing team members for a requisition. | Yes |

| Function | Function Description | Response |
|---|---|---|
| Interview team notifications | Ability to send an email notification (including a calendar meeting request) to the interview team members when scheduling the interview within the system (including interview packets, resumes, etc. when sending the email request). | Yes |
| Storage of interviewer comments | Ability to configure an online interview feedback form to capture the comments from each interviewer. | Yes |
| Interviewer attachments | Ability to include attachments to the interviewer notifications (e.g. interview guidelines, interview schedule, resume, etc.) | Yes |
| **Offer Management and Onboarding** | | |
| Approval routing and status tracking | Select a list of approvers, route for approval via email. In addition, the status of the approval process is tracked and displayed real-time on the offer in the application and in the subsequent emails that go to the second and third approver, etc. | Yes |
| Pre-defined approval routing lists | Lists of approvers can be created, saved, and/or assigned to a user or requisition. | Yes |
| Approvals can take place directly from an email | When approving an offer, the approver can take action directly from the email notification without having to log into the application. | Yes |
| Offer letters can be generated by merging fields into letter templates. | Data can be merged from the candidate record, the requisition and the offer terms into offer letter templates. | Yes |

| Function | Function Description | Response |
|---|---|---|
| Offer letters can be edited at the user level | Users can make edits to the offer letter at the time of generation and distribution. | Yes |
| Specific Onboarding Module | Does the product offer a specific On-boarding module, allowing clients to define required notifications at hire and send notifications through the system (e.g. provisioning, IT for user account setup, new hire, manager checklist, etc.)? | Yes |
| Onboarding Docu-mentation Manage-ment | Electronically provide new hire paper-work and track completion of key docu-ments (I-9, Non Disclosures, Benefits Paperwork). | Yes |
| **Global Capabilities & Compliance** | | |
| EEO Compliance data collection | Configurable notification and collection of EEO compliance information at vari-able points in the process. | Yes |
| Global - in-country data collection based on regula-tions | Configurable data requests based on in-country requirements. Example: Ger-many, martial status, number of children. | Yes |
| Ability to present Career Sections in Multiple Languages | Ability to present Career Sections in Multiple Languages. | Yes |
| Ability to present the Recruiter and Manager Portals in multiple languages | Ability to present the Recruiter and Man-ager Portals in multiple languages. | Yes |
| Data Segregation by country, region or predefined type | Data Segregation, i.e. preventing users from a particular country or location from seeing candidates who are in another country or location. | Yes |

| Function | Function Description | Response |
|---|---|---|
| OFCCP Compliance tools to enable search and applicant declaration | Functionality consistent with the new OFCCP definition of Internet Applicant (record keeping for searches, candidate submissions, etc.) | Yes |
| Privacy Policy acknowledgements | Ability to require that candidates agree with the privacy policy before they submit. | Yes |
| Compliance with Data Privacy | Ability for customers to remove a candidate's data at that candidate's request. | Yes |
| Tax Credit Screening & Processing | Provides automatic Tax ID and SSN validation. Automatically transmits request to conduct tax credit screening for WOTC, WTW and more through to screening partners. Displays those results within the candidate profile for review and processing upon hire. | Yes |
| **Reporting & Integration** | | |
| Standard reports are delivered with the system | System is delivered with a minimum of 10 standard reports. | Yes |
| Ad-hoc reporting capability | System is delivered with an ad-hoc report-writing tool so that clients can create their own reports as needed. | Yes |
| Reporting Security | Ability to enable field-level security and access to report creation, output and distribution. | Yes |
| Reporting Distribution | Ability to generate scheduled reports and distribute through email. | Yes |
| Real-Time Reporting | Ability to report on data in the application in real time (not based on a refresh of data in a reporting environment.) | Yes |

| Function | Function Description | Response |
|---|---|---|
| HRIS Integration | Ability to create bi-directional integrations from an HRIS to the ATS. | Yes |
| Integration - Client Self-Service Tools | Ability for clients to create their own integration touch points as needed (and make them operational). | Yes |
| Integration - API capability | Ability to allow clients to create integrations through APIs. | Yes |

## Performance Management

| Performance Dashboard | | |
|---|---|---|
| Dashboard configuration | Ability to configure dashboard based on user preference. | Yes |
| Create and display reports | Display reports that can be generated (i.e. review completion progress, goal progress). | Yes |
| Create and display charts and graphs | Display charts and graphs that are available to show planning actions. | Yes |
| Display help and reference tools | Display and view help and reference tools that can be selected by link or mouse hover. | Yes |
| Employee Information Review (Data Import from HRIS/LMS) | | |
| Import and display employee information | Display name, address, phone, email, location, photo, education (typically pulled from HRIS). | Yes |
| Import and display employee position information | Display current job title, job summary, job family, job level/grade, job code, FLSA, shift, status (FT/PT) (typically pulled through HRIS). | Yes |
| Create and display work history | Display created previous work history (i.e. name of company, job title, responsibilities/duties, employment dates). | Yes |

| Function | Function Description | Response |
|---|---|---|
| Create and display years in management | Display created years of management experience (manually entered or via integration). | Yes |
| Create and display years in industry | Display created years of experience in industry (primarily entered manually). | Yes |
| Import, create and display employee language(s) | Display employee languages (i.e. read, written, fluent) (primarily entered manually). | Yes |
| Import, create and display employee affiliations | Display employee affiliation memberships. | Yes |
| Import, create and display employee certifications | Display employee certifications and dates. | Yes |
| Import, create and display employee licenses | Display employee licenses and dates (usually a text box); include expiration dates (could be for transportation, professional licenses, healthcare licenses, etc.) | Yes |
| Import and display organizational information | Display company name, company division, company department (typically imported from HRIS). | Yes |
| Import and display management hierarchy information | Display multiple levels of management names and information (i.e. Executive Management, Division Head, Department Head, Direct Manager, Employee). | Yes |
| Import and display direct reports | Display name and information of employee direct reports. | Yes |
| Import and display matrix manager hierarchy information | Display multiple levels of matrix management names and information (i.e. Employee has dotted line reporting relationships). | Yes |

| Function | Function Description | Response |
|---|---|---|
| Import and display multiple manager hierarchy information | Display multiple levels of numerous management names and information (i.e. Employee reports to more than one manager directly). | Yes |
| Organizational Chart View | Organizational information can be displayed in an Org Chart view (note how this is displayed visually). | Yes |
| Organizational Change Requests | Due to potential errors within HRMS, manager has the ability to request an employee change in hierarchy (i.e. manager name, organization, location, job role); changes can be configured to require approval. | Yes |
| Import and display employee current and past compensation | Display employee's past and current base salary, bonus, equity, commission, etc. | Yes |
| Import and display employee most recent performance measures | Display employee's current competencies, goals, skills, projects, performance rating, development plan and personal improvement plan. | Yes |
| Import and display employee previous performance measures | Display employee's previous competencies, goals, skills, projects, performance rating, development plan and personal improvement plan. | Yes |
| Complete and display employee training | Display employee's completed and assigned training (i.e. mandatory/development); Note if there is any integration with LMS. | Yes |
| External Identifier | Ability to have an external identifier field to bring in content on goals from a third-party application (i.e. description, start date, critical, public goal); can be configured to be read-only for imports. | Yes |

| Function | Function Description | Response |
|---|---|---|
| UDFs | Available user-defined fields for employee profile. | No |
| **Career Planning / Personal Development (Employee)** | | |
| Create and display future career plan scenarios | Display multiple future career plans (vertical, horizontal, both). Where does the employee want to go next? (lateral, promotion, etc.) | Yes |
| Select and display positions, job families and organizations/divisions of interest | Display selected positions and organizations of interest from import of job list and organization list (mentorships and cross-training); gives the employee the opportunity to identify a position, job-family or organization of interest. | Yes |
| Create and display training requests | Display developmental training requests (entered by an employee or manager); this could be an integration point to the LMS. | Yes |
| Create and display executive/professional requests | Display various executive/professional requests (i.e. executive coaching, cross-training, job shadowing, speaking engagements, writing submittals, managing people, presentations, mentoring, apprenticeships). | Yes |
| Create and display organization affiliations and/or conferences/seminars | Display employee organization/affiliation or conference/seminar requests to join or attend. | Yes |
| Select and display competency development | Display selected desired competencies (entered by employee). | Yes |
| Create self-asses job readiness | Display selected self-readiness from list of options (i.e. Now, 0-3 months, 3-6 months, 6-9 months, 9-12 months, 12 months +). | Yes |

| Function | Function Description | Response |
|---|---|---|
| Display position Gap % | Display gap % of employee readiness to ideal position as well as required training, license(s), education, certification(s). This could be automatically calculated by the system (key differentiator). This is a gap analysis on the underlying competencies (most recent performance rating vs. competencies required for next position). | Yes |
| Select and display willingness to relocate | Display selected willingness to relocate (i.e. yes, no, maybe, comments). | Yes |
| Display career prerequisites | Display required training, education, certification(s), license(s) for position of interest. | Yes |
| Submit development requests for approval | Submit development self-assessments to direct manager for review, feedback and approval (areas where the development needs to occur, as well as specific courses/ conferences to help meet these development areas). Could be an integration point with LMS. | Yes |
| **Career Development (Manager)** | | |
| Create or select and display employee training goals | Display created or selected employee completed training, assigned training (mandatory/development), scheduled training and employee training requests. This is the manager identifying training goals for an employee. | Yes |
| Competency Development | Display assigned professional/leadership competencies. | Yes |

| Function | Function Description | Response |
|---|---|---|
| Create and display executive/professional assignments | Display various executive/ professional recommendations (i.e. executive coaching, cross training, job shadowing, speaking engagements, writing submittals, managing people, presentations, mentoring, apprenticeships). | Yes |
| Create and display organization affiliations and/or conferences/seminars | Display employee organization/affiliation or conference/seminar recommendations. | Yes |
| **Individual Goal / Self Assessment (Employee)** | | |
| Select, create and display individual development goals | Display selected or created completed training, improvement competencies, executive coaching, promotion, cross training. | Yes |
| Select competency development | Display selected development competencies. This is where the employee selects competencies to develop for his/her career on the annual review. | Yes |
| Submit goal/competency assessment for approval | Submit manual or automatic goal/competency assessment to direct manager. | Yes |
| Solicit and display feedback | Select employees (i.e. managers, matrix managers, peers) to solicit performance feedback (i.e. 360, peer review, business review) and display results. | Yes |
| Create and display self-performance notes | Display created performance notes (i.e. kudos) throughout the review cycle (manually entered by employee or can solicit feedback throughout project). | Yes |
| Create and display self goal assessment progress | Display created self-goal progress (i.e. quantitative % of completion, qualitative to include customer satisfaction, timeline to include start/completion date). | Yes |

| Function | Function Description | Response |
|---|---|---|
| Submit goal/competency review for approval | Submit manual or automatic goal/competency assessment to direct manager and higher levels. | Yes |
| UDFs | Available user-defined fields for employee goals. | No |
| **Review Process (Employee and Manager)** | | |
| Select and display competencies | Display selected professional or leadership competencies. | Yes |
| Select and display goals/objectives | Display selected goals/objectives (i.e. quantitative and/or qualitative). | Yes |
| Select and display goal alignment | Display selected goal alignment to company, organization, department, and/or manager goals (cascading goals). | Yes |
| Select or create and display projects | Display selected or created projects. | Yes |
| Select and display project alignment to goals | Display selected project alignment to company, organization, department and/or manager goals. | Yes |
| Select or create and display skills | Display selected or created company, organization, department, employee skills. | Yes |
| Create and display employee performance notes | Display created performance notes (positive or negative) throughout the review cycle. These are notes created by the manager. | Yes |
| Solicit and display feedback | Select employees (i.e. managers, matrix managers, peers) to solicit performance feedback (i.e. 360, peer review, business review) and display. Pay particular attention to how this feedback is gathered and entered into the system. | Yes |

| Function | Function Description | Response |
|---|---|---|
| Create and display employee goal assessment review | Display created employee goal progress (i.e. quantitative % of completion, qualitative to include customer satisfaction, timeline to include start/completion date). This is the manager entering the assessment. | Yes |
| Performance review filtering | Manager can filter performance review information based on approval status, assigned to, author/owner, manager, employee, organization, location, job field, job role, review cycle, review group, review group owner, overall rating; filtering can be cumulative. | Yes |
| Batch activities | Manager can take group actions on multiple employees simultaneously. | Yes |
| UDFs | Available user-defined fields for employee competencies. | No |
| **Workflow** | | |
| Review cycles | Ability to configure multiple review cycles and tie to various reviews. | Yes |
| Review groups | Ability to define review recipients based on dates, job function, organization, job code, etc. | Yes |
| Workflow Order | Ability to configure order of workflow (i.e. self-assessments can be configured to be completed first). | Yes |
| Notifications | Ability to push reviews to employees and managers. | Yes |
| Reminders | Ability to send reminders to employees and managers via email (manual and automatic). | Yes |

| Function | Function Description | Response |
|---|---|---|
| Acknowledgements | Ability to send auto-acknowledgements triggered by event/activity. | Yes |
| Next Level Approval | Ability to auto/manually route to multiple levels of approval. | Yes |
| Configurable work-flow | Ability to: configure various steps of the review process; make review steps mandatory; use manager override; display/hide visual graphic workflow diagram. | Yes |
| Auto/Manual Progression | Ability to automatically or manually progress through the review process. | Yes |
| Review form | Exportable and printable review form. | Yes |
| **System Admin** | | |
| Review sections | Ability to configure multiple review sections, including goals, competencies, comments, rating models, etc. | Yes |
| Configurable rating models | Does it configure and display alpha and numeric values? Can values be rounded (up/down/both), value ranges, number of decimals (1-5)? | Yes |
| Comments | Display and made available in individual review sections and overall review. Can they be configured to be mandatory and overridden by management? | Yes |
| Goals | Ability to link organizational, divisional, departmental and individual goals into sections and ability to display goal progress. | Yes |
| Competencies | Ability to link competencies into sections. | Yes |
| Weightings | Ability to weigh employee performance based on goals and competencies. | Yes |

| Function | Function Description | Response |
|---|---|---|
| **Search Functionality** | | |
| Basic Employee Search | Basic search by employee name (i.e. first or last name or a combination of both). | Yes |
| Job/Position Basic Search | Basic search by job role or position title, etc. | Yes |
| Competency Basic Search | Basic search by competency name. | Yes |
| Advanced Search | More detailed search capabilities that combine various search criteria or fields; may include optional weighting to determine which employees are retrieved in a search as well as each person's rank in the search results. | Yes |
| Succession Planning Search | Search functionality that dynamically generates the criteria used to match employees who would make good succession candidates with a specific position profile (could have various levels of "fit"). | Yes |
| **Employee View / Navigation / Help / Other** | | |
| List View | Display employee goals, business goals or projects; the list mode is a list of items with information on key dates and progress. | Yes |
| Card View | Display employee goals, business goals or projects using the card mode. The card mode provides details on one item at a time and offers the possibility of editing progress. This can also include employee photos. | Yes |
| Timeline / Gantt | Display employee goals, business goals or projects using the timeline mode; the timeline mode provides a timeline view of an item's start and due dates. | Yes |

| Function | Function Description | Response |
|---|---|---|
| Org Chart | Managers can access and manage information on their direct reports for all functionalities activated; the organizational chart will provide key data (i.e. risk of loss or most recent performance rating) for each of the manager's direct reports. | Yes |
| Mini-Org Chart | Displays a single analytic data point at a time; the manager can drill down into all layers of his organization and can view key metrics (i.e. performance reviews, goals, succession). | Yes |
| Graphs | Graphical display of various information (i.e. Gap Analysis, goal progress and review completion progress). | Yes |
| Help Links | Online help, FAQs, customer support, product version. | Yes |
| Attach Documents | Ability to attach reference documents to various sections within the system. | Yes |
| Browser capabilities | Supported by general Internet access (works with standard browsers: IE, Safari, Mozilla, Opera). | Yes |
| Mouse-Over Hover | Additional tooltips or descriptions that display when users hover mouse pointer over various graphics or words within the system. | Yes |
| Web 2.0 | Ability to utilize Web 2.0 functionality, i.e. social networking. | Yes |
| **Security** | | |
| Logging In | Various login options (i.e. manual, SSO, LDAP). | Yes |

| Function | Function Description | Response |
|---|---|---|
| File Transfer | Various file transfer protocol (i.e. FTP, sFTP, vendor-specific transfer import/export tool). | Yes |
| Encryption | Various data encryption ability (i.e. PGP). | Yes |
| Roles / Permissions | Configurable list of permission-based roles with detailed access rights to various organizations, levels, etc. Typically employees only view within their own organization hierarchy. | Yes |
| Integration | Ability to integrate organizational data i.e. HRIS/ATS/LMS and employee data including competencies, training, development plans, etc. | Yes |
| **Reporting** | | |
| Standard reports are delivered with the system | System is delivered with a set number of standard reports. | Yes |
| Ad-hoc reporting capability | System is delivered with an ad-hoc report-writing tool so that clients can create their own reports as needed. | Yes |
| Advanced Value metrics | Data analysis of employee review process status and goal progress by hierarchy. | Yes |
| Reporting Security | Ability to enable field-level security and access to report creation, output and distribution. | Yes |
| Reporting UDFs | Ability to report user-defined fields. | Yes |
| Exporting reports | Reports can easily be exported to other applications (i.e. .xls, .pdf, .txt). | Yes |

| Function | Function Description | Response |
|---|---|---|

## Succession Planning

| Succession Planning (Manager - Planning of Individual Talent Matched to Critical Roles) | | |
|---|---|---|
| Create and display critical roles for today | Display critical job roles (i.e. title, level, location, division, organization). | Yes |
| Create and display critical roles for future | Display critical job roles (i.e. title, level, location, division, organization) for future (workforce planning-like tools). | Yes |
| Calculate and display performance rating | Performance rating is automatically averaged from various sections of the performance review and displayed (current and past). | Yes |
| Calculate and display performance ranking | High potential employees will be automatically ranked according to order of fit with critical role (i.e. 9-box grid, numeric ranking, high performer, high potential) - can be ranked by position, organization, etc. | Yes |
| Multi-dimensional matrix | Matrix that can be configured up to various # of cells (i.e. 9-box, 12-box, 16-box, 25-box); text within grid is configurable. | Yes |
| Various dimensions of matrix | Matrix displays employee performance, potential, number of succession plans for each, years in management, years in industry. | Yes |
| Navigation from multi-dimensional matrix | Manager can select an employee within the matrix and navigate to employee information (i.e. Performance review, talent profile, employee goals, career plan). | Yes |

| Function | Function Description | Response |
|---|---|---|
| Display employee comparisons | Display comparison of multiple high potential employees according to fit to critical role (i.e. # of employees to compare, comparable data, fit gap analysis, ranking analysis, bench strength). | Yes |
| Create and display role readiness | Manager can create and display high potential employee role readiness (i.e. now, 0-3 months, 3-6 months, 6-9 months, 9-12 months, 12+ months). | Yes |
| Create and display retention risk | Manager can create and display high potential employee retention/loss/flight risk (i.e. high, medium, low, comments). | Yes |
| Create and display role willingness | Manager can create and display high potential employee role willingness (i.e. yes, no, comments). | Yes |
| Create and display willingness to relocate | Manager can create and display high potential employee willingness to relocate (i.e. yes, no, maybe, comments). | Yes |
| Create and display willingness to travel | Manager can create and display high potential employee willingness to travel (i.e. none, 25-50%, 50-75%, 75-100%). | Yes |
| Create and display interest in international assignment | Manager can create and display high potential employee interest in international assignment (i.e. yes, no, maybe). | Yes |
| Create and display interim replacement for critical role | Manager can create and display high potential interim replacement for critical roles. | Yes |
| Display of gap analysis | Automatically calculate and display high potential employee's fit gap analysis to the next position and ranking analysis. | Yes |
| UDFs | Available user-defined fields for succession planning. | No |

| Function | Function Description | Response |
|----------|---------------------|----------|
| **Succession Pooling (Manager - Planning of a Talent Pool for Critical Roles)** | | |
| Display high potential pool | Display nominated and/or approved high potential pool (i.e. employee information, designated nominators, designated approvers, approvals, rejections, role readiness, rejection comments). | Yes |
| Calculate and display performance rating | Performance rating is automatically averaged from various sections of the performance review and displayed (current and past). | Yes |
| Calculate and display performance ranking | Pool of high potential employees will be automatically ranked according to order of fit with critical role (i.e. 9-box grid, numeric ranking, high performer, high potential). | Yes |
| Display employee comparisons | Display comparison of multiple high potential employees according to fit to critical role (i.e. # of employees to compare, comparable data, fit gap analysis, ranking analysis, bench strength). | Yes |
| Create and display role readiness | Manager can create and display high potential employee role readiness (i.e. now, 0-3 months, 3-6 months, 6-9 months, 9-12 months, 12+ months). | Yes |
| Create and display retention risk | Manager can create and display high potential employee retention/loss/flight risk (i.e. high, medium, low, comments). | Yes |
| Create and display role willingness | Manager can create and display high potential employee role willingness (i.e. yes, no, comments). | Yes |
| Create and display willingness to relocate | Manager can create and display high potential employee willingness to relocate (i.e. yes, no, maybe, comments). | Yes |

| Function | Function Description | Response |
|---|---|---|
| Create and display willingness to travel | Manager can create and display high potential employee willingness to travel (i.e. none, 25-50%, 50-75%, 75-100%). | Yes |
| Create and display interest in international assignment | Manager can create and display high potential employee interest in international assignment (i.e. yes, no, maybe). | Yes |
| Create and display interim replacement for critical role | Manager can create and display high potential interim replacement for critical roles. | Yes |
| Display of gap analysis | Automatically calculate and display high potential employees' fit gap analysis to position and ranking analysis of employees to position. | Yes |
| UDFs | Available user-defined fields for succession pooling. | No |
| **Workflow** | | |
| Succession approval workflow | Ability to define or edit approvers, add/ remove users and roles, ability to change the approval order and ability to reject with comments. | Yes |
| Nominations for succession pool | Ability to nominate, reject and enter comments on nominated HiPo employees. | Yes |
| **Reporting** | | |
| Standard reports are delivered with the system | System is delivered with a set number of standard reports. | Yes |
| Ad-hoc reporting capability | System is delivered with an ad-hoc report writing tool so that clients can create their own reports as needed. | Yes |

| Function | Function Description | Response |
|---|---|---|
| Advanced Value metrics | Data analysis of high performers / high potential employees, identified gaps and critical roles. | Yes |
| Reporting Security | Ability to enable field-level security and access to report creation, output and distribution. | Yes |
| Reporting UDFs | Ability to report user-defined fields. | Yes |
| Exporting reports | Reports can easily be exported to other applications (i.e. .xls, .pdf, .txt). | Yes |

## Compensation Management

| Compensation Dashboard | | |
|---|---|---|
| Dashboard configuration | Ability to configure dashboard based on user preference. | Yes |
| Create and display a compensation worksheet | Display a compensation worksheet that will provide individual and org planning status and detail. | Yes |
| Create and display reports | Display reports that can be generated, i.e. budget usage by merit, bonus, equity, adjustment and percent of planning completed. | Yes |
| Create and display charts and graphs | Display charts and graphs that are available to show planning actions. | Yes |
| Import and display allocation guidelines | Display compensation allocation guidelines for merit, bonus, equity and adjustments - also refer to the time allocation/ workflow to complete this process. | Yes |
| Import and display eligibility guidelines | Display employee eligibility guidelines for planning, i.e. FT, PT, commission, LOA, new hire, etc. Guidelines are input by compensation department. | Yes |

| Function | Function Description | Response |
|---|---|---|
| Display help and reference tools | Display and view help and reference tools that can be selected by link or mouse hover. | Yes |
| **Compensation Budget** | | |
| Import and display multiple aggregate planning budget by org | Display multiple approved allocated budgets by diverse business groups on all pages (usually imported from financial system). | Yes |
| Import and display aggregate merit budget by org | Display approved allocated merit budget by diverse business groups on all pages. | Yes |
| Import and display aggregate bonus budget by org | Display approved allocated bonus by diverse business groups on all pages. | Yes |
| Import and display aggregate equity budget by org | Display approved allocated equity budget by diverse business groups on all pages. | Yes |
| Import and display aggregate adjust-ment budget by org | Display approved allocated adjustment budget by diverse business groups on all pages. | Yes |
| **Employee Information Review** | | |
| Import and display employee Informa-tion | Display name, location, photo, org, direct manager (typically imported from PM tool). | Yes |
| Import and display employee position | Display current job title, job code and level/grade. | Yes |
| Import and display employee prior compensation plan-ning period data | Display current hourly rate, annual rate, bonus percent, bonus amount, equity allocation and total compensation. | Yes |

| Function | Function Description | Response |
|---|---|---|
| Import and display employee prior performance rating | Display prior performance rating. | Yes |
| Import and display new employee performance rating | Display new performance rating. | Yes |
| Import and display employee's position salary range | Display employee's salary range. | Yes |
| Import and display salary penetration % based on position wage range | Display % of penetration that employee's salary falls within the range. | Yes |
| **Promotion** | | |
| Display position information | Ability to select and display job titles, job codes and job level/grades. | Yes |
| Import and display corporate promotion guidelines | Ability to display promotion guidelines per position, including salary range and percent increase guidelines. | Yes |
| Promotion amount | Ability to enter promotion percent or amount. | Yes |
| Auto-calculate promotion amount | System to auto-populate promotion amount based on percent increase. | Yes |
| Ability to calculate hourly rate | System to auto-populate new hourly rate based on promotion increase. | Yes |
| Ability to auto-calculate annual rate | System to auto-populate new annual rate based on promotion increase. | Yes |
| Promotion approval chain | TBD. | Yes |

| Function | Function Description | Response |
|---|---|---|
| Develop documentation | Ability to document the promotion justification. | Yes |
| **Adjustment** | | |
| Import and display adjustment guidelines | Ability to display adjustment allocation guidelines, including salary range and percent increase guidelines. | Yes |
| Adjustment allocation | Ability to enter and submit an adjustment percent or amount. | Yes |
| Auto-calculate hourly amount | System to auto-populate new hourly rate based on adjustment percent increase. | Yes |
| Auto-calculate adjustment amount | System to auto-populate new annual rate based on adjustment percent increase. | Yes |
| Adjustment approvals | Display adjustment approvals. | Yes |
| Develop documentation | Ability to document the adjustment justification. | Yes |
| **Merit** | | |
| Import and display merit guidelines | Ability to display merit allocation guidelines, including salary range and percent increase guidelines. | Yes |
| Performance-based recommendations | Merit allocation can be based on performance rating. | Yes |
| Merit allocation | Ability to enter and submit a merit percent or amount. | Yes |
| Import and display proration of merit based on hire date | System to auto-calculate merit increase based on hire date, i.e. less than one year would be calculated by months employed. | Yes |

| Function | Function Description | Response |
|---|---|---|
| Auto-calculate hourly amount | System to auto-populate new hourly rate based on merit percent increase. | Yes |
| Auto-calculate adjustment amount | System to auto-populate new annual rate based on merit percent increase. | Yes |
| Merit approvals | | Yes |
| Develop documentation | Ability to document the merit justification. | Yes |
| **Bonus** | | |
| Import and display bonus allocation guidelines | Ability to display bonus allocation guidelines. | Yes |
| Performance-based recommendations | Bonus allocation can be based on performance rating. | Yes |
| Bonus allocation | Ability to enter and submit a bonus percent or amount. | Yes |
| Bonus adjustment | Auto-Proration of bonus based on hired or leave, i.e. severance date. | Yes |
| Bonus approvals | Ability to obtain appropriate approvals (workflow to select appropriate approvers). | Yes |
| Develop documentation | Ability to document the merit justification. | Yes |
| **Equity** | | |
| Import and display equity allocation guidelines | Ability to display equity allocation guidelines. | Yes |
| Performance-based recommendations | Equity allocation can be based on performance rating. | Yes |

| Function | Function Description | Response |
|---|---|---|
| Equity allocation | Ability to enter and submit equity percent or amount. | Yes |
| Equity allocation adjustment | Auto-Proration of equity allocation based on hire date. | Yes |
| Equity approvals | Show equity approvals. | Yes |
| Develop documen-tation | Ability to document the merit justification. | Yes |
| **Other** | | |
| Ability to assign a delegate | Ability to assign a delegate to complete compensation planning, i.e. Admin. | Yes |
| Employee Filter | Ability to sort by employee name or data, i.e. first name, last name, employee ID, etc. | Yes |
| Employee Search | Ability to search throughout the tool by employee name or data, i.e. first name, last name, employee ID, etc. | Yes |
| Revert or change functionality | Ability for planning administrators to revert or change submitted data. | Yes |
| Collaborative work-flow | Ability for managers, compensation and HR partners to collaborate on various compensation workflows. | Yes |
| Display out-of-guideline entries | Ability to display out-of-guideline entries made within adjustments, merit, bonus and equity. | Yes |
| **Reporting** | | |
| Standard reports are delivered with the system | System is delivered with a set number of standard reports. | Yes |

| Function | Function Description | Response |
|---|---|---|
| Ad-hoc reporting capability | System is delivered with an ad-hoc report-writing tool so that clients can create their own reports as needed. | Yes |
| Advanced-Value metrics | Data analysis of comp gaps based on roles and hierarchy. | Yes |
| Reporting Security | Ability to enable field-level security and access to report creation, output and distribution. | Yes |
| **Security** | | |
| Logging In | Various login options (i.e. manual, SSO, LDAP). | Yes |
| File Transfer | Various file transfer protocol (i.e. FTP, sFTP, vendor-specific transfer import/export tool). | Yes |
| Encryption | Various data encryption ability (i.e. PGP). | Yes |
| Roles / Permissions | Configurable list of permission-based roles with detailed access rights to various organizations, levels, etc. Typically employees only view within their own organization hierarchy. | Yes |
| Integration | Ability to Integrate organizational data with appropriate org system, i.e. HRIS/Payroll, employee data, including employee salaries, levels, performance rating, etc. | Yes |
| Reporting UDFs | Ability to report user-defined fields. | Yes |
| Exporting reports | Reports can easily be exported to other applications (i.e. .xls, .pdf, .txt). | Yes |

| Function | Function Description | Response |
|---|---|---|

## Learning Management

| Content Management and Delivery | | |
|---|---|---|
| Application Simulation | Client content owners can create application simulations for use in training (i.e. "Show Me"/"Try Me" Flash-type simulations). | Yes |
| Assign learning content-based employee data | Learning content assigned to employees based on their job function or organizational data (not specific to position, but job family or organization). | Yes |
| Catalogs | Employees can search through and browse course catalogs to identify courses in which they are interested. | Yes |
| Competency Management - Third-Party Defined | Courses and learning plans can be built around competencies, driven by integration with a third-party vendor. | Yes |
| Competency Management - Customer-Defined | Courses and learning plans can be built around competencies as determined by the customer. | Yes |
| Offline Capabilities | Learning content can be downloaded for completion even if the user is not connected to the Internet/network. Can also upload results. | Yes |
| Employee Profile Management | System can house employee profiles that can be used for learning plan assignment, development plan creation and management (could be integration point). | Yes |
| External Content Integration | Employees can access, review and register for courses in systems and online portals that are integrated with the LMS. | Yes |

| Function | Function Description | Response |
|---|---|---|
| Internal Content Authoring | WYSIWYG (what you see is what you get) editor is built into the system for creation of learning materials within the system by client content owners. | Yes |
| Learning Plans | Customer can create learning plans for employees. Employees can manage their progress, review schedules, register for courses and access online courses from plans. Collaboration with employees and managers to create this learning plan (and appropriate workflow). Could be an integration point from PM tool. | Yes |
| Multiple Languages | System supports multiple languages for global implementations. | Yes |
| PowerPoint Conversion | System allows for uploading of PowerPoint files as learning content. | Yes |
| Repository | Digital repository for management of draft and active content is available in the system. Content managers would use this functionality (and allows for collaboration). | Yes |
| Scheduling | Users can book resources, locations, and structures from within the system. This is an integration point as well. | Yes |
| Single Sign-On | Standard SSO capability for integration with client Intranet. | Yes |
| Version Control | Content owners have the ability to manage content versioning. | Yes |
| Virtual Classrooms | System provides virtual classroom functionality for live, remote learning sessions. | Yes |

| Function | Function Description | Response |
|---|---|---|
| **Testing and Tracking** | | |
| General Assessments | System allows for creation of assessments that aren't tied to particular training content. Could be tied to competencies. | Yes |
| Content Test Completion | Users can complete tests online as assigned. Could be offline as well. | Yes |
| Content Test Creation | System allows for creation of tests for learning content. | Yes |
| Polling | Polling can be conducted through one or more channels (e.g. Content, User Home Page Interface, etc.) | Yes |
| Test Completion Tracking | User test completion status and rates can be tracked. | Yes |
| Test Score Tracking | User test scores can be stored and tracked. | Yes |
| **Reporting** | | |
| Ad-hoc reporting capability | System is delivered with an ad-hoc report-writing tool so that clients can create their own reports as needed. | Yes |
| Data analysis | System provides functionality for advanced data analysis and dashboarding. | Yes |
| Reporting Security | Ability to enable field-level security and access to report creation, output and distribution. | Yes |
| Standard reports are delivered with the system | System is delivered with a minimum of 10 standard reports. | Yes |

| Function | Function Description | Response |
|---|---|---|
| **Integration** | | |
| Employee Profile Integration | System allows for employee profile integration with other talent management solutions (e.g., Performance, Succession, Compensation, Recruitment, etc.) | Yes |
| Integration | Ability to allow clients to create integrations through APIs, XML, flat files, etc. | Yes |
| **Web 2.0 Features** | | |
| Blogs | System allows for creation of blogs for content delivery. | Yes |
| Forums | System allows for creation and maintenance of forums to capture user-generated content and enable collaborative learning activities. | Yes |
| Other Collaborative Learning Tools | Additional collaborative learning tools are available. | Yes |
| Podcasting | System allows for creation of podcasts for content delivery. | Yes |
| RSS Feeds | System allows users to identify content "tracks" that they wish to monitor on a regular basis and displays updates in an RSS-like format. | Yes |
| Wikis | System allows for creation and maintenance of wikis to capture user-generated content and enable collaborative learning activities. | Yes |
| **User Communication** | | |
| Completion Date Reminders | Users can be notified when they are approaching a target content completion date. | Yes |

| Function | Function Description | Response |
|---|---|---|
| Completion Reminders | Users can be reminded to complete content that has been saved in progress. | Yes |
| Content Notifications | Users can be notified when new content is added to their learning plan or a track in which they are interested. | Yes |
| Manager Notifications | User managers and/or learning administrators can be notified when certain activities are completed. | Yes |
| Workflow | System allows for creation of workflow to communicate user status to content and people managers. | Yes |

# StepStone Solutions

## Company Information (provided by StepStone)

**Company Name:**              StepStone Solutions

**Corporate URL:**             www.stepstonesolutions.com

**Headquarters Address:**      Thunes vei 2 0274 Oslo, Norway

**Type of Business or Areas of Focus:**

StepStone provides Total Talent Management solutions for global organizations. These solutions include e-Recruitment, Performance Management, Succession Planning and Career Development, Learning and Compensation (as well as "HR Core functionality"). Solutions can be deployed individually or as an integrated suite.

**Number of Employees:**       990+

**Year Founded:**              1996

**Stock Symbol (If Applicable):**  Oslo Stock Exchange (OSE): STP
London Stock Exchange (LSE): STPS

## Company Description and History:

A pioneer in the e-Recruitment market since 1997, StepStone delivers a unique "one-stop shop" for customers seeking competitive advantage in the attraction, retention and development of talent, through its talent networks and human capital management solutions.

StepStone helps it customers gain this competitive advantage by:

- Leveraging an online platform to increase effectiveness in attracting, integrating, managing, motivating, developing and retaining talent;

- Managing activity across different countries and continents;
- Providing scalable solutions that can be deployed module-by-module across business units;
- Reducing cost and administrative time by automating basic HCM tasks; thereby, increasing time to focus on value-added activities;
- Enabling compliance with increasingly complex employment regulations and data protection legislation.

Global customers of StepStone exploiting this competitive advantage include: Deutsche Telekom, Aviva, PricewaterhouseCoopers, AstraZeneca, ThyssenKrupp, Fiat and Telefonica.

StepStone's unique combination of talent networks and human capital management solutions enable it to deliver a comprehensive, multilingual suite of talent management solutions to its customers.

These solutions are available under the hosted software as a service ("SaaS") model and delivered from its hosting centers in Europe, the United States and the Far East.

## Products/Services/Solutions:

StepStone Solutions provides Total Talent Management Solutions for global organizations. These solutions include e-Recruitment, Performance Management, Succession Planning and Career Development, Learning and Compensation (as well as "HR Core functionality")—these solutions can be deployed individually or as an integrated suite.

StepStone's Total Talent Management Solution features a consistent user interface, a single point of access and cross-application workflows that bridge the gap between recruiting and talent management functions.

For managers, these enhanced capabilities help users post and manage job requisitions, review applications and evaluate an internal applicant's candidacy based on the availability of prior performance data—all from a centralized console. From this console, they can also initiate performance reviews, allocate bonuses and assess bench strength for key positions. For employees, having a single tool to apply for jobs, set goals and objectives and participate in the performance appraisal process provides a more consistent user experience, better insight into the skills and competencies required for advancement and greater control over achieving specific career goals.

StepStone's Total Talent Management Suite is comprised of the following solutions:

## 1. StepStone e-Recruitment (i-GRasp)

StepStone i-GRasp is a fully globalized e-Recruitment solution suite that integrates every part of an employer's recruitment process, from job posting through candidate application, screening and selection, agency and job board management, to HR system integration, management reporting and on-boarding. Uniquely, i-GRasp provides support for ALL types of candidate applications including integration with the client's corporate Web site and intranet as well as e-mail, paper and job board applicants. At the click of a button, in-depth reporting for all aspects of the recruitment process is always available—clients can readily track cost per hire, time to hire and other key indicators. Additionally, StepStone's e-Recruitment solution includes feature/functionality to support the following recruiting initiatives:

- Permanent Recruitment and Internal Mobility
- Temporary Staff and Contractor Management
- Campus and Graduate Recruitment
- Web-based surveys (e.g., candidate experience, hiring manager satisfaction)
- Campaign Management

## 2. StepStone Talent Management (ETWeb)

StepStone ETWeb is a fully globalized talent management solution that includes feature/functionality to support the following HR initiatives:

- Performance Management
- Succession Planning
- Career Development
- Learning
- Compensation
- HR "Core" Management

StepStone ETWeb's sophisticated decision support tools provide at-a-glance charts, graphs and reports that allow employers to quantify macro trends and "hot spots" across functional areas and geographic locations. Drill down functionality enables users to view details of specific employee groups (or individuals) while a business intelligence engine automatically correlates multi-disciplinary data based on pre-defined objectives and key performance metrics, recommending critical actions and next steps.

StepStone ETWeb can be deployed both as a modular and as a standalone solution. Using the Self-Service technology, users can access relevant information pertinent to their specific role (employee, manager, HR department) and update it as needed. ETWeb™ is currently available in over 20 languages, making it easy for employees of different nationalities to work with the application in their preferred language (including Russian, Chinese and Arabic).

### 3. StepStone EasyCruit

StepStone EasyCruit is a full-featured, fully globalized On Demand e-Recruitment solution that is targeted at employers in the SMG market segment—this solution is primarily sold in the Nordic region. EasyCruit is integrated with a wide range of online talent sites, including StepStone's leading European job boards.

## Additional Notes/Comments:

### StepStone's Global Capabilities

StepStone's solutions were designed from the ground up to manage multinational implementations. Features supporting its multinational approach include: full multilingual support for candidates and recruiters through all system interfaces and communications to all participants in the process, multi-currency support for cost-per-hire reporting and contingent worker tracking and billing and the ability to support multiple career portals per iteration of the product. It offers 24/7 support for clients as required from centers in Europe/UK, the U.S. and Singapore. The strategy is to provide local country support across Europe, the U.S. and in the Asia Pacific region.

### StepStone's Key Differentiators
- Financial strength and stability
  — Public, profitable company (e.g., transparency)
  — 20 consecutive quarters of revenue growth
- Market leading global capabilities with local support
  — 1500+ customers

— Deep domain expertise at the local level
— Experience with complex, global deployments requiring support for multiple brands, languages, currencies, level of access control and regional regulatory compliance
— Most comprehensive global infrastructure
- Breadth and depth of talent management offering
  — Integrated Total Talent Management suite
  — Best-in-breed Talent Management solutions
  — Total Talent Management Consulting Services
    – StepChange (Change Management Consulting)
    – Selection Decision Improvement Consulting
    – Employer Branding and Candidate Experience Audits
    – Star Performers (identifying "X-Factor" in high performing employees)
    – Global Resourcing Model Analysis

# Author's StepStone Functionality Matrix

| Function | Function Description | Response |
|----------|--------------------|----------|

Talent Acquisition

| Requisition Management & Posting | | |
|---|---|---|
| Multiple requisition forms allowed (Example: hourly, internal transfer, business unit specific, reoccurring, sourcing, college) | More than one requisition form/template can be configured in a client's database to accommodate variance in business units or type of recruiting. (Example: A user from the Manufacturing group can enter a requisition and only see and populate fields that are applicable to Mfg. A different user from the Services group can enter a requisition and only see the fields designated for a Services requisition within the same database. | Yes |
| Data Segregation | Ability to segregate requisitions and candidates by hire type (executive, HR, etc.) or organization. | Yes |

| Function | Function Description | Response |
|----------|---------------------|----------|
| Requisition approval routing workflow and approval status indicator | Select a list of approvers, route for approval via email. Approvals should be able to be sent in parallel or sequentially. | Yes |
| Approval status tracking | The status of the approval process is tracked and displayed real-time on the requisition in the application as well as in the subsequent emails that go to the second and third approver, etc. | Yes |
| Pre-defined approval routing lists | Lists of approvers can be created, saved, and/or assigned to a user or requisition, or defined by the organizational structure automatically. | Yes |
| Approvals can take place directly from an email | When approving a requisition, the approver can take action directly from the email notification without having to log into the application. | Yes |
| Pre-qualifying questions based on position/job needs, including weighting to filter for top candidates | Questions developed, defined and delivered to a candidate in the online application process and tied directly to the job posting/requirements, including weighting to filter for top candidates. | Yes |
| Knock-out questions | Ability to establish certain questions to be disqualifiers, where if the candidate does not answer correctly, the process is ended. | Yes |
| Job posting scheduling | Check a box to select the appropriate career site(s) for the job to appear. Scheduling of start and end dates of posting to any given site to allow for staggered posting. | Yes |

| Function | Function Description | Response |
|---|---|---|
| Advanced job descriptions - Formatting and Spell Checking | Ability to edit and format job descriptions and marketing messages with MS Word, like functions for Bolding, Underlining, and Spell Checking. | Yes |
| Electronic job board relationship management (facilitation of job positing to all e-media providers) | Ability to identify and post job opportunities to an unlimited number of electronic job boards and other end destinations. Ability to multi-select boards and push positions out to the market. | Yes |
| **Candidate Experience** | | |
| Unlimited Career Site portals | Ability to establish an unlimited number of integrated career sites for different purposes - such as college recruiting, location-specific kiosks, or for a specific job family like Sales or Engineering. Determine if there are additional costs per Career Section. | Yes |
| Online profile form(s) defined by the client | Data collection form(s) that can be pushed to a candidate to gather needed information for relationship management and interested resume submissions. Customers can tailor the form to their specification, adding or removing fields. | Yes |
| User-defined secure login user name and password. | User-created login and password authentication for accessing profile and career management activities. | Yes |
| Candidate login optional | Candidate can submit resume and apply to jobs without establishing a password-protected user account. | No |
| Resume submission via upload of file - Candidate | Candidate can browse hard drive for formatted resume and upload to candidate resume repository. | Yes |

| Function | Function Description | Response |
|---|---|---|
| Resume submission via upload of file - Recruiter/Manager | Recruiter/Manager can browse hard drive for formatted resume and upload to candidate resume repository. | Yes |
| Resume builder functionality | Ability for candidates without a formal resume to submit a resume via a "Resume Builder." | No |
| Extraction of data from resume to create profile | Extraction engine behind the text or uploaded resume for population of fielded data in the candidate profile. | Yes |
| Candidate defined Job Agents | Candidates can establish job search parameters and be notified when jobs are posted which meet their preferences. | Yes |
| Candidate status check | Candidates can login to check the status of their resume submissions. | Yes |
| Ability to upload attachments | | Yes |
| Ability for candidate to save a submission as a draft | | Yes |
| Candidate self-withdrawal | Ability for candidates to remove themselves from consideration for a position. | Yes |
| Conceptual search for the candidate when scaning for jobs | Candidates can use "free form" language to search for jobs. | Yes |
| Sourcing/CRM | | |
| Specific job referral and general referrals | Employees can submit a resume as a general referral or to a specific job. | Yes |
| Notifications to the referring employee and the referred candidate | Email notifications are automatically sent to the employee making the referral and to the candidate who was referred. | Yes |

| Function | Function Description | Response |
|---|---|---|
| Referral status check | Employees can review a list of candidates they have referred and check their status. | Yes |
| Tracking steps and status searches | Recruiters can search for candidates based on their tracking steps and status against requisitions. | Yes |
| Keyword search against free-form text and fielded data | Keyword search against text records from candidate and fielded data in the same search. | Yes |
| Search criteria highlighted for relevance in record review | Search results with indicators for criteria matching and relevance in the results. | No |
| Configurable search results list | The column headers that are displayed in a search results list can be configured with different data elements from the candidate record. (Example: Education, Work History, Phone Number). | Yes |
| Ability to search file attachments | Keyword searching will search the resumes that have been submitted as file attachments as well as text fields. | Yes |
| Ability to create "overnight" searches | | Yes |
| Conceptual search engine to match resumes | Ability to use the requisition's job description or a large text phrase to find matching resumes using a conceptual search or natural language search engine. Conceptual searches should also be able to be conducted with fielded search. | No |
| "More like this" searching | Ability to take a resume and conduct a search to find other resumes that are similar to it (more like it). | No |

| Function | Function Description | Response |
|---|---|---|
| Library of candidate correspondence/ communication templates | Ability for clients to create a library of correspondence templates that can be sent to candidates at the user's discretion. | Yes |
| Editable correspondence at the user level | Users can make edits to the correspondence at the time of generation and distribution. | Yes |
| Agency Portal | Functionality designed for the management of third-party staffing agencies. Includes the ability to push requisitions to one or more suppliers and receive agency resume submissions. | Yes |
| Contingent Labor Management | Functionality designed specifically for the requisition and management of contract labor including the distribution of job requirements to multiple vendors, submission and review of resumes, tracking of assignment, time reporting and billing. | Yes |
| Candidate Pool Generation (Leads/ Prospective Candidates) | Able to enter limited candidate information (less required fields than regular candidate profile without comprising the configuration of the candidate profile) and develop target candidate pool for key skills. | Yes |
| Marketing Campaigns (Leads/Prospective Candidates) | Includes proactive candidate pool in messaging, advertising campaigns or special event invitations. This should include the ability to send emails to thousands of candidates (as necessary). | Yes |
| Sending resumes to a manager | Ability to send a "Formatted Resume" to a Hiring Manager. | Yes |

| Function | Function Description | Response |
|----------|---------------------|----------|
| **Assessment and Interview Management** | | |
| Customer-defined workflow steps and status | Customer can set up steps and status for tracking a candidate through the recruiting process, with ability to tailor it for required and desired steps. | Yes |
| Customer can define multiple process workflows (Example: employee referral, internal transfers, etc.) | Ability to create multiple applicant workflows (set of tracking steps & status) to be selected at the requisition level. | Yes |
| Workflow triggered alerts | Alerts can be set up in the system to drive the next step in the process or to function as reminders. | Yes |
| Ability to create a "tree-structure" workflow (i.e. step A can be followed by step B, C, D or E) | | No |
| Volume hiring updates | The ability to change the status for a group of candidates to hired in a single step (e.g. mass hiring in one step). | Yes |
| Integrated Assessments | Ability to store and/or integrate validated assessment tools into the recruiting workflow for certain jobs. | Yes |
| Assessment Triggers | Ability for Assessment to automatically be presented to candidates based on their responses to pre-screening questions or other data in their profile. | Yes |
| Assessment on demand | Ability to push an online assessment to a candidate on demand via email link. | Yes |
| Interview team member history | Ability to select and record a list of interviewing team members for a requisition. | Yes |

| Function | Function Description | Response |
|---|---|---|
| Interview team notifications | Ability to send an email notification (including a calendar meeting request) to the interview team members when scheduling the interview within the system (including interview packets, resumes, etc. when sending the email request). | Yes |
| Storage of interviewer comments | Ability to configure an online interview feedback form to capture the comments from each interviewer. | Yes |
| Interviewer attachments | Ability to include attachments to the interviewer notifications (e.g. interview guidelines, interview schedule, resume, etc.) | Yes |
| **Offer Management and Onboarding** | | |
| Approval routing and status tracking | Select a list of approvers, route for approval via email. In addition, the status of the approval process is tracked and displayed real-time on the offer in the application as well as in the subsequent emails that go to the second and third approver, etc. | Yes |
| Pre-defined approval routing lists | Lists of approvers can be created, saved, and/or assigned to a user or requisition. | Yes |
| Approvals can take place directly from an email | When approving an offer, the approver can take action directly from the email notification without having to log into the application. | Yes |
| Offer letters can be generated by merging fields into letter templates. | Data can be merged from the candidate record, the requisition and the offer terms into offer letter templates. | Yes |

| Function | Function Description | Response |
|----------|---------------------|----------|
| Offer letters can be edited at the user level | Users can make edits to the offer letter at the time of generation and distribution. | Yes |
| Specific Onboarding Module | Does the product offer a specific On-boarding module, allowing clients to define required notifications at hire and send notifications through the system? (e.g. provisioning, IT for user account setup, new hire, manager checklist, etc.) | Yes |
| Onboarding Docu-mentation Manage-ment | Electronically provide new hire paper-work and track completion of key docu-ments (I-9, Non Disclosures, Benefits Paperwork). | Yes |
| **Global Capabilities & Compliance** | | |
| EEO Compliance data collection | Configurable notification and collection of EEO compliance information at vari-able points in the process. | Yes |
| Global – in-coun-try data collection based on regula-tions | Configurable data requests based on in-country requirements. Example: Ger-many, martial status, number of children. | Yes |
| Ability to present Career Sections in Multiple Languages | Ability to present Career Sections in multiple languages. | Yes |
| Ability to present the Recruiter and Manager Portals in multiple languages | Ability to present the Recruiter and Man-ager Portals in multiple languages. | Yes |
| Data Segregation by country, region or predefined type | Data Segregation, i.e. preventing users from a particular country or location from seeing candidates who are in another country or location. | Yes |

| Function | Function Description | Response |
|----------|---------------------|----------|
| OFCCP Compliance tools to enable search and applicant declaration | Functionality consistent with the new OFCCP definition of Internet Applicant (record keeping for searches, candidate submissions, etc.) | Yes |
| Privacy Policy acknowledgements | Ability to require that candidates agree with the privacy policy before they submit. | Yes |
| Compliance with Data Privacy | Ability for customers to remove a candidate's data at that candidate's request. | Yes |
| Tax Credit Screening & Processing | Provides automatic Tax ID and SSN validation. Automatically transmits request to conduct tax credit screening for WOTC, WTW, and more through to screening partners and display those results within the candidate profile for review and processing upon hire. | No |
| **Reporting & Integration** | | |
| Standard reports are delivered with the system | System is delivered with a minimum of 10 standard reports. | Yes |
| Ad-hoc reporting capability | System is delivered with an ad-hoc report-writing tool so that clients can create their own reports as needed. | Yes |
| Reporting Security | Ability to enable field-level security and access to report creation, output and distribution. | No |
| Reporting Distribution | Ability to generate scheduled reports and distribute through email. | Yes |
| Real-Time Reporting | Ability to report on data in the application in real time (not based on a refresh of data in a reporting environment). | Yes |

| Function | Function Description | Response |
|---|---|---|
| HRIS Integration | Ability to create bi-directional integrations from an HRIS to the ATS. | Yes |
| Integration - Client Self-Service Tools | Ability for clients to create their own integration touchpoints as needed (and make them operational). | No |
| Integration - API capability | Ability to allow clients to create integrations through APIs. | Yes |

## Performance Management

| Performance Dashboard | | |
|---|---|---|
| Dashboard configuration | Ability to configure dashboard based on user preference. | Yes |
| Create and display reports | Display reports that can be generated (i.e. review completion progress, goal progress). | Yes |
| Create and display charts and graphs | Display charts and graphs that are available to show planning actions. | Yes |
| Display help and reference tools | Display and view help and reference tools that can be selected by link or mouse hover. | Yes |
| **Employee Information Review (Data Import from HRIS/LMS)** | | |
| Import and display employee information | Display name, address, phone, email, location, photo, education (typically pulled from HRIS). | Yes |
| Import and display employee position information | Display current job title, job summary, job family, job level/grade, job code, FLSA, shift, status (FT/PT) (typically pulled through HRIS). | Yes |
| Create and display work history | Display created previous work history (i.e. name of company, job title, responsibilities/duties, employment dates). | Yes |

| Function | Function Description | Response |
|----------|---------------------|----------|
| Create and display years in management | Display created years of management experience (manually entered or via integration). | Yes |
| Create and display years in industry | Display created years of experience in industry (primarily entered manually). | Yes |
| Import, create and display employee language(s) | Display employee languages (i.e. read, written, fluent) (primarily entered manually). | Yes |
| Import, create and display employee affiliations | Display employee affiliation memberships. | Yes |
| Import, create and display employee certifications | Display employee certifications and dates. | Yes |
| Import, create and display employee licenses | Display employee licenses and dates (usually a text box) - important to include expiration dates (could be for transportation, professional licenses, healthcare licenses, etc.) | Yes |
| Import and display organizational information | Display company name, company division, company department (typically imported from HRIS). | Yes |
| Import and display management hierarchy information | Display multiple levels of management names and information (i.e. Executive Management, Division Head, Department Head, Direct Manager, Employee). | Yes |
| Import and display direct reports | Display name and information of employee direct reports. | Yes |
| Import and display matrix manager hierarchy information | Display multiple levels of matrix management names and information (i.e. Employee has dotted line reporting relationships). | Yes |

| Function | Function Description | Response |
|----------|---------------------|----------|
| Import and display multiple manager hierarchy information | Display multiple levels of numerous management names and information (i.e. Employee reports to more than one manager directly). | Yes |
| Organizational Chart View | Organizational information can be displayed in an Org Chart view (note how this is displayed visually). | Yes |
| Organizational Change Requests | Due to potential errors within HRMS, manager has the ability to request an employee change in hierarchy (i.e. manager name, organization, location, job role); changes can be configured to require approval. | Yes |
| Import and display employee current and past compensation | Display employee's past and current base salary, bonus, equity, commission, etc. | Yes |
| Import and display employee's most recent performance measures | Display employee's current competencies, goals, skills, projects, performance rating, development plan, personal improvement plan. | Yes |
| Import and display employee previous performance measures | Display employee's previous competencies, goals, skills, projects, performance rating, development plan, personal improvement plan. | Yes |
| Complete and display employee training | Display employee's completed and assigned training (i.e. mandatory/development). Note if there is any integration with LMS. | Yes |
| External Identifier | Ability to have an external identifier field to bring in content on goals from a third-party application (i.e. description, start date, critical, public goal); can be configured to be read-only for imports. | Yes |

| Function | Function Description | Response |
|----------|---------------------|----------|
| UDFs | Available user-defined fields for employee profile. | Yes |
| **Career Planning / Personal Development (Employee)** | | |
| Create and display future career plan scenarios | Display multiple future career plans (vertical, horizontal, both). Where does the employee want to go next? (lateral, promotion, etc.) | Yes |
| Select and display positions, job families and organizations/divisions of interest | Display selected positions and organizations of interest from import of job list and organization list (mentorships and cross-training) - gives the employee the opportunity to identify a position, job-family or organization of interest. | Yes |
| Create and display training requests | Display developmental training requests (entered by an employee or manager). This could be an integration point to the LMS. | Yes |
| Create and display executive/professional requests | Display various executive/professional requests (i.e. executive coaching, cross-training, job shadowing, speaking engagements, writing submittals, managing people, presentations, mentoring, apprenticeships). | Yes |
| Create and display organization affiliations and/or conferences/seminars | Display employee organization/affiliation or conference/seminar requests to join or attend. | Yes |
| Select and display competency development | Display selected desired competencies (entered by employee). | Yes |
| Create self-asses job readiness | Display selected self-readiness from list of options (i.e. Now, 0-3 months, 3-6 months, 6-9 months, 9-12 months, 12 months +). | Yes |

| Function | Function Description | Response |
|---|---|---|
| Display position Gap % | Display gap % of employee readiness to ideal position as well as required training, license(s), education, certification(s). This could be automatically calculated by the system (key differentiator). This is a gap analysis on the underlying competencies (most recent performance rating vs. competencies required for next position). | Yes |
| Select and display willingness to relocate | Display selected willingness to relocate (i.e. yes, no, maybe, comments). | Yes |
| Display career pre-requisites | Display required training, education, certification(s), license(s) for position of interest. | Yes |
| Submit development requests for approval | Submit development self-assessments to direct manager for review, feedback and approval (areas where the development needs to occur, as well as specific courses and conferences to help meet these development areas). Could be an integration point with LMS. | Yes |
| **Career Development (Manager)** | | |
| Create or select and display employee training goals | Display created or selected employee completed training, assigned training (mandatory/development), scheduled training and employee training requests. This is the manager identifying training goals for an employee. | Yes |
| Competency Development | Display assigned professional/leadership competencies. | Yes |

| Function | Function Description | Response |
|---|---|---|
| Create and display executive/professional assignments | Display various executive/professional recommendations (i.e. executive coaching, cross-training, job shadowing, speaking engagements, writing submittals, managing people, presentations, mentoring, apprenticeships). | Yes |
| Create and display organization affiliations and/or conferences/seminars | Display employee organization/affiliation or conference/seminar recommendations. | Yes |
| **Individual Goal / Self-Assessment (Employee)** | | |
| Select, create and display individual development goals | Display selected or created completed training, improvement competencies, executive coaching, promotion, cross-training. | Yes |
| Select competency development | Display selected development competencies. This is where employees select competencies they want to develop for their career on annual review. | Yes |
| Submit goal/competency assessment for approval | Submit manual or automatic goal/competency assessment to direct manager. | Yes |
| Solicit and display feedback | Select employees (i.e. managers, matrix managers, peers) to solicit performance feedback (i.e. 360, peer review, business review) and display results. | Yes |
| Create and display self-performance notes | Display created performance notes (i.e. kudos) throughout the review cycle (manually entered by employee or can solicit feedback throughout project). | Yes |
| Create and display self-goal assessment progress | Display created self-goal progress (i.e. quantitative % of completion, qualitative to include customer satisfaction, timeline to include start/completion date). | Yes |

| Function | Function Description | Response |
|---|---|---|
| Submit goal/competency review for approval | Submit manual or automatic goal/competency assessment to direct manager and higher levels. | Yes |
| UDFs | Available user-defined fields for employee goals. | Yes |
| **Review Process (Employee and Manager)** | | |
| Select and display competencies | Display selected professional or leadership competencies. | Yes |
| Select and display goals/objectives | Display selected goals/objectives (i.e. quantitative and/or qualitative). | Yes |
| Select and display goal alignment | Display selected goal alignment to company, organization, department and/or manager goals (cascading goals). | Yes |
| Select or create and display projects | Display selected or created projects. | Yes |
| Select and display project alignment to goals | Display selected project alignment to company, organization, department and/or manager goals. | Yes |
| Select or create and display skills | Display selected or created company, organization, department, employee skills. | Yes |
| Create and display employee performance notes | Display created performance notes (positive or negative) throughout the review cycle. These are notes created by the manager. | Yes |
| Solicit and display feedback | Select employees (i.e. managers, matrix managers, peers) to solicit performance feedback (i.e. 360, peer review, business review) and display. Pay particular attention to how this feedback is gathered and entered into the system. | Yes |

| Function | Function Description | Response |
|----------|--------------------|----------|
| Create and display employee goal assessment review | Display created employee goal progress (i.e. quantitative % of completion, qualitative to include customer satisfaction, timeline to include start/completion date); this is the manager entering the assessment. | No |
| Performance review filtering | Manager can filter performance review information based on approval status, assigned to, author/owner, manager, employee, organization, location, job field, job role, review cycle, review group, review group owner, overall rating; filtering can be cumulative. | Yes |
| Batch activities | Manager can take group actions on multiple employees simultaneously. | No |
| UDFs | Available user-defined fields for employee competencies. | Yes |
| **Workflow** | | |
| Review cycles | Ability to configure multiple review cycles and tie to various reviews. | Yes |
| Review groups | Ability to define review recipients based on dates, job function, organization, job code, etc. | Yes |
| Workflow Order | Ability to configure order of workflow (i.e. self-assessments can be configured to be completed first). | Yes |
| Notifications | Ability to push reviews to employees and managers. | Yes |
| Reminders | Ability to send reminders to employees and managers via email (manual and automatic). | Yes |

| Function | Function Description | Response |
|---|---|---|
| Acknowledgements | Ability to send auto-acknowledgements triggered by event/activity. | Yes |
| Next Level Approval | Ability to auto/manually route to multiple levels of approval. | Yes |
| Configurable work-flow | Ability to: configure various steps of the review process; make review steps mandatory; have manager override ability; display/hide visual graphic workflow diagram. | Yes |
| Auto/Manual Progression | Ability to automatically or manually progress through the review process. | Yes |
| Review form | Exportable and printable review form. | Yes |
| **System Admin** | | |
| Review sections | Ability to configure multiple review sections, including goals, competencies, comments, rating models, etc. | Yes |
| Configurable rating models | Does it configure and display alpha and numeric values? Can values be rounded (up/down/both), value ranges, number of decimals (1-5)? | Yes |
| Comments | Displayed and available in individual review sections and overall review. Can they be configured to be mandatory and be overridden by management? | Yes |
| Goals | Ability to link organizational, divisional, departmental, individual goals into sections and to display goal progress. | Yes |
| Competencies | Ability to link competencies into sections. | Yes |
| Weightings | Ability to weigh employee performance based on goals and competencies. | Yes |

| Function | Function Description | Response |
|---|---|---|
| **Search Functionality** | | |
| Basic Employee Search | Basic search by employee name (i.e. first or last name or a combination of both). | Yes |
| Job/Position Basic Search | Basic search by job role or position title, etc. | Yes |
| Competency Basic Search | Basic search by competency name. | Yes |
| Advanced Search | More detailed search capabilities that combine various search criteria or fields; may include optional weighting to determine which employees are retrieved in a search as well as each person's rank in the search results. | Yes |
| Succession Planning Search | Search functionality that dynamically generates the criteria used to match employees who would make good succession candidates with a specific position profile (could have various levels of "fit"). | Yes |
| **Employee View / Navigation / Help / Other** | | |
| List View | Display employee goals, business goals or projects; the list mode is a list of items with information on key dates and progress. | Yes |
| Card View | Display employee goals, business goals or projects using the card mode; the card mode provides details on one item at a time and offers the possibility of editing progress. This can also include employee photos. | Yes |
| Timeline / Gantt | Display employee goals, business goals or projects using the timeline mode; the timeline mode provides a timeline view of an item's start and due dates. | No |

| Function | Function Description | Response |
|---|---|---|
| Org Chart | Managers can access and manage information on their direct reports for all functionalities activated; the organizational chart will provide key data (i.e. risk of loss or most recent performance rating) for each of the manager's direct reports. | Yes |
| Mini-Org Chart | Displays a single analytic data point at a time; the manager can drill down into all layers of his organization and can view key metrics (i.e. performance reviews, goals, succession). | Yes |
| Graphs | Graphical display of various information (i.e. Gap Analysis, goal progress, review completion progress). | Yes |
| Help Links | Online help, FAQs, customer support, product version. | Yes |
| Attach Documents | Ability to attach reference documents to various sections within the system. | Yes |
| Browser capabilities | Supported by general Internet access (works with standard browsers: IE, Safari, Mozilla, Opera). | Yes |
| Mouse-Over Hover | Additional tooltips or descriptions that display when user hovers the mouse pointer over various graphics or words within the system. | Yes |
| Web 2.0 | Ability to utilize Web 2.0 functionality, i.e. social networking. | Yes |
| Security | | |
| Logging In | Various login options (i.e. manual, SSO, LDAP). | Yes |

| Function | Function Description | Response |
|---|---|---|
| File Transfer | Various file transfer protocol (i.e. FTP, sFTP, vendor-specific transfer import/export tool). | Yes |
| Encryption | Various data encryption ability (i.e. PGP). | Yes |
| Roles / Permissions | Configurable list of permission-based roles with detailed access rights to various organizations, levels, etc. Typically employees only view within their own organization hierarchy. | Yes |
| Integration | Ability to integrate organizational data i.e. HRIS/ATS/ LMS and employee data including competencies, training, development plans, etc. | Yes |
| **Reporting** | | |
| Standard reports are delivered with the system | System is delivered with a set number of standard reports. | Yes |
| Ad-hoc reporting capability | System is delivered with an ad-hoc report-writing tool so that clients can create their own reports as needed. | Yes |
| Advanced Value metrics | Data analysis of employee review process status, goal progress by hierarchy. | Yes |
| Reporting Security | Ability to enable field-level security and access to report creation, output and distribution. | Yes |
| Reporting UDFs | Ability to report user-defined fields. | Yes |
| Exporting reports | Reports can easily be exported to other applications (i.e. .xls, .pdf, .txt). | Yes |

| Function | Function Description | Response |
|----------|---------------------|----------|

## Succession Planning

| Succession Planning (Manager - Planning of Individual Talent Matched to Critical Roles) | | |
|---|---|---|
| Create and display critical roles for today | Display critical job roles (i.e. title, level, location, division, organization). | Yes |
| Create and display critical roles for future | Display critical job roles (i.e. title, level, location, division, organization) for future (workforce planning-like tools). | Yes |
| Calculate and display performance rating | Performance rating is automatically averaged from various sections of the performance review and displayed (current and past). | Yes |
| Calculate and display performance ranking | High potential employees will be automatically ranked according to order of fit with critical role (i.e. 9-box grid, numeric ranking, high performer, high potential) - can be ranked by position, organization, etc. | Yes |
| Multi-dimensional matrix | Matrix that can be configured up to various # of cells (i.e. 9-box, 12-box, 16-box, 25-box); text within grid is configurable. | Yes |
| Various dimensions of matrix | Matrix displays employee performance, potential, number of succession plans an employee is on, years in management, years in industry. | Yes |
| Navigation from multi-dimensional matrix | Manager can select an employee within the matrix and navigate to employee information (i.e. Performance review, talent profile, employee goals, career plan). | No |

| Function | Function Description | Response |
|---|---|---|
| Display employee comparisons | Display comparison of multiple high potential employees according to fit to critical role (i.e. # of employees to compare, comparable data, fit gap analysis, ranking analysis, bench strength). | Yes |
| Create and display role readiness | Manager can create and display high potential employee role readiness (i.e. now, 0-3 months, 3-6 months, 6-9 months, 9-12 months, 12+ months). | Yes |
| Create and display retention risk | Manager can create and display high potential employee retention/loss/flight risk (i.e. high, medium, low, comments). | Yes |
| Create and display role willingness | Manager can create and display high potential employee role willingness (i.e. yes, no, comments). | Yes |
| Create and display willingness to relocate | Manager can create and display high potential employee willingness to relocate (i.e. yes, no, maybe, comments). | Yes |
| Create and display willingness to travel | Manager can create and display high potential employee willingness to travel (i.e. none, 25-50%, 50-75%, 75-100%). | Yes |
| Create and display interest in international assignment | Manager can create and display high potential employee interest in international assignment (i.e. yes, no, maybe). | Yes |
| Create and display interim replacement for critical role | Manager can create and display high potential interim replacement for critical roles. | Yes |
| Display of gap analysis | Automatically calculate and display high potential employees' fit gap analysis to the next position and ranking analysis of employee to that next position. | Yes |

| Function | Function Description | Response |
|---|---|---|
| UDFs | Available user-defined fields for succession planning. | Yes |
| **Succession Pooling (Manager - Planning of a Talent Pool for Critical Roles)** | | |
| Display high potential pool | Display nominated and/or approved high potential pool (i.e. employee information, designated nominators, designated approvers, approvals, rejections, role readiness, rejection comments). | Yes |
| Calculate and display performance rating | Performance rating is automatically averaged from various sections of the performance review and displayed (current and past). | Yes |
| Calculate and display performance ranking | Pool of high potential employees will be automatically ranked according to order of fit with critical role (i.e. 9-box grid, numeric ranking, high performer, high potential). | Yes |
| Display employee comparisons | Display comparison of multiple high potential employees according to fit to critical role (i.e. # of employees to compare, comparable data, fit gap analysis, ranking analysis, bench strength). | Yes |
| Create and display role readiness | Manager can create and display high potential employee role readiness (i.e. now, 0-3 months, 3-6 months, 6-9 months, 9-12 months, 12+ months). | Yes |
| Create and display retention risk | Manager can create and display high potential employee retention/loss/flight risk (i.e. high, medium, low, comments). | Yes |
| Create and display role willingness | Manager can create and display high potential employee role willingness (i.e. yes, no, comments). | Yes |

| Function | Function Description | Response |
|---|---|---|
| Create and display willingness to relocate | Manager can create and display high potential employee willingness to relocate (i.e. yes, no, maybe, comments). | Yes |
| Create and display willingness to travel | Manager can create and display high potential employee willingness to travel (i.e. none, 25-50%, 50-75%, 75-100%). | Yes |
| Create and display interest in international assignment | Manager can create and display high potential employee interest in international assignment (i.e. yes, no, maybe). | Yes |
| Create and display interim replacement for critical role | Manager can create and display high potential interim replacement for critical roles. | Yes |
| Display of gap analysis | Automatically calculate and display high potential employees' fit gap analysis of employee to position and ranking analysis of employee to position. | Yes |
| UDFs | Available user-defined fields for succession pooling. | Yes |
| **Workflow** | | |
| Succession approval workflow | Ability to define or edit approvers, to add/remove users and roles, to change the approval order, to reject with comments. | Yes |
| Nominations for succession pool | Ability to nominate, reject and enter comments on nominated HiPo employees. | Yes |
| **Reporting** | | |
| Standard reports are delivered with the system | System is delivered with a set number of standard reports. | Yes |
| Ad-hoc reporting capability | System is delivered with an ad-hoc report-writing tool so that clients can create their own reports as needed. | Yes |

| Function | Function Description | Response |
|----------|---------------------|----------|
| Advanced Value metrics | Data analysis of high performers / high potential employees, identified gaps, critical roles. | Yes |
| Reporting Security | Ability to enable field-level security and access to report creation, output and distribution. | Yes |
| Reporting UDFs | Ability to report user-defined fields. | Yes |
| Exporting reports | Reports can easily be exported to other applications (i.e. .xls, .pdf, .txt). | Yes |

## Compensation Management

| Compensation Dashboard | | |
|------------------------|---|---|
| Dashboard configuration | Ability to configure dashboard based on user preference. | Yes |
| Create and display a compensation worksheet | Display a compensation worksheet that will provide individual and org planning status and detail. | Yes |
| Create and display reports | Display reports that can be generated, i.e. budget usage by merit, bonus, equity, adjustment and percent of planning completed. | Yes |
| Create and display charts and graphs | Display charts and graphs that are available to show planning actions. | Yes |
| Import and display allocation guidelines | Display compensation allocation guidelines for merit, bonus, equity and adjustments - also refer to the time allocation/workflow to complete this process. | Yes |
| Import and display eligibility guidelines | Display employee eligibility guidelines for planning, i.e. FT, PT, commission, LOA, new hire, etc. Guidelines are input by compensation department. | Yes |

| Function | Function Description | Response |
|---|---|---|
| Display help and reference tools | Display and view help and reference tools that can be selected by link or mouse hover. | Yes |
| **Compensation Budget** | | |
| Import and display multiple aggregate planning budget by org | Display multiple approved allocated budget by diverse business groups on all pages (usually imported from financial system). | Yes |
| Import and display aggregate merit budget by org | Display approved allocated merit budget by diverse business groups on all pages. | Yes |
| Import and display aggregate bonus budget by org | Display approved allocated bonus by diverse business groups on all pages. | Yes |
| Import and display aggregate equity budget by org | Display approved allocated equity budget by diverse business groups on all pages. | No |
| Import and display aggregate adjust-ment budget by org | Display approved allocated adjustment budget by diverse business groups on all pages. | Yes |
| **Employee Information Review** | | |
| Import and display employee Informa-tion | Display name, location, photo, org, direct manager (typically imported from PM tool). | Yes |
| Import and display employee position | Display current job title, job code, level/grade. | Yes |
| Import and display employee prior compensation plan-ning period data | Display current hourly rate, annual rate, bonus percent, bonus amount, equity allocation, total compensation. | Yes |

| Function | Function Description | Response |
|---|---|---|
| Import and display employee prior per-formance rating | Display prior performance rating. | Yes |
| Import and display new employee per-formance rating | Display new performance rating. | Yes |
| Import and display employee's position salary range | Display employee's salary range. | Yes |
| Import and display salary penetration percentage based on position salary range | Display percentage of penetration that employee's salary falls within the range. | Yes |
| **Promotion** | | |
| Display position information | Ability to select and display job titles, job codes, job level/grades. | Yes |
| Import and display corporate promotion guidelines | Ability to display promotion guidelines per position, including salary range and percent increase guidelines. | Yes |
| Promotion amount | Ability to enter promotion percent or amount. | Yes |
| Auto-calculate pro-motion amount | System to auto-populate promotion amount based on percent increase. | Yes |
| Ability to calculate hourly rate | System to auto-populate new hourly rate based on promotion increase. | Yes |
| Ability to auto-calcu-late annual rate | System to auto-populate new annual rate based on promotion increase. | Yes |
| Promotion approval chain | TBD. | No |

| Function | Function Description | Response |
|---|---|---|
| Develop documentation | Ability to document the promotion justification. | No |
| **Adjustment** | | |
| Import and display adjustment guidelines | Ability to display adjustment allocation guidelines, including salary range and percent increase guidelines. | Yes |
| Adjustment allocation | Ability to enter and submit an adjustment percent or amount. | Yes |
| Auto-calculate hourly amount | System to auto-populate new hourly rate based on adjustment percent increase. | Yes |
| Auto-calculate adjustment amount | System to auto-populate new annual rate based on adjustment percent increase. | Yes |
| Adjustment approvals | | Yes |
| Develop documentation | Ability to document the adjustment justification. | Yes |
| **Merit** | | |
| Import and display promotion guidelines | Ability to display merit allocation guidelines, including salary range and percent increase guidelines. | Yes |
| Performance-based recommendations | Merit allocation can be based on performance rating. | Yes |
| Merit allocation | Ability to enter and submit a merit percent or amount. | Yes |
| Import and display proration of merit based on hire date | System to auto-calculate merit increase based on hire date, i.e. less than one year would be calculated by months employed. | Yes |

| Function | Function Description | Response |
|---|---|---|
| Auto-calculate hourly amount | System to auto populate new hourly rate based on merit percent increase. | Yes |
| Auto-calculate adjustment amount | System to auto-populate new annual rate based on merit percent increase. | Yes |
| Merit approvals | | Yes |
| Develop documentation | Ability to document the merit justification. | Yes |
| **Bonus** | | |
| Import and display bonus allocation guidelines | Ability to display bonus allocation guidelines. | Yes |
| Performance based recommendations | Bonus allocation can be based on performance rating. | Yes |
| Bonus allocation | Ability to enter and submit a bonus percent or amount. | Yes |
| Bonus adjustment | Auto-Proration of bonus based on hired or leave, i.e. severance date. | No |
| Bonus approvals | Ability to obtain appropriate approvals (workflow to select appropriate approvers). | Yes |
| Develop documentation | Ability to document the merit justification. | Yes |
| **Equity** | | |
| Import and display equity allocation guidelines | Ability to display equity allocation guidelines. | No |
| Performance-based recommendations | Equity allocation can be based on performance rating. | No |

| Function | Function Description | Response |
|---|---|---|
| Equity allocation | Ability to enter and submit equity percent or amount. | No |
| Equity allocation adjustment | Auto-Proration of equity allocation based on hire date. | No |
| Equity approvals | | No |
| Develop documentation | Ability to document the merit justification. | No |
| **Other** | | |
| Ability to assign a delegate | Ability to assign a delegate to complete compensation planning, i.e. Admin. | Yes |
| Employee Filter | Ability to sort by employee name or data, i.e. first name, last name, employee ID, etc. | Yes |
| Employee Search | Ability to search throughout the tool by employee name or data, i.e. first name, last name, employee ID, etc. | Yes |
| Revert or change functionality | Ability for planning administrators to revert or change submitted data. | Yes |
| Collaborative workflow | Ability for managers, compensation and HR Partners to collaborate on various compensation workflows. | Yes |
| Display out-of-guideline entries | Ability to display out-of-guideline entries made within adjustments, merit, bonus, equity. | Yes |
| **Reporting** | | |
| Standard reports are delivered with the system | System is delivered with a set number of standard reports. | Yes |

| Function | Function Description | Response |
|---|---|---|
| Ad-hoc reporting capability | System is delivered with an ad-hoc report-writing tool so that clients can create their own reports as needed. | Yes |
| Advanced Value metrics | Data analysis of comp gaps based on roles, hierarchy. | Yes |
| Reporting Security | Ability to enable field-level security and access to report creation, output and distribution. | Yes |
| **Security** | | |
| Logging In | Various login options (i.e. manual, SSO, LDAP). | Yes |
| File Transfer | Various file transfer protocol (i.e. FTP, sFTP, vendor-specific transfer import/export tool). | Yes |
| Encryption | Various data encryption ability (i.e. PGP). | Yes |
| Roles / Permissions | Configurable list of permission-based roles with detailed access rights to various organizations, levels, etc. Typically employees only view within their own organization hierarchy. | Yes |
| Integration | Ability to Integrate organizational data with appropriate org system, i.e. HRIS/Payroll, employee data including employee salaries, levels, performance rating, etc. | Yes |
| Reporting UDFs | Ability to report user-defined fields. | Yes |
| Exporting reports | Reports can easily be exported to other applications (i.e. .xls, .pdf, .txt). | Yes |

| Function | Function Description | Response |
|---|---|---|

## Learning Management

| | | |
|---|---|---|
| **Content Management and Delivery** | | |
| Application Simulation | Client content owners can create application simulations for use in training (i.e. "Show Me"/"Try Me" Flash-type simulations). | No |
| Assign learning content-based employee data | Learning content can be assigned to employees based on their job function or organizational data (not specific to position, but job family or organization). | Yes |
| Catalogs | Employees can search through and browse course catalogs to identify courses in which they are interested. | Yes |
| Competency Management – Third-Party Defined | Courses and learning plans can be built around competencies, driven by integration with a third-party vendor. | Yes |
| Competency Management – Customer-Defined | Courses and learning plans can be built around competencies as determined by the customer. | Yes |
| Offline Capabilities | Learning content can be downloaded for completion even if the user is not connected to the Internet/network. Can also upload results. | No |
| Employee Profile Management | System can house employee profiles that can be used for learning plan assignment, development plan creation and management (could be integration point). | Yes |
| External Content Integration | Employees can access, review and register for courses in systems and online portals that are integrated with the LMS. | Yes |

| Function | Function Description | Response |
|---|---|---|
| Internal Content Authoring | WYSIWYG (what you see is what you get) editor is built into the system for creation of learning materials within the system by client content owners. | No |
| Learning Plans | Customer can create learning plans for employees. Employees can manage their progress, review schedules, register for courses and access online courses from plans. Collaboration with employees and managers to create this learning plan (and appropriate workflow). Could be an integration point from PM tool. | Yes |
| Multiple Languages | System supports multiple languages for global implementations. | Yes |
| PowerPoint Conversion | System allows for uploading of PowerPoint files as learning content. | Yes |
| Repository | Digital repository for management of draft and active content is available in the system. Content managers would use this functionality (and allows for collaboration). | No |
| Scheduling | Users can book resources, locations and structures from within the system. This is an integration point as well. | Yes |
| Single Sign-On | Standard SSO capability for integration with client Intranet. | Yes |
| Version Control | Content owners have the ability to manage content versioning. | No |
| Virtual Classrooms | System provides virtual classroom functionality for live, remote learning sessions. | No |

| Function | Function Description | Response |
|---|---|---|
| **Testing and Tracking** | | |
| General Assessments | System allows for creation of assessments that aren't tied to particular training content. Could be tied to competencies. | Yes |
| Content Test Completion | Users can complete tests online as assigned. Could be offline as well. | No |
| Content Test Creation | System allows for creation of tests for learning content. | No |
| Polling | Polling can be conducted through one or more channels (e.g. Content, User Home Page Interface, etc.) | Yes |
| Test Completion Tracking | User test completion status and rates can be tracked. | Yes |
| Test Score Tracking | User test scores can be stored and tracked. | Yes |
| **Reporting** | | |
| Ad-hoc reporting capability | System is delivered with an ad-hoc report-writing tool so that clients can create their own reports as needed. | Yes |
| Data analysis | System provides functionality for advanced data analysis and dashboarding. | Yes |
| Reporting Security | Ability to enable field-level security and access to report creation, output and distribution. | Yes |
| Standard reports are delivered with the system | System is delivered with a minimum of 10 standard reports. | Yes |

| Function | Function Description | Response |
|---|---|---|
| **Integration** | | |
| Employee Profile Integration | System allows for employee profile integration with other talent management solutions (e.g. Performance, Succession, Compensation, Recruitment, etc.) | Yes |
| Integration | Ability to allow clients to create integrations through APIs, XML, flat files, etc. | Yes |
| **Web 2.0 Features** | | |
| Blogs | System allows for creation of blogs for content delivery. | Yes |
| Forums | System allows for creation and maintenance of forums to capture user-generated content and enable collaborative learning activities. | No |
| Other Collaborative Learning Tools | Additional collaborative learning tools are available. | No |
| Podcasting | System allows for creation of podcasts for content delivery. | No |
| RSS Feeds | System allows users to identify content "tracks" that they wish to monitor on a regular basis, and displays updates in an RSS-like format. | No |
| Wikis | System allows for creation and maintenance of wikis to capture user-generated content and enable collaborative learning activities. | Yes |
| **User Communication** | | |
| Completion Date Reminders | Users can be notified when they are approaching a target content completion date. | Yes |

| Function | Function Description | Response |
|----------|---------------------|----------|
| Completion Reminders | Users can be reminded to complete content that has been saved in progress. | No |
| Content Notifications | Users can be notified when new content is added to their learning plan or a track in which they are interested. | Yes |
| Manager Notifications | User managers and/or learning administrators can be notified when certain activities are completed. | Yes |
| Workflow | System allows for creation of workflow to communicate user status to content and people managers. | Yes |

# SuccessFactors

## Company Information (provided by SuccessFactors)

**Company Name:**          SuccessFactors

**Corporate URL:**         www.successfactors.com

**Main Phone:**            (800) 809-9920

**Headquarters Address:**  1500 Fashion Island Blvd., Suite 300, San Mateo, CA 94404

**Type of Business or Areas of Focus:**
Integrated performance and talent management solutions.

**Number of Employees:**   Not provided

**Stock Symbol:**          SFSF

## Company Description and History:

SuccessFactors is one of the fastest growing public software companies and the leading provider of on-demand employee performance and talent management solutions. The company enables organizations of every size, and across every industry and geography, to achieve high-performing workforces through goal alignment and execution, talent development and planning and pay-for-performance initiatives. From 92 customers and approximately 282,000 end users in 2003 to more than 2,500 customers and 4.5 million end users today, SuccessFactors' solutions are widely deployed across 60 industries in over 185 countries in 31 languages. Founded in 2001 with offices around the world, the company employs passionate people focused on revolutionizing the future of work.

## Products/Services/Solutions:

1. **Goal Management**—*Align all employees around a common set of goals.*
Create, align and monitor goals across the organization to ensure on-strategy execution.

2. **Performance Management**—*Identify engage, motivate and retain high performers.*
Measure employee and give meaningful feedback, all while automating and streamlining performance reviews.

3. **360 Degree Reviews**—*Get a more complete picture of performance.*
Collect feedback from superiors, subordinates, peers and external parties to better understand competency gaps and development needs.

4. **Compensation Management**—*Reward employees based on their individual performance.*
Award salary raises, bonuses and stock to high performers; streamline compensation planning and ensure compliance.

5. **Learning & Development**—*Develop employees to tap their full potential.*
Ensure employees have the skills they need to meet organizational objectives and give them the tools to chart a successful career path.

6. **Succession Management**—*Ensure adequate bench strength across the organization.*
Reveal potential leadership gaps and leverage tools to find and compare succession candidates across the organization.

7. **Recruiting Management**—*Recruit the right talent to fill organizational gaps.*
Maximize return on recruiting by strategically sourcing the right talent based on a clear understanding of performance.

8. **Employee Profile**—*Know the employees and keep them connected.*
Create a corporate social network that paints a more complete picture of the employees and promotes collaboration and knowledge sharing.

9. **Analytics & Reporting**—*Gain insights to drive organizational performance.*
Optimize decision-making by capturing strategic insights about workforce performance and talent management processes.

# Author's SuccessFactors Functionality Matrix

| Function | Function Description | Response |
|---|---|---|

## Talent Acquisition

| Requisition Management & Posting | | |
|---|---|---|
| Multiple requisition forms allowed (Example: hourly, internal transfer, business unit specific, reoccurring, sourcing, college) | More than one requisition form/template can be configured in a client's database to accommodate variance in business units or type of recruiting. (Example: A user from the Manufacturing group can enter a requisition and only see and populate fields that are applicable to Mfg. A different user from the Services group can enter a requisition and only see the fields designated for a Services requisition within the same database. | Yes |
| Data Segregation | Ability to segregate requisitions and candidates by hire type (executive, HR, etc.) or organization. | Yes |
| Requisition approval routing workflow and approval status indicator | Select a list of approvers and route for approval via email. Approvals should be able to be sent in parallel or sequentially. | Yes |

| Function | Function Description | Response |
|---|---|---|
| Approval status tracking | The status of the approval process is tracked and displayed real-time on the requisition in the application as well as in the subsequent emails that go to the second and third approver, etc. | Yes |
| Pre-defined approval routing lists | Lists of approvers can be created, saved and/or assigned to a user or requisition or defined by the organizational structure automatically. | Yes |
| Approvals can take place directly from an email | When approving a requisition, the approver can take action directly from the email notification without having to log into the application. | No |
| Pre-qualifying questions based on position/job needs, including weighting to filter for top candidates | Questions developed, defined and delivered to a candidate in the online application process tied directly to the job posting/requirements, including weighting to filter for top candidates. | Yes |
| Knock-out questions | Ability to establish certain questions to be disqualifiers, where if the candidate does not answer correctly, the process is ended. | Yes |
| Job posting scheduling | Check a box to select the appropriate career site(s) for the job to appear. Scheduling of start and end dates of posting to any given site to allow for staggered posting. | Yes |
| Advanced job descriptions - Formatting and Spell Checking | Ability to edit and format job descriptions and marketing messages with MS Word, like functions for Bolding, Underlining and Spell Checking. | Yes |

| Function | Function Description | Response |
|---|---|---|
| Electronic job board relationship management (facilitation of job positing to all e-media providers) | Ability to identify and post job opportunities to an unlimited number of electronic job boards and other end destinations. Ability to multi-select boards and push positions out to the market. | Yes |
| **Candidate Experience** | | |
| Unlimited Career Site Portals | Ability to establish an unlimited number of integrated career sites for different purposes - such as college recruiting, location-specific kiosks or for a specific job family like Sales or Engineering. Determine if there are additional costs per Career Section. | No |
| Online profile form(s) defined by the client | Data collection form(s) that can be pushed to a candidate to gather needed information for relationship management and interested resume submissions. Customers can tailor the form to their specification, adding or removing fields. | Yes |
| User-defined secure login user name and password. | User-created login and password authentication for accessing profile and career management activities. | Yes |
| Candidate login optional | Candidate can submit resume and apply to jobs without establishing a password-protected user account. | Yes |
| Resume submission via upload of file - Candidate | Candidates can browse hard drive for formatted resume and upload to candidate resume repository. | No |
| Resume submission via upload of file - Recruiter/Manager | Recruiter/Managers can browse hard drive for formatted resume and upload to candidate resume repository. | No |
| Resume builder functionality | Ability for candidates without a formal resume to submit a resume via a "Resume Builder" | Yes |

| Function | Function Description | Response |
|---|---|---|
| Extraction of data from resume to create profile | Extraction engine behind the text or uploaded resume for population of fielded data in the candidate profile. | No |
| Candidate defined Job Agents | Candidate can establish job search parameters and be notified when jobs are posted which meet their preferences. | No |
| Candidate status check | Candidates can login to check the status of their resume submissions. | Yes |
| Ability to upload attachments | Ability to upload attachments. | No |
| Ability for candidate to save a submission as a draft | Ability for candidate to save a submission as a draft. | Yes |
| Candidate self-withdrawal | Ability for candidates to remove themselves from consideration for a position. | Yes |
| Conceptual search for the candidate when searching for jobs | Candidate can use "free form" language to search for jobs. | No |
| Sourcing/CRM | | |
| Specific job referral and general referrals | Employees can submit a resume as a general referral or to a specific job. | No |
| Notifications to the referring employee and the referred candidate | Email notifications are automatically sent to the referring employee and to the candidate who was referred. | No |
| Referral status check | Employees can review a list of candidates they have referred and check their status. | No |
| Tracking steps and status searches | Recruiters can search for candidates based on their tracking steps and status against requisitions. | No |

| Function | Function Description | Response |
|---|---|---|
| Keyword search against free form text and fielded data | Keyword search against text records from candidate and fielded data in the same search. | Yes |
| Search criteria highlighted for relevance in record review | Search results with indicators for criteria matching and relevance in the results. | No |
| Configurable search results list | The column headers that are displayed in a search results list can be configured with different data elements from the candidate record. (Example: Education, Work History, Phone Number). | No |
| Ability to search file attachments | Keyword searching will scan the resumes that have been submitted as file attachments as well as text fields. | No |
| Ability to create "overnight" searches | Ability to create "overnight" searches. | No |
| Conceptual search engine to match resumes | Ability to use the requisition's job description or a large text phrase to find matching resumes using a conceptual search or natural language search engine. Conceptual searches should also be able to be conducted with fielded search. | No |
| "More like this" searching | Ability to take a resume and conduct a search to find other resumes that are similar to it (more like it). | No |
| Library of candidate correspondence/ communication templates | Ability for clients to create a library of correspondence templates that can be sent to candidates at the user's discretion. | No |
| Editable correspondence at the user level | Users can make edits to the correspondence at the time of generation and distribution. | No |

| Function | Function Description | Response |
|---|---|---|
| Agency Portal | Functionality designed for the management of third-party staffing agencies. Includes the ability to push requisitions to one or more suppliers and receive agency resume submissions. | No |
| Contingent Labor Management | Functionality designed specifically for requisition and management of contract labor including the distribution of job requirements to multiple vendors, submission and review of resumes, tracking of assignment, time reporting and billing. | No |
| Candidate Pool Generation (Leads/ Prospective Candidates) | Able to enter limited applicant info (less required fields than regular candidate profile without comprising the configuration of the candidate profile) and develop target candidate pool for key skills. | Yes |
| Marketing Campaigns (Leads/Prospective Candidates) | Include proactive candidate pool in messaging, advertising campaigns or special event invitations. This should include the ability to send emails to thousands of candidates (as necessary). | No |
| Sending resumes to a manager | Ability to send a "Formatted Resume" to a Hiring Manager. | No |
| **Assessment and Interview Management** | | |
| Customer-defined workflow steps and status | Customer can set up steps and status for tracking a candidate through the recruiting process, with ability to tailor it for required and desired steps. | Yes |
| Customer can define multiple process workflows (Example: employee referral, internal transfers, etc.) | Ability to create multiple applicant workflows (set of tracking steps & status) to be selected at the requisition level. | No |

| Function | Function Description | Response |
| --- | --- | --- |
| Workflow triggered alerts | Alerts can be set up in the system to drive the next step in the process or to function as reminders. | No |
| Ability to create a "tree-structure" workflow (i.e. step A can be followed by step B, C, D or E) | Ability to create a "tree-structure" work-flow (i.e. step A can be followed by step B, C, D or E). | No |
| Volume hiring updates | The ability to change the status for a group of candidates to hired in a single step (e.g. mass hiring in one step). | No |
| Integrated Assess-ments | Ability to store and/or integrate validated assessment tools into the recruiting workflow for certain jobs. | No |
| Assessment Trig-gers | Ability for Assessment to automatically be presented to candidates based on their responses to pre-screening ques-tions or other data in their profile. | No |
| Assessment on demand | Ability to push an online assessment to a candidate on demand via email link. | No |
| Interview team member history | Ability to select and record a list of inter-viewing team members for a requisition. | No |
| Interview team notifi-cations | Ability to send an email notification (including a calendar meeting request) to the interview team members when scheduling it within the system (including interview packets, resumes, etc. when sending the email request). | Yes |
| Storage of interview-er comments | Ability to configure an online interview feedback form to capture the comments from each interviewer. | No |

| Function | Function Description | Response |
|---|---|---|
| Interviewer attachments | Ability to include attachments to the interviewer notifications (e.g. interview guidelines, interview schedule, resume, etc.) | No |
| **Offer Management and Onboarding** | | |
| Approval routing and status tracking | Select a list of approvers, route for approval via email. The status of the approval process is tracked and displayed real-time on the offer in the application, as well as in the subsequent emails that go to the second and third approver, etc. | No |
| Pre-defined approval routing lists | Lists of approvers can be created, saved and/or assigned to a user or requisition. | No |
| Approvals can take place directly from an email | When approving an offer, the approver can take action directly from the email notification without having to log into the application. | No |
| Offer letters can be generated by merging fields into letter templates | Data can be merged from the candidate record, the requisition and the offer terms into offer letter templates. | No |
| Offer letters can be edited at the user level | Users can make edits to the offer letter at the time of generation and distribution. | No |
| Specific Onboarding Module | Does the product offer a specific Onboarding module, allowing clients to define required notifications at hire and send them through the system? (e.g. provisioning, IT for user account setup, new hire, manager checklist, etc.) | No |
| Onboarding Documentation Management | Electronically provide new hire paperwork and track completion of key documents (I-9, Non Disclosures, Benefits Paperwork). | Yes |

| Function | Function Description | Response |
|---|---|---|
| **Global Capabilities & Compliance** | | |
| EEO Compliance data collection | Configurable notification and collection of EEO compliance information at variable points in the process. | Yes |
| Global – in-country data collection based on regulations | Configurable data requests based on in-country requirements. Example: Germany, martial status, number of children. | Yes |
| Ability to present Career Sections in Multiple Languages | Ability to present Career Sections in multiple languages. | No |
| Ability to present the Recruiter and Manager Portals in Multiple Languages | Ability to present the Recruiter and Manager Portals in multiple languages. | Yes |
| Data Segregation by country, region or predefined type | Data Segregation, i.e. preventing users from a particular country or location from seeing candidates who are in another country or location. | Yes |
| OFCCP Compliance tools to enable search and applicant declaration | Functionality consistent with the new OFCCP definition of Internet Applicant (record-keeping for searches, candidate submissions, etc.) | No |
| Privacy Policy acknowledgements | Ability to require that candidates agree with the privacy policy before they submit. | Yes |
| Compliance with Data Privacy | Ability for customers to remove a candidate's data at that candidate's request. | No |
| Tax Credit Screening & Processing | Provides automatic Tax ID and SSN validation. Automatically transmit request to conduct tax credit screening for WOTC, WTW and more through to screening partners and display those results within the Candidate Profile for review and processing upon hire. | No |

| Function | Function Description | Response |
|---|---|---|
| **Reporting & Integration** | | |
| Standard reports are delivered with the system | System is delivered with a minimum of 10 standard reports. | Yes |
| Ad-hoc reporting capability | System is delivered with an ad-hoc re-port-writing tool so that clients can create their own reports as needed. | Yes – GA March 09 |
| Reporting Security | Ability to enable field-level security and access to report creation, output and distribution. | Yes |
| Reporting Distribu-tion | Ability to generate scheduled reports and distribute through email | No |
| Real-Time Reporting | Ability to report on data in the application in real time (not based on a refresh of data in a reporting environment). | Yes |
| HRIS Integration | Ability to create bi-directional integrations from an HRIS to the ATS. | Yes |
| Integration - Client Self-Service Tools | Ability for clients to create their own integration touch points as needed (and make them operational). | No |
| Integration - API capability | Ability to allow clients to create integra-tions through APIs. | No |

## Performance Management

| Function | Function Description | Response |
|---|---|---|
| **Performance Dashboard** | | |
| Dashboard configu-ration | Ability to configure dashboard based on user preference. | Yes |
| Create and display reports | Display reports that can be generated (i.e. review completion and goal prog-ress). | Yes |

| Function | Function Description | Response |
|---|---|---|
| Create and display charts and graphs | Show charts and graphs that are available to display planning actions. | Yes |
| Display help and reference tools | Display/view help and reference tools that can be selected by link or mouse hover. | Yes |
| **Employee Information Review (Data Import from HRIS/LMS)** | | |
| Import and display employee information | Display name, address, phone, email, location, photo, education (typically pulled from HRIS). | Yes |
| Import and display employee position information | Display current job title, job summary, job family, job level/grade, job code, FLSA, shift, status (FT/PT) (typically pulled through HRIS). | Yes |
| Create and display work history | Display created previous work history (i.e. name of company, job title, responsibilities/duties, employment dates). | Yes |
| Create and display years in management | Display created years of management experience (manually entered or via integration). | Yes |
| Create and display years in industry | Display created years of experience in industry (primarily entered manually). | Yes |
| Import, create and display employee language(s) | Display employee languages i.e. read, written and fluent (primarily entered manually). | Yes |
| Import, create and display employee affiliations | Display employee affiliation memberships. | Yes |
| Import, create and display employee certifications | Display employee certifications and dates. | Yes |

| Function | Function Description | Response |
|---|---|---|
| Import, create and display employee licenses | Display employee licenses and dates (usually a text box) - important to include expiration dates (could be for transportation, professional licenses, healthcare licenses, etc.) | Yes |
| Import and display organizational information | Display company name, company division, company department (typically imported from HRIS). | Yes |
| Import and display management hierarchy information | Display multiple levels of management names and information (i.e. Executive Management, Division Head, Department Head, Direct Manager, Employee). | Yes |
| Import and display direct reports | Display name and information of employee direct reports. | Yes |
| Import and display matrix manager hierarchy information | Display multiple levels of matrix management names and information (i.e. Employee has dotted line reporting relationships). | Yes |
| Import and display multiple manager hierarchy information | Display multiple levels of numerous management names and information (i.e. Employee reports to more than one manager directly). | Yes |
| Organizational Chart View | Organizational information displayed in an Org Chart view; note how displayed visually. | Yes |
| Organizational Change Requests | Due to potential errors within HRMS, manager has the ability to request an employee change in hierarchy (i.e. manager name, organization, location, job role); changes can be configured to require approval. | Yes by configuration |

| Function | Function Description | Response |
|----------|---------------------|----------|
| Import and display employee current and past compensation | Display employee's past and current base salary, bonus, equity, commission, etc. | Yes |
| Import and display employee's most recent performance measures | Display employee's current competencies, goals, skills, projects, performance rating, development plan and personal improvement plan. | Yes |
| Import and display employee previous performance measures | Display employee's previous competencies, goals, skills, projects, performance rating, development plan and personal improvement plan. | Yes |
| Complete and display employee training | Display employee's completed and assigned training (i.e. mandatory/development); Note if there is any integration with LMS. | Yes |
| External Identifier | Ability to have an external identifier field to bring in content on goals from a third-party application (i.e. description, start date, critical, public goal); can be configured to be read-only for imports. | can be configured |
| UDFs | Available user-defined fields for employee profile. | Yes |
| **Career Planning / Personal Development (Employee)** | | |
| Create and display future career plan scenarios | Display multiple future career plans (vertical, horizontal, both). Where does the employee want to go next? (lateral, promotion, etc.) | Yes |
| Select and display positions, job families and organizations/divisions of interest | Display selected positions and organizations of interest from import of job list and organization list (mentorships and cross-training); gives the employee the opportunity to identify a position, job-family or organization of interest. | Yes |

| Function | Function Description | Response |
|---|---|---|
| Create and display training requests | Display developmental training requests (entered by an employee or manager). This could be an integration point to the LMS. | Yes |
| Create and display executive/profes-sional requests | Display various executive/profes-sional requests (i.e. executive coaching, cross-training, job shadowing, speaking engagements, writing submittals, man-aging people, presentations, mentoring, apprenticeships). | Yes |
| Create and display organization affilia-tions and/or confer-ences/seminars | Display employee organization/affiliation or conference/seminar requests to join or attend. | Yes |
| Select and display competency devel-opment | Display selected desired competencies (entered by employee). | Yes |
| Create self-asses job readiness | Display selected self-readiness from list of options (i.e. Now, 0-3 months, 3-6 months, 6-9 months, 9-12 months, 12 months +). | Yes |
| Display position Gap % | Display gap % of employee readiness to ideal position as well as required train-ing, license(s), education, certification(s). This could be automatically calculated by the system (key differentiator). This is a gap analysis on the underlying competencies (most recent performance rating vs. competencies required for next position). | Yes |
| Select and dis-play willingness to relocate | Display selected willingness to relocate (i.e. yes, no, maybe, comments). | Yes |

| Function | Function Description | Response |
|---|---|---|
| Display career pre-requisites | Display required training, education, certification(s), license(s) for position of interest. | Yes |
| Submit development requests for approval | Submit development self- assessments to direct manager for review, feedback and approval (areas where the development needs to occur, as well as specific courses and conferences to help meet these development areas). Could be an integration point with LMS. | Yes |
| **Career Development (Manager)** | | |
| Create or select and display employee training goals | Display created or selected employee completed training, assigned training (mandatory/development), scheduled training and employee training requests. This is the manager identifying training goals for an employee. | Yes |
| Competency Development | Display assigned professional/leadership competencies. | Yes |
| Create and display executive/professional assignments | Display various executive/professional recommendations (i.e. executive coaching, cross-training, job shadowing, speaking engagements, writing submittals, managing people, presentations, mentoring, apprenticeships). | Yes |
| Create and display organization affiliations and/or conferences/seminars | Display employee organization/affiliation or conference/seminar recommendations. | Yes |
| **Individual Goal / Self Assessment (Employee)** | | |
| Select, create and display individual development goals | Display selected or created completed training, improvement competencies, executive coaching, promotion and cross training. | Yes |

| Function | Function Description | Response |
|---|---|---|
| Select competency development | Display selected development competencies. This is where employees select competencies they want to develop for their careers on the annual review. | Yes |
| Submit goal/competency assessment for approval | Submit manual or automatic goal/competency assessment to direct manager. | Yes |
| Solicit and display feedback | Select employees (i.e. managers, matrix managers, peers) to solicit performance feedback (i.e. 360, peer review, business review) and display results. | Yes |
| Create and display self-performance notes | Display created performance notes (i.e. kudos) throughout the review cycle (manually entered by employee or can solicit feedback throughout project). | Yes |
| Create and display self-goal assessment progress | Display created self-goal progress (i.e. quantitative % of completion, qualitative to include customer satisfaction, timeline to include start/completion date). | Yes |
| Submit goal/competency review for approval | Submit manual or automatic goal/competency assessment to direct manager and higher levels. | Yes |
| UDFs | Available user-defined fields for employee goals. | Yes |
| **Review Process (Employee and Manager)** | | |
| Select and display competencies | Display selected professional or leadership competencies. | Yes |
| Select and display goals/objectives | Display selected goals/objectives (i.e. quantitative and/or qualitative). | Yes |
| Select and display goal alignment | Display selected goal alignment to company, organization, department and/or manager goals (cascading goals). | Yes |

| Function | Function Description | Response |
|----------|---------------------|----------|
| Select or create and display projects | Display selected or created projects. | Yes |
| Select and display project alignment to goals | Display selected project alignment to company, organization, department and/or manager goals. | Yes |
| Select or create and display skills | Display selected or created company, organization, department, employee skills. | Yes |
| Create and display employee performance notes | Display created performance notes (positive or negative) throughout the review cycle. Notes created by the manager. | Yes |
| Solicit and display feedback | Select employees (i.e. managers, matrix managers, peers) to solicit performance feedback (i.e. 360, peer review, business review) and display. Pay particular attention to how this feedback is gathered and entered into the system. | Yes |
| Create and display employee goal assessment review | Display created employee goal progress (i.e. quantitative % of completion, qualitative to include customer satisfaction, timeline to include start/ completion date). This is the manager entering the assessment. | Yes |
| Performance review filtering | Manager can filter performance review information based on approval status, assigned to, author/owner, manager, employee, organization, location, job field, job role, review cycle, review group, review group owner, overall rating; filtering can be cumulative. | Yes |
| Batch activities | Manager can take group actions on multiple employees simultaneously. | Yes |
| UDFs | Available user-defined fields for employee competencies. | Yes |

| Function | Function Description | Response |
|----------|---------------------|----------|
| **Workflow** | | |
| Review cycles | Ability to configure multiple review cycles and tie to various reviews. | Yes |
| Review groups | Ability to define review recipients based on dates, job function, organization, job code, etc. | Yes |
| Workflow Order | Ability to configure order of workflow (i.e. self-assessments can be configured to be completed first). | Yes |
| Notifications | Ability to push reviews to employees and managers. | Yes |
| Reminders | Ability to send reminders to employees and managers via email (manual and automatic). | Yes |
| Acknowledgements | Ability to send auto-acknowledgements triggered by event/activity. | Yes |
| Next Level Approval | Ability to auto/manually route to multiple levels of approval. | Yes |
| Configurable work-flow | Ability to: configure various steps of the review process; make review steps mandatory; have manager override; display/hide visual graphic workflow diagram. | Yes |
| Auto/Manual Progression | Ability to automatically or manually progress through the review process. | Yes |
| Review form | Exportable and printable review form. | Yes |
| **System Admin** | | |
| Review sections | Ability to configure multiple review sections, including goals, competencies, comments, rating models, etc. | Yes |

| Function | Function Description | Response |
|---|---|---|
| Configurable rating models | Does it configure and display alpha and numeric values? Can values be rounded (up/down/both), value ranges, number of decimals (1-5)? | Yes |
| Comments | Displayed and available in individual review sections and overall review. Can they be configured to be mandatory and overridden by management? | Yes |
| Goals | Ability to link organizational, divisional, departmental, individual goals into sections and to display goal progress. | Yes |
| Competencies | Ability to link competencies into sections. | Yes |
| Weightings | Ability to weigh employee performance based on goals and competencies. | Yes |
| **Search Functionality** | | |
| Basic Employee Search | Basic search by employee name (i.e. first or last name or a combination of both). | Yes |
| Job/Position Basic Search | Basic search by job role or position title, etc. | Yes |
| Competency Basic Search | Basic search by competency name. | Yes |
| Advanced Search | More detailed search capabilities that combine various search criteria or fields. May include optional weighting to determine which employees are retrieved in a search as well as each person's rank in the search results. | Yes |
| Succession Planning Search | Search functionality that dynamically generates the criteria used to match employees who would make good succession candidates with a specific position profile (could have various levels of "fit"). | Yes |

| Function | Function Description | Response |
|---|---|---|
| **Employee View / Navigation / Help / Other** | | |
| List View | Display employee goals, business goals or projects; the list mode is a list of items with information on key dates and progress. | Yes |
| Card View | Display employee goals, business goals or projects using the card mode; the card mode provides details on one item at a time and offers the possibility of editing progress. This can also include employee photos. | Yes |
| Timeline / Gantt | Display employee goals, business goals or projects using the timeline mode; the timeline mode provides a timeline view of an item's start and due dates. | No |
| Org Chart | Managers can access and manage information on their direct reports for all functionalities activated; the organizational chart will provide key data (i.e. risk of loss or most recent performance rating) for each of the manager's direct reports. | Yes |
| Mini-Org Chart | Displays a single analytic data point at a time; the manager can drill down into all layers of his organization and can view key metrics (i.e. performance reviews, goals, succession). | Yes |
| Graphs | Graphical display of various information (i.e. Gap Analysis, goal progress, review completion progress). | Yes |
| Help Links | Online help, FAQs, customer support, product version. | Yes |
| Attach Documents | Ability to attach reference documents to various sections within the system. | Yes |

| Function | Function Description | Response |
|---|---|---|
| Browser capabilities | Supported by general Internet access (works with standard browsers: IE, Safari, Mozilla, Opera). | Yes |
| Mouse-Over Hover | Additional tooltips or descriptions that display when user hovers the mouse pointer over various graphics or words within the system. | Yes |
| Web 2.0 | Ability to utilize Web 2.0 functionality, i.e. social networking. | Yes |
| **Security** | | |
| Logging In | Various login options (i.e. manual, SSO, LDAP). | Yes |
| File Transfer | Various file transfer protocol (i.e. FTP, sFTP, vendor-specific transfer import/export tool). | Yes |
| Encryption | Various data encryption ability (i.e. PGP). | Yes |
| Roles / Permissions | Configurable list of permission-based roles with detailed access rights to various organizations, levels, etc. Typically employees only view within their own organization hierarchy. | Yes |
| Integration | Ability to integrate organizational data i.e. HRIS/ATS/ LMS and employee data including competencies, training, development plans, etc. | Yes |
| **Reporting** | | |
| Standard reports are delivered with the system | System is delivered with a set number of standard reports. | Yes |

| Function | Function Description | Response |
|---|---|---|
| Ad-hoc reporting capability | System is delivered with an ad-hoc report-writing tool so that clients can create their own reports as needed. | No |
| Advanced Value metrics | Data analysis of employee review process status, goal progress by hierarchy. | Yes |
| Reporting Security | Ability to enable field-level security and access to report creation, output and distribution. | Yes |
| Reporting UDFs | Ability to report user-defined fields | Yes |
| Exporting reports | Reports can easily be exported to other applications (i.e. .xls, .pdf, .txt). | Yes |

## Succession Planning

| Succession Planning (Manager - Planning of Individual Talent Matched to Critical Roles) | | |
|---|---|---|
| Create and display critical roles for today | Display critical job roles (i.e. title, level, location, division, organization). | Yes |
| Create and display critical roles for future | Display critical job roles (i.e. title, level, location, division, organization) for future (workforce planning-like tools). | Yes |
| Calculate and display performance rating | Performance rating is automatically averaged from various sections of the performance review and displayed (current and past). | Yes |
| Calculate and display performance ranking | High potential employees will be automatically ranked according to order of fit with critical role (i.e. 9-box grid, numeric ranking, high performer, high potential); can be ranked by position, organization, etc. | Yes |

| Function | Function Description | Response |
|---|---|---|
| Multi-dimensional matrix | Matrix that can be configured up to various # of cells (i.e. 9-box, 12-box, 16-box, 25-box); text within grid is configurable. | Yes |
| Various dimensions of matrix | Matrix displays employee performance, potential, number of succession plans for employee, years in management, years in industry. | Yes |
| Navigation from multi-dimensional matrix | Manager can select an employee within the matrix and navigate to employee information (i.e. Performance review, talent profile, employee goals, career plan). | Yes |
| Display employee comparisons | Display comparison of multiple high potential employees according to fit to critical role (i.e. # of employees to compare, comparable data, fit gap analysis, ranking analysis, bench strength). | Yes |
| Create and display role readiness | Manager can create and display high potential employee role readiness (i.e. now, 0-3 months, 3-6 months, 6-9 months, 9-12 months, 12+ months). | Yes |
| Create and display retention risk | Manager can create and display high potential employee retention/loss/flight risk (i.e. high, medium, low, comments). | Yes |
| Create and display role willingness | Manager can create and display high potential employee role willingness (i.e. yes, no, comments) | Yes |
| Create and display willingness to relocate | Manager can create and display high potential employee willingness to relocate (i.e. yes, no, maybe, comments). | Yes |
| Create and display willingness to travel | Manager can create and display high potential employee willingness to travel (i.e. none, 25-50%, 50-75%, 75-100%). | Yes |

| Function | Function Description | Response |
|---|---|---|
| Create and display interest in international assignment | Manager can create and display high potential employee interest in international assignment (i.e. yes, no, maybe). | Yes |
| Create and display interim replacement for critical role | Manager can create and display high potential interim replacement for critical roles. | Yes |
| Display of gap analysis | Automatically calculate and display high potential employees' fit gap analysis to the next position and ranking analysis of employees to that next position. | Yes |
| UDFs | Available user-defined fields for succession planning. | Yes |
| **Succession Pooling (Manager - Planning of a Talent Pool for Critical Roles)** | | |
| Display high potential pool | Display nominated and/or approved high potential pool (i.e. employee information, designated nominators, designated approvers, approvals, rejections, role readiness, rejection comments). | Yes |
| Calculate and display performance rating | Performance rating is automatically averaged from various sections of the performance review and displayed (current and past). | Yes |
| Calculate and display performance ranking | Pool of high potential employees will be automatically ranked according to order of fit with critical role (i.e. 9-box grid, numeric ranking, high performer, high potential). | Yes |
| Display employee comparisons | Display comparison of multiple high potential employees according to fit to critical role (i.e. # of employees to compare, comparable data, fit gap analysis, ranking analysis, bench strength). | Yes |

| Function | Function Description | Response |
|----------|---------------------|----------|
| Create and display role readiness | Manager can create and display high potential employee role readiness (i.e. now, 0-3 months, 3-6 months, 6-9 months, 9-12 months, 12+ months). | Yes |
| Create and display retention risk | Manager can create and display high potential employee retention/loss/flight risk (i.e. high, medium, low, comments). | Yes |
| Create and display role willingness | Manager can create and display high potential employee role willingness (i.e. yes, no, comments). | Yes |
| Create and display willingness to relocate | Manager can create and display high potential employee willingness to relocate (i.e. yes, no, maybe, comments). | Yes |
| Create and display willingness to travel | Manager can create and display high potential employee willingness to travel (i.e. none, 25-50%, 50-75%, 75-100%). | Yes |
| Create and display interest in international assignment | Manager can create and display high potential employee interest in international assignment (i.e. yes, no, maybe). | Yes |
| Create and display interim replacement for critical role | Manager can create and display high potential interim replacement for critical roles. | Yes |
| Display of gap analysis | Automatically calculate and display high potential employees' fit gap analysis of employee to position and ranking analysis of employee to position. | Yes |
| UDFs | Available user-defined fields for succession pooling. | Yes |
| **Workflow** | | |
| Succession approval workflow | Ability to: define or edit approvers; add/remove users and roles; change the approval order and reject with comments. | Yes |

| Function | Function Description | Response |
|---|---|---|
| Nominations for succession pool | Ability to nominate, reject and enter comments on nominated HiPo employees. | Yes |
| **Reporting** | | |
| Standard reports are delivered with the system | System is delivered with a set number of standard reports. | Yes |
| Ad-hoc reporting capability | System is delivered with an ad-hoc report-writing tool so that clients can create their own reports as needed. | No – Planned Q2 09 |
| Advanced Value metrics | Data analysis of high performers / high potential employees, identified gaps, critical roles. | Yes |
| Reporting Security | Ability to enable field-level security and access to report creation, output and distribution. | Yes |
| Reporting UDFs | Ability to report user-defined fields. | Yes |
| Exporting reports | Reports can easily be exported to other applications (i.e. .xls, .pdf, .txt). | Yes |

## Compensation Management

| Function | Function Description | Response |
|---|---|---|
| **Compensation Dashboard** | | |
| Dashboard configuration | Ability to configure dashboard based on user preference. | Yes |
| Create and display a compensation worksheet | Display a compensation worksheet that will provide individual and org planning status and detail. | Yes |
| Create and display reports | Display reports that can be generated, i.e. budget usage by merit, bonus, equity, adjustment and percent of planning completed. | Yes |

| Function | Function Description | Response |
|----------|--------------------|----------|
| Create and display charts and graphs | Display available charts and graphs to show planning actions. | Yes |
| Import and display allocation guidelines | Display compensation allocation guidelines for merit, bonus, equity and adjustments. Also refer to the time allocation/ workflow to complete this process. | Yes |
| Import and display eligibility guidelines | Display employee eligibility guidelines for planning, i.e. FT, PT, commission, LOA, new hire, etc. Guidelines are input by compensation department. | Yes |
| Display help and reference tools | Display and view help and reference tools that can be selected by link or mouse hover. | Yes |
| **Compensation Budget** | | |
| Import and display multiple aggregate planning budget by org | Display multiple approved allocated budgets by diverse business groups on all pages (usually imported from financial system). | Yes |
| Import and display aggregate merit budget by org | Display approved allocated merit budget by diverse business groups on all pages. | Yes |
| Import and display aggregate bonus budget by org | Display approved allocated bonus by diverse business groups on all pages. | Yes |
| Import and display aggregate equity budget by org | Display approved allocated equity budget by diverse business groups on all pages. | Yes |
| Import and display aggregate adjustment budget by org | Display approved allocated adjustment budget by diverse business groups on all pages. | Yes |

| Function | Function Description | Response |
|---|---|---|
| **Employee Information Review** | | |
| Import and display employee Information | Display name, location, photo, org, direct manager (typically imported from PM tool). | Yes |
| Import and display employee position | Display current job title, job code and level/grade. | Yes |
| Import and display employee prior compensation planning period data | Display current hourly rate, annual rate, bonus percent, bonus amount, equity allocation and total compensation. | Yes |
| Import and display employee prior performance rating | Display prior performance rating. | Yes |
| Import and display new employee performance rating | Display new performance rating. | Yes |
| Import and display employee's position salary range | Display employee's salary range. | Yes |
| Import and display salary penetration percentage based on position salary range | Display percentage of penetration that employee's salary falls within the range. | Yes |
| **Promotion** | | |
| Display position information | Ability to select and display job titles, job codes and job level/grades. | Yes |
| Import and display corporate promotion guidelines | Ability to display promotion guidelines per position, including salary range and percent increase guidelines. | Yes |

| Function | Function Description | Response |
|----------|--------------------|----------|
| Promotion amount | Ability to enter promotion percent or amount. | Yes |
| Auto-calculate promotion amount | System to auto-populate promotion amount based on percent increase. | Yes |
| Ability to calculate hourly rate | System to auto-populate new hourly rate based on promotion increase. | Yes |
| Ability to auto-calculate annual rate | System to auto-populate new annual rate based on promotion increase | Yes |
| Promotion approval chain | Ability to obtain appropriate approvals (workflow to select appropriate approvers). | Yes |
| Develop documentation | Ability to document the promotion justification. | Yes |
| **Adjustment** | | |
| Import and display adjustment guidelines | Ability to display adjustment allocation guidelines, including salary range and percent increase guidelines. | Yes |
| Adjustment allocation | Ability to enter and submit an adjustment percent or amount. | Yes |
| Auto-calculate hourly amount | System to auto-populate new hourly rate based on adjustment percent increase. | Yes |
| Auto-calculate adjustment amount | System to auto-populate new annual rate based on adjustment percent increase. | Yes |
| Adjustment approvals | Ability to obtain appropriate approvals (workflow to select appropriate approvers). | Yes |
| Develop documentation | Ability to document the adjustment justification. | Yes |

| Function | Function Description | Response |
|---|---|---|
| **Merit** | | |
| Import and display promotion guide-lines | Ability to display merit allocation guide-lines, including salary range and percent increase guidelines. | Yes |
| Performance-based recommendations | Merit allocation can be based on perfor-mance rating. | Yes |
| Merit allocation | Ability to enter and submit a merit per-cent or amount. | Yes |
| Import and display proration of merit based on hire date | System to auto-calculate merit increase based on hire date, i.e. less than one year would be calculated by months employed. | Yes |
| Auto-calculate hourly amount | System to auto-populate new hourly rate based on merit percent increase. | Yes |
| Auto-calculate ad-justment amount | System to auto-populate new annual rate based on merit percent increase. | Yes |
| Merit approvals | Ability to obtain appropriate approvals (workflow to select appropriate approv-ers). | Yes |
| Develop documen-tation | Ability to document the merit justification. | Yes |
| **Bonus** | | |
| Import and display bonus allocation guidelines | Ability to display bonus allocation guide-lines. | Yes |
| Performance-based recommendations | Bonus allocation can be based on per-formance rating. | Yes |
| Bonus allocation | Ability to enter and submit a bonus per-cent or amount. | Yes |

| Function | Function Description | Response |
|---|---|---|
| Bonus adjustment | Auto-Proration of bonus based on hired or leave, i.e. severance date. | Yes |
| Bonus approvals | Ability to obtain appropriate approvals (workflow to select appropriate approvers). | Yes |
| Develop documentation | Ability to document the merit justification. | Yes |
| **Equity** | | |
| Import and display equity allocation guidelines | Ability to display equity allocation guidelines. | Yes |
| Performance-based recommendations | Equity allocation can be based on performance rating. | Yes |
| Equity allocation | Ability to enter and submit equity percent or amount. | Yes |
| Equity allocation adjustment | Auto-Proration of equity allocation based on hire date. | Yes |
| Equity approvals | Ability to obtain appropriate approvals (workflow to select appropriate approvers). | Yes |
| Develop documentation | Ability to document the merit justification. | Yes |
| **Other** | | |
| Ability to assign a delegate | Ability to assign a delegate to complete compensation planning, i.e. Admin. | Yes |
| Employee Filter | Ability to sort by employee name or data, i.e. first name, last name, employee ID, etc. | Yes |

| Function | Function Description | Response |
|----------|---------------------|----------|
| Employee Search | Ability to search throughout the tool by employee name or data, i.e. first name, last name, employee ID, etc. | Yes |
| Revert or change functionality | Ability for planning administrators to revert/ change submitted data. | Yes |
| Collaborative work-flow | Ability for managers, compensation and HR partners to collaborate on various compensation workflows. | Yes |
| Display out-of-guideline entries | Ability to display out-of-guideline entries made within adjustments, merit, bonus and equity. | Yes |
| **Reporting** | | |
| Standard reports are delivered with the system | System is delivered with a set number of standard reports. | Yes |
| Ad-hoc reporting capability | System is delivered with an ad-hoc report-writing tool so that clients can create their own reports as needed. | No |
| Advanced Value metrics | Data analysis of comp gaps based on roles, hierarchy. | Yes |
| Reporting Security | Ability to enable field-level security and access to report creation, output and distribution. | Yes |
| **Security** | | |
| Logging In | Various login options (i.e. manual, SSO, LDAP). | Yes |
| File Transfer | Various file transfer protocol (i.e. FTP, sFTP, vendor-specific, transfer import/export tool). | Yes |
| Encryption | Various data encryption ability (i.e. PGP). | Yes |

| Function | Function Description | Response |
|---|---|---|
| Roles / Permissions | Configurable list of permission-based roles with detailed access rights to various organizations, levels, etc. Typically employees only view within their own organization hierarchy. | Yes |
| Integration | Ability to Integrate organizational data with appropriate org system, i.e. HRIS/Payroll, employee data, including employee salaries, levels, performance rating, etc. | Yes |
| Reporting UDFs | Ability to report user-defined fields. | Yes |
| Exporting reports | Reports can easily be exported to other applications (i.e. .xls, .pdf, .txt). | Yes |

# Taleo

## Company Information (provided by Taleo)

**Company Name:**          Taleo Corporation

**Corporate URL:**         www.taleo.com

**Main Phone:**            (925) 452-3000

**Main Email:**            info@taleo.com

**Headquarters Address:**  4140 Dublin Blvd., Suite 400,
                           Dublin, CA 94568

**Type of Business or Areas of Focus:**

Leading organizations of all sizes worldwide use Taleo on-demand talent management solutions to assess, acquire, develop and align their workforce for improved business performance. We offer solutions for three distinct market segments based on organization size. These segments are: Large Enterprise for companies with over 10,000 employees; Enterprise for companies with up to 10,000 employees and Small and Medium-Sized Business (SMB) for companies up to 3,000 employees. Taleo also serves virtually all industry segments with a strong presence in healthcare, retail, financial services, manufacturing and the public sector.

**Number of Employees:**   Approximately 900

**Year Founded:**          1998

**Stock Symbol:**          TLEO

## Company Description and History:

Taleo was founded in 1998 as Recruitsoft and has had a long history of innovation and industry leadership.

Taleo combines software, best practices and services so organizations can increase process efficiency, improve workforce quality, reduce risk and drive financial results. Taleo provides a full suite of talent management solutions including sourcing, recruiting, onboarding, performance management, succession planning, goals management, compensation management and development planning. All solutions are built on a unified talent management platform and share a common talent profile and common solutions for integration, reporting, analytics, organization management and competency management. Taleo's open, unified, on-demand platform and talent management applications are at the heart of the Taleo Talent Grid which ties together over 100 million talent profiles, 3,800 companies and over 50 best of breed partners through three marketplaces—the Taleo Talent Exchange, Taleo Solution Exchange and the Taleo Knowledge Exchange.

Taleo's first customers included Hewlett-Packard and Bombardier who selected Taleo for its new approach to recruiting using a standard talent profile instead of the resume. This profile-based approach was Taleo's first major innovation and fundamentally changed the game in recruiting. Since then, Taleo has been the first to market with several more innovations, including self-service system administration, SmartOrg, a single unified platform, Taleo Connect and the new Taleo Performance Suite. Taleo has won numerous awards including the HR Tech Product of the Year for its Reporting/Analytics and Onboarding solutions and was in the leaders' quadrant of the Gartner E-Recruitment Magic Quadrant in 2006 and 2008. Taleo was an early pioneer in the Software-as-a-Service delivery model and is currently one of the largest SaaS vendors in the world. Taleo is a publicly-traded, profitable company with a senior leadership team that has decades of experience running some of the most respected technology companies including, IBM, Oracle, Peoplesoft and SAP. More than 2.5 million users from 3,800 organizations use Taleo to manage their talent in over 200 countries/territories in 26 languages.

## Products/Services/Solutions:

The Taleo Talent Management Solutions presented below are all part of the Taleo Enterprise Edition product suite for organizations with more than 3,000 employees. This does not cover any functionality in the Taleo Business Edition Solution, which also includes recruiting and performance management functionality. In this document the solutions will be presented in three distinct groups: Taleo Recruiting, Taleo Performance and Taleo Platform modules.

## Taleo Recruiting Modules

### 1. Taleo Recruiting

Taleo Recruiting is an industry-leading, e-recruitment system designed to source, screen, track and hire all types of talent including salaried professionals, hourly workers and contingent labor on a single platform. Taleo also supports campus recruiting and internal mobility programs. Highlights include: requisition management; single click job posting; sourcing tracking and analysis; Web 2.0 candidate portal capabilities; candidate communication agent; 4-tier screening and assessment with ACE methodology; offer management; support for 26 languages; functionality for EEO/AA/OFCCP and international regulatory compliance; SmartOrg, self-service configuration to enable companies to manage complex, global recruiting operations and remote system administration to support the needs of smaller companies.

### 2. Taleo TalentReach powered by AIRS

Taleo TalentReach is the talent CRM functionality that includes a whole suite of sourcing products for building a talent pipeline and sourcing passive candidates. Capabilities include: contact management; employment marketing campaign management; consolidated Internet search and spidering capabilities; automated searches; access to over 40 million passive candidate profiles; OFCCP compliance capabilities and sourcing reporting and analytics.

### 3. Taleo Assessment

Taleo Assessment is a testing platform and authoring tool that supports assessment content, customer-owned content or third party content as a seamless part of the selection process. Assessment results are embedded in the candidate's profiles and can automatically generate interview guides based on them. The Taleo Assessment authoring tool is designed to enable I/O psychologists to build and manage assessment content and interview guides. Taleo has a team of I/O psychologists that have developed validated assessment content for campus recruiting, call centers, retail hourly, customer service, retail management, healthcare and cultural fit that can be tailored to each client's specifications.

## 4. Taleo Onboarding

Taleo Onboarding™ improves the bottom line by providing new employees with the tools they need to be productive faster. Taleo's new hire portal ensures that new hires hit the ground running. The system pays for itself quickly by eliminating printing and mailing costs while improving compliance with pre-populated forms. The powerful workflow engine manages provisioning of equipment like phones, computers and security badges. It streamlines new hire paperwork with electronic forms management and I-9 checking. The hiring manager's dashboard makes tracking the process simple. Tight integration with both Taleo Recruiting and internal systems makes the entire process seamless.

## Taleo Performance Modules

## 5. Performance Management

Taleo Performance Management brings together the information needed for managers to objectively and accurately evaluate their employees. With a unified design approach, all relevant information, such as a current goals achievement, and Multi-rater feedback are automatically pulled into the review and scored and weighted for the manager. Competencies can also be incorporated into the review and can be predefined or dynamically generated based upon the employee's job role, organization, job level or job family. Other key functionality includes calibration capabilities to help managers compare individual performance to corporate standards and peers within the team or throughout the company.

## 6. Taleo Goals Management

Taleo Goals Management helps define, track and evaluate goals at the organization, project or employee level. Organizational goals can be cascaded down, ensuring corporate alignment with key initiatives. Project-based goals give cross-functional groups the option to work on specific, targeted objectives. Employee goals can be aligned to organizational goals, project goals or even other employee goals. All goal management functionality is supported by role-based workflows, and the Taleo Inbox Outlook plug-in complements this process by allowing goal plan updates to be made within Outlook without the need to access the Taleo application.

## 7. Taleo Succession Planning

Taleo Succession Planning helps define succession plans for any position from senior executives to key high potential talent. Succession plans are based on positions, rather than individuals, ensuring that plans are retained when individuals move into new roles. Because Taleo Recruiting and Taleo Performance are built on a unified platform, succession plans can include both internal and external candidates. Other key highlights of Taleo Succession Planning include: timeline views; talent cards; organization charts; readiness and risk assessment; nomination process management and retention management; hi-potential identification and a unique multi-dimensional matrix, which is more flexible than the traditional 9-box.

## 8. Taleo Career Management

Taleo Career Management increases employee retention by providing visibility into current opportunities and future career options within the organization. Employees are able to model an unlimited number of multi-position career paths based upon personal interest or the results of best fit search technology that suggests options based upon an employee's qualifications. Employees can also search for new jobs using criteria like keywords, job families, competencies or locations. Based on projected career path, employees are presented with a gap analysis highlighting strengths, areas for improvement and other skills needed. They then can solicit feedback from their personal network or manager.

### 9. Taleo Development Planning

Development Planning is a key outcome of the goal and performance evaluation processes, and Taleo Performance currently provides the ability to capture customer-specific employee developmental information. With release 8.0 in 2009, the company will launch Taleo Development Planning and deliver a truly unique learning management solution that will enable employees to continuously develop new skills to fill identified gaps and support their career goals. This solution will integrate with multiple LMS but will move beyond traditional LMS systems to incorporate other types of learning, including recommended reading, mentorship opportunities, job shadowing, stretch projects, practice communities, cross-functional assignments and self directed e-learning courses.

### 10. Compensation Management (Worldwide Compensation)

Worldwide Compensation includes a unique Global Rewards Library and highly configurable Global Compensation Platform designed to localize total compensation plans by country, subsidiary, business unit or critical skills, while centralizing financial controls. The Global Rewards Library is a Web-based tool which provides compensation practice information for over 50 countries, including major emerging markets. The Global Compensation Platform provides extensive configuration capabilities and helps manage multiple compensation components, including merit, adjustments, promotions, allowances, bonuses and equity plans such as stock options, restricted stocks and stock appreciation rights. Other highlights include comprehensive reporting, planning cycle management and standard access to Mercer's ePrism market data. Taleo has made an equity investment with an exclusive option to acquire Worldwide Compensation.

## Taleo Platform Modules

### 11. Taleo Connect

Taleo Connect™ is designed to integrate Taleo with other corporate systems like HRIS, data warehouses and internal HR portals. The Taleo Connect integration suite is part of the company's unified platform that supports both Taleo Recruiting and Performance and includes Taleo Connect Client, Taleo Connect Broker and Taleo Connect

Web Services. Clients can use Taleo Connect Client or Taleo Connect Web Services to build, monitor and maintain their own integrations to back-end systems. The Taleo Connect Broker solution is designed for clients with limited IT where Taleo builds the integration scripts, then monitors and manages the integrations for the client.

### 12. Taleo Passport

Taleo Passport works with both Taleo Recruiting and Taleo Performance and provides "turnkey" integration access to Taleo Passport Certified partners in multiple categories, including sourcing, background checking, assessments, drug screening, tax credits, I-9 and reference checking. Taleo works with its partners to build certified, reusable integrations that can be rolled out to multiple customers. This saves the client's time and money compared to traditional integration projects. With Taleo Passport, clients only need to select their vendor of choice. Taleo activates and configures the integration and access to the service, and results are embedded into the selection process.

### 13. Taleo Anywhere

Taleo Anywhere is a set of integration capabilities that are part of the unified talent management platform that work with both Taleo Recruiting and Taleo Performance products. Taleo Anywhere integration solutions open up the Taleo platform through standard Web services API's and RSS feeds to integrate with mobile devices like Blackberry, desktop productivity tools like Microsoft outlook and popular social networking tools like Facebook.

### 14. Taleo Reporting & Analytics

Taleo Reporting and Analytics work with both Taleo Recruiting and Taleo Performance and are built on the Business Objects XIR2 platform. Taleo offers several standard reports for both recruiting and performance that cover key metrics for sourcing, compliance, recruiter and process efficiency, employee performance ratings, succession plans, goals alignment and performance. Advanced reporting enables clients to build their own customized reports with drill down capabilities. Taleo Analytics provides standard dashboards on the most common talent management analytics and includes dashboard authoring tools. Taleo also offers expert reporting and analytics services.

## Additional Notes/Comments:

### Taleo Unified Talent Management Platform

According to Taleo, one of the major differentiators that separates it from the competition is its unified Talent Management Platform. Taleo has developed an advanced component-based, services oriented solution architecture that has enabled it to build talent management solutions for recruiting and performance management that share common elements. These common elements include: a common data model; organizational model; workflows; search; system configuration tools; integration tools; reporting and global capabilities. The platform also includes Taleo's secure, scalable and reliable software-as-a-service infrastructure.

### Taleo Talent Grid

Recently, at TaleoWORLD 2008, Taleo announced its vision for creating the Talent Grid. Taleo was a pioneer in the on-demand, software-as-a-service delivery model, which is a form of cloud computing. Taleo is now leveraging its cloud computing expertise and position in the marketplace to bring together over 50 best of breed talent management partners, 3,600 customers, 100 million candidates and many other talent management experts in new and exciting ways through its unified talent management platform. The Talent Grid is analogous to the power grid that provides energy to homes, charges cell phones and keeps the economy running smoothly. For businesses, the Talent Grid provides the infrastructure and resources to power an organization's main source of innovation and execution: its talent. Companies who plug into the Talent Grid get all the benefits of Taleo and its ecosystem of partners and customers. The Talent Grid will be populated by third-party solutions such as background checks, assessments and salary data, as well as content from customers' talent pools, social networks, talent management best practices and successful methodologies. Combined, this will offer anyone who plugs into the grid the ability to radically change and improve the way he/she assesses, acquires, engages and retains talent to drive business performance.

At the core of the talent grid is the Taleo talent management platform and applications. Throughout 2009, Taleo will continue to open up access to the talent grid through innovative integration solutions;

its new MyTaleo portal technology and development of its online talent management marketplaces—solution exchange, talent exchange and knowledge exchange.

# Author's Taleo Functionality Matrix

| Function | Function Description | Response |
|---|---|---|

## Talent Acquisition

| Requisition Management & Posting | | |
|---|---|---|
| Multiple requisition forms allowed (Example: hourly, internal transfer, business unit specific, reoccurring, sourcing, college) | More than one requisition form/template can be configured in a client's database to accommodate variance in business units or type of recruiting. (Example: A user from the Manufacturing group can enter a requisition and only see and populate fields that are applicable to Mfg. A different user from the Services group can enter a requisition and only see the fields designated for a Services requisition within the same database. | Yes |
| Data Segregation | Ability to segregate requisitions and candidates by hire type (executive, HR, etc.) or organization. | Yes |
| Requisition approval routing workflow and approval status indicator | Select a list of approvers, route for approval via email. Approvals should be able to be sent in parallel or sequentially. | Yes |
| Approval status tracking | The status of the approval process is tracked and displayed real-time on the requisition in the application as well as in the subsequent emails that go to the second and third approver, etc. | Yes |

| Function | Function Description | Response |
|---|---|---|
| Pre-defined approval routing lists | Lists of approvers can be created, saved and/or assigned to a user or requisition, or defined by the organizational structure automatically. | Yes |
| Approvals can take place directly from an email | When approving a requisition, the approver can take action directly from the email notification without having to log into the application. | Yes |
| Pre-qualifying questions based on position/job needs, including weighting to filter for top candidates | Questions developed, defined and delivered to a candidate in the online application process are tied directly to the job posting/requirements, including weighting to filter top candidates. | Yes |
| Knock-out questions | Ability to establish certain questions to be disqualifiers, where if the candidate does not answer correctly, the process is ended. | Yes |
| Job posting scheduling | Check a box to select the appropriate career site(s) for the job to appear. Scheduling of start and end dates of posting to any given site to allow for staggered posting. | Yes |
| Advanced job descriptions - Formatting and Spell Checking | Ability to edit and format job descriptions and marketing messages with MS Word, like functions for Bolding, Underlining and Spell Checking. | Yes |
| Electronic job board relationship management (facilitation of job positing to all e-media providers) | Ability to identify and post job opportunities to an unlimited number of electronic job boards and other end destinations. Ability to multi-select boards and push positions out to the market. | Yes |

| Function | Function Description | Response |
|----------|---------------------|----------|
| **Candidate Experience** | | |
| Unlimited Career Site portals | Ability to establish an unlimited number of integrated career sites for different purposes - such as college recruiting, location-specific kiosks or for a specific job family like Sales or Engineering. Determine if there are additional costs per Career Section. | Yes |
| Online profile form(s) defined by the client | Data collection form(s) that can be pushed to a candidate to gather needed information for relationship management and interested resume submissions. Customers can tailor the form to their specification, adding or removing fields. | Yes |
| User-defined secure login user name and password. | User-created login and password authentication for accessing profile and career management activities. | Yes |
| Candidate login optional | Candidate can submit resume and apply to jobs without establishing a password-protected user account. | No |
| Resume submission via upload of file - Candidate | Candidates can browse hard drive for formatted resume and upload to candidate resume repository. | Yes |
| Resume submission via upload of file - Recruiter/Manager | Recruiter/Manager can browse hard drive for formatted resume and upload to candidate resume repository. | Yes |
| Resume builder functionality | Ability for candidates without a formal resume to submit a resume via a "Resume Builder." | Yes |
| Extraction of data from resume to create profile | Extraction engine behind the text or uploaded resume for population of fielded data in the candidate profile. | Yes |

| Function | Function Description | Response |
|----------|---------------------|----------|
| Candidate-defined Job Agents | Candidate can establish job search parameters and be notified when jobs are posted which meet their preferences. | Yes |
| Candidate status check | Candidates can login to check the status of their resume submissions. | Yes |
| Ability to upload attachments | Ability to upload attachments. | Yes |
| Ability for candidate to save a submission as a draft | Ability for candidate to save a submission as a draft. | Yes |
| Candidate self-withdrawal | Ability for candidates to remove themselves from consideration for a position. | Yes |
| Conceptual search for the candidate when searching for jobs | Candidates can use "free form" language to search for jobs. | No |
| **Sourcing/CRM** | | |
| Specific job referral and general referrals | Employees can submit a resume as a general referral or to a specific job. | Yes |
| Notifications to the referring employee and the referred candidate | Email notifications are automatically sent to the employee making the referral and to the candidate who was referred. | Yes |
| Referral status check | Employees can review a list of candidates they have referred and check their status. | Yes |
| Tracking steps and status searches | Recruiters can search for candidates based on their tracking steps and status against requisitions. | Yes |

| Function | Function Description | Response |
|---|---|---|
| Keyword search against free form text and fielded data | Keyword search against text records from candidate and fielded data in the same search. | Yes |
| Search criteria highlighted for relevance in record review | Search results with indicators for criteria matching and relevance in the results. | Yes |
| Configurable search results list | Column headers that are displayed in a search results list can be configured with different data elements from the candidate record. (Example: Education, Work History, Phone Number). | Yes |
| Ability to search file attachments | Keyword searching will scan the resumes that have been submitted as file attachments as well as text fields. | Yes |
| Ability to create "overnight" searches | Ability to create "overnight" searches. | Yes |
| Conceptual search engine to match resumes | Ability to use the requisition's job description or a large text phrase to find matching resumes using a conceptual search or natural language search engine. Conceptual searches should also be able to be conducted with fielded search. | Yes |
| "More like this" searching | Ability to take a resume and conduct a search to find others that are similar to it (more like it). | Yes |
| Library of candidate correspondence/ communication templates | Ability for clients to create a library of correspondence templates that can be sent to candidates at the user's discretion. | Yes |
| Editable correspondence at the user level | Users can make edits to the correspondence at the time of generation and distribution. | Yes |

| Function | Function Description | Response |
|---|---|---|
| Agency Portal | Functionality designed for the management of third-party staffing agencies. Includes the ability to push requisitions to one or more suppliers and receive agency resume submissions. | Yes |
| Contingent Labor Management | Functionality designed specifically for the requisition and management of contract labor including the distribution of job requirements to multiple vendors, submission and review of resumes, tracking of assignment, time reporting and billing. | Yes |
| Candidate Pool Generation (Leads/Prospective Candidates) | Able to enter limited candidate information (less required fields than regular candidate profile without comprising the configuration of the candidate profile) and develop target candidate pool for key skills. | Yes |
| Marketing Campaigns (Leads/Prospective Candidates) | Include proactive candidate pool in messaging, advertising campaigns or special event invitations. This should include the ability to send emails to thousands of candidates (as necessary). | Yes |
| Sending resumes to a manager | Ability to send a "Formatted Resume" to a Hiring Manager. | Yes |
| **Assessment and Interview Management** | | |
| Customer-defined workflow steps and status | Customer can set up steps and status for tracking a candidate through the recruiting process, with ability to tailor it for required and desired steps. | Yes |
| Customer can define multiple process workflows (Example: employee referral, internal transfers, etc.) | Ability to create multiple applicant workflows (set of tracking steps & status) to be selected at the requisition level. | Yes |

| Function | Function Description | Response |
|----------|---------------------|----------|
| Workflow triggered alerts | Alerts can be set up in the system to drive the next step in the process or to function as reminders. | Yes |
| Ability to create a "tree-structure" workflow (i.e. step A can be followed by step B, C, D or E) | | No |
| Volume hiring updates | The ability to change the status for a group of candidates to be hired in a single step (e.g. mass hiring in one step). | No |
| Integrated Assessments | Ability to store and/or integrate validated assessment tools into the recruiting workflow for certain jobs. | Yes |
| Assessment Triggers | Ability for assessment to automatically be presented to a candidate based on responses to pre-screening questions or other data in his/her profile. | Yes |
| Assessment on demand | Ability to push an online assessment to a candidate on demand via email link. | Yes |
| Interview team member history | Ability to select and record a list of interviewing team members for a requisition. | No |
| Interview team notifications | Ability to send an email notification (including a calendar meeting request) to the interview team members when scheduling the interview within the system (including interview packets, resumes, etc. when sending the email request). | Yes |
| Storage of interviewer comments | Ability to configure an online interview feedback form to capture the comments from each interviewer. | No |

| Function | Function Description | Response |
|---|---|---|
| Interviewer attachments | Ability to include attachments to the interviewer notifications (e.g. interview guidelines, interview schedule, resume, etc.) | Yes |
| **Offer Management and Onboarding** | | |
| Approval routing and status tracking | Select a list of approvers and route for approval via email. Status of the approval process is tracked and displayed real-time on the offer in the application as well as in the subsequent emails that go to the second and third approver, etc. | Yes |
| Pre-defined approval routing lists | Lists of approvers can be created, saved and/or assigned to a user or requisition. | Yes |
| Approvals can take place directly from an email | When approving an offer, the approver can take action directly from the email notification without having to log into the application. | Yes |
| Offer letters can be generated by merging fields into letter templates. | Data can be merged from the candidate record, the requisition and the offer terms into offer letter templates. | Yes |
| Offer letters can be edited at the user level | Users can make edits to the offer letter at the time of generation and distribution. | Yes |
| Specific Onboarding Module | Does the product offer a specific Onboarding module, allowing clients to define required notifications at hire and send notifications through the system? (e.g. provisioning, IT for user account setup, new hire, manager checklist, etc.) | Yes |
| Onboarding Documentation Management | Electronically provide new hire paperwork and track completion of key documents (I-9, Non Disclosures, Benefits Paperwork). | Yes |

| Function | Function Description | Response |
|----------|---------------------|----------|
| **Global Capabilities & Compliance** | | |
| EEO Compliance data collection | Configurable notification and collection of EEO compliance information at variable points in the process. | Yes |
| Global – in-country data collection based on regulations | Configurable data requests based on in-country requirements. Example: Germany, martial status, number of children. | Yes |
| Ability to present Career Sections in Multiple Languages | Ability to present career sections in multiple languages. | Yes |
| Ability to present the Recruiter and Manager Portals in Multiple Languages | Ability to present the recruiter and manager portals in multiple languages. | Yes |
| Data Segregation by country, region or predefined type | Data segregation, i.e. preventing users from a particular country or location from seeing candidates who are in another country or location. | Yes |
| OFCCP Compliance tools to enable search and applicant declaration | Functionality consistent with the new OFCCP definition of Internet Applicant (record keeping for searches, candidate submissions, etc.) | Yes |
| Privacy Policy acknowledgements | Ability to require that candidates agree with the privacy policy before they submit. | Yes |
| Compliance with Data Privacy | Ability for customers to remove a candidate's data at that candidate's request. | Yes |

| Function | Function Description | Response |
|---|---|---|
| Tax Credit Screening & Processing | Provides automatic Tax ID and SSN validation. Automatically transmits request to conduct tax credit screening for WOTC, WTW and more through to screening partners and displays those results within the candidate profile for review and processing upon hire. | Yes |
| **Reporting & Integration** | | |
| Standard reports are delivered with the system | System is delivered with a minimum of 10 standard reports. | Yes |
| Ad-hoc reporting capability | System is delivered with an ad-hoc report-writing tool so that clients can create their own reports as needed. | Yes |
| Reporting Security | Ability to enable field-level security and access to report creation, output and distribution. | Yes |
| Reporting Distribution | Ability to generate scheduled reports and distribute through email. | Yes |
| Real-Time Reporting | Ability to report on data in the application in real time (not based on a refresh of data in a reporting environment). | Yes |
| HRIS Integration | Ability to create bi-directional integrations from an HRIS to the ATS. | Yes |
| Integration - Client Self-Service Tools | Ability for clients to create their own integration touch points as needed (and make them operational). | Yes |
| Integration - API capability | Ability to allow clients to create integrations through APIs. | Yes |

| Function | Function Description | Response |
|---|---|---|

## Performance Management

| Performance Dashboard | | |
|---|---|---|
| Dashboard configuration | Ability to configure dashboard based on user preference. | Yes – via reporting |
| Create and display reports | Display reports that can be generated (i.e. review completion progress, goal progress). | Yes |
| Create and display charts and graphs | Display charts and graphs that are available for planning actions. | Yes |
| Display help and reference tools | Display and view help and reference tools that can be selected by link or mouse hover. | Yes |
| **Employee Information Review (Data Import from HRIS/LMS)** | | |
| Import and display employee information | Display name, address, phone, email, location, photo, education (typically pulled from HRIS). | Yes |
| Import and display employee position information | Display current job title, job summary, job family, job level/grade, job code, FLSA, shift, status (FT/PT) (typically pulled through HRIS). | Yes |
| Create and display work history | Display created previous work history (i.e. name of company, job title, responsibilities/duties, employment dates). | Yes |
| Create and display years in management | Display created years of management experience (manually entered or via integration). | Yes |
| Create and display years in industry | Display created years of experience in industry (primarily entered manually). | Yes |

| Function | Function Description | Response |
|---|---|---|
| Import, create and display employee language(s) | Display employee languages (i.e. read, written, fluent) primarily entered manually. | Yes |
| Import, create and display employee affiliations | Display employee affiliation memberships. | Yes |
| Import, create and display employee certifications | Display employee certifications and dates. | Yes |
| Import, create and display employee licenses | Display employee licenses and dates (usually a text box). Important to include expiration dates (for transportation, professional licenses, healthcare licenses, etc.) | Yes |
| Import and display organizational information | Display company name, division, department (typically imported from HRIS). | Yes |
| Import and display management hierarchy information | Display multiple levels of management names and information (i.e. Executive Management, Division Head, Department Head, Direct Manager, Employee). | Yes |
| Import and display direct reports | Display name and information of employee direct reports. | Yes |
| Import and display matrix manager hierarchy information | Display multiple levels of matrix management names and information (i.e. Employee has dotted line reporting relationships). | No |
| Import and display multiple manager hierarchy information | Display multiple levels of numerous management names and information (i.e. Employee reports to more than one manager directly). | No |
| Organizational Chart View | Organizational information can be displayed in an Org Chart view. (Note how this is displayed visually). | Yes |

| Function | Function Description | Response |
|----------|--------------------|----------|
| Organizational Change Requests | Due to potential errors within HRMS, manager has the ability to request an employee change in hierarchy (i.e. manager name, organization, location, job role); changes can be configured to require approval. | Yes |
| Import and display employee current and past compensation | Display employee's past and current base salary, bonus, equity, commission, etc. | Yes |
| Import and display employee most recent performance measures | Display employee's current competencies, goals, skills, projects, performance rating, development plan and personal improvement plan. | Yes |
| Import and display employee previous performance measures | Display employee's previous competencies, goals, skills, projects, performance rating, development plan and personal improvement plan. | Yes |
| Complete and display employee training | Display employee's completed and assigned training (i.e. mandatory/development). Note if there is any integration with LMS. | Yes |
| External Identifier | Ability to have an external identifier field to bring in content on goals from a third-party application (i.e. description, start date, critical, public goal). Can be configured to be read-only for imports. | Yes |
| UDFs | Available user-defined fields for employee profile. | Yes |
| **Career Planning / Personal Development (Employee)** | | |
| Create and display future career plan scenarios | Display multiple future career plans (vertical, horizontal, both). Where does the employee want to go next? (lateral, promotion, etc.) | Yes |

| Function | Function Description | Response |
|---|---|---|
| Select and display positions, job families and organizations/divisions of interest | Display selected positions and organizations of interest from import of job and organization lists (mentorships and cross-training).Gives the employee the opportunity to identify a position, job-family or organization of interest. | Yes |
| Create and display training requests | Display developmental training requests (entered by an employee or manager). This could be an integration point to the LMS. | Yes |
| Create and display executive/professional requests | Display various executive/ professional requests (i.e. executive coaching, cross-training, job shadowing, speaking engagements, writing submittals, managing people, presentations, mentoring, apprenticeships). | Yes |
| Create and display organization affiliations and/or conferences/seminars | Display employee organization/ affiliation or conference/seminar requests to join or attend. | Yes |
| Select and display competency development | Display selected desired competencies (entered by employee). | Yes |
| Create self-asses job readiness | Display selected self-readiness from list of options (i.e. Now, 0-3 months, 3-6 months, 6-9 months, 9-12 months, 12 months +). | Yes |
| Display position Gap % | Display gap % of employee readiness to ideal position as well as required training, license(s), education, certification(s). Could be automatically calculated by the system (key differentiator). This is gap analysis on the underlying competencies (most recent performance rating vs. competencies required for next position). | Yes |

| Function | Function Description | Response |
|---|---|---|
| Select and display willingness to relocate | Display selected willingness to relocate (i.e. yes, no, maybe, comments). | Yes |
| Display career prerequisites | Display required training, education, certification(s), license(s) for position of interest. | Yes |
| Submit development requests for approval | Submit development self-assessments to direct manager for review, feedback and approval (areas where the development needs to occur, as well as specific courses and conferences to help meet these development areas). Could be an integration point with LMS. | Yes |
| **Career Development (Manager)** | | |
| Create or select and display employee training goals | Display created or selected employee completed training, assigned training (mandatory/ development), scheduled training and employee training requests. This is the manager identifying training goals for an employee. | Yes |
| Competency Development | Display assigned professional/ leadership competencies. | Yes |
| Create and display executive/professional assignments | Display various executive/professional recommendations (i.e. executive coaching, cross-training, job shadowing, speaking engagements, writing submittals, managing people, presentations, mentoring, apprenticeships.) | Yes |
| Create and display organization affiliations and/or conferences/seminars | Display employee organization/ affiliation or conference/seminar recommendations. | Yes |

| Function | Function Description | Response |
|----------|--------------------|----------|
| **Individual Goal / Self-Assessment (Employee)** | | |
| Select, create and display individual development goals | Display selected or created completed training, improvement competencies, executive coaching, promotion and cross-training. | Yes |
| Select competency development | Display selected development competencies. This is where employees selects competencies they want to develop for their career on the annual review. | Yes |
| Submit goal/competency assessment for approval | Submit manual or automatic goal/competency assessment to direct manager. | Yes |
| Solicit and display feedback | Select employees (i.e. managers, matrix managers, peers) to solicit performance feedback (i.e. 360, peer review, business review) and display results. | Yes |
| Create and display self-performance notes | Display created performance notes (i.e. kudos) throughout the review cycle (manually entered by employee or can solicit feedback throughout project). | Yes |
| Create and display self-goal assessment progress | Display created self-goal progress (i.e. quantitative % of completion, qualitative to include customer satisfaction, timeline to include start/completion date). | Yes |
| Submit goal/competency review for approval | Submit manual or automatic goal/competency assessment to direct manager and higher levels. | Yes |
| UDFs | Available user-defined fields for employee goals. | Yes |
| **Review Process (Employee and Manager)** | | |
| Select and display competencies | Display selected professional or leadership competencies. | Yes |

| Function | Function Description | Response |
|---|---|---|
| Select and display goals/objectives | Display selected goals/objectives (i.e. quantitative and/or qualitative). | Yes |
| Select and display goal alignment | Display selected goal alignment to company, organization, department and/or manager goals (cascading goals). | Yes |
| Select or create and display projects | Display selected or created projects. | Yes |
| Select and display project alignment to goals | Display selected project alignment to company, organization, department and/or manager goals. | Yes |
| Select or create and display skills | Display selected or created company, organization, department, employee skills. | Yes |
| Create and display employee performance notes | Display created performance notes (positive or negative) throughout the review cycle. Notes created by the manager. | Yes |
| Solicit and display feedback | Select employees (i.e. managers, matrix managers, peers) to solicit performance feedback (i.e. 360, peer review, business review) and display. Note how this feedback is gathered and entered into the system. | Yes |
| Create and display employee goal assessment review | Display created employee goal progress (i.e. quantitative % of completion, qualitative to include customer satisfaction, timeline to include start/completion date). This is the manager entering the assessment. | Yes |
| Performance review filtering | Manager can filter performance review information based on approval status, assigned to, author/owner, manager, employee, organization, location, job field, job role, review cycle, review group, review group owner, overall rating; filtering can be cumulative. | No |

| Function | Function Description | Response |
|---|---|---|
| Batch activities | Manager can take group actions on multiple employees simultaneously. | Yes – Small batches, 20 – 40 employees |
| UDFs | Available user-defined fields for employee competencies. | Yes |
| **Workflow** | | |
| Review cycles | Ability to configure multiple review cycles/tied to various reviews. | Yes |
| Review groups | Ability to define review recipients based on dates, job function, organization, job code, etc. | Yes |
| Workflow Order | Ability to configure order of workflow (i.e. self-assessments can be configured to be completed first). | Yes |
| Notifications | Ability to push reviews to employees and managers. | Yes |
| Reminders | Ability to send reminders to employees and managers via email (manual and automatic). | No |
| Acknowledgements | Ability to send auto-acknowledgements triggered by event/activity. | Yes |
| Next Level Approval | Ability to auto/manually route to multiple levels of approval. | Yes |
| Configurable workflow | Ability to: configure various steps of the review process; make review steps mandatory; have manager override;display/hide visual graphic workflow diagram. | Yes |
| Auto/Manual Progression | Ability to automatically or manually progress through the review process. | Yes |

| Function | Function Description | Response |
|---|---|---|
| Review form | Exportable and printable review form. | Yes |
| **System Admin** | | |
| Review sections | Ability to configure multiple review sections, including goals, competencies, comments, rating models, etc. | Yes |
| Configurable rating models | Does it configure and display alpha and numeric values? Can values be rounded (up/down/ both), value ranges, number of decimals (1-5)? | Yes |
| Comments | Displayed and available in individual and overall review sections. Can they be configured to be mandatory and have ability to be overridden by management? | Yes |
| Goals | Ability to link organizational, divisional, departmental, individual goals into sections and to display goal progress. | Yes |
| Competencies | Ability to link competencies into sections. | Yes |
| Weightings | Ability to weigh employee performance based on goals and competencies. | Yes |
| **Search Functionality** | | |
| Basic Employee Search | Basic search by employee name (i.e. first or last name or a combination of both). | Yes |
| Job/Position Basic Search | Basic search by job role or position title, etc. | Yes |
| Competency Basic Search | Basic search by competency name. | Yes |

| Function | Function Description | Response |
|---|---|---|
| Advanced Search | More detailed search capabilities that combine various search criteria or fields. May include optional weighting to determine which employees are retrieved in a search as well as each person's rank in the search results. | Yes |
| Succession Planning Search | Search functionality that dynamically generates the criteria used to match employees who would make good succession candidates with a specific position profile (could have various levels of "fit"). | Yes |
| **Employee View / Navigation / Help / Other** | | |
| List View | Display employee goals, business goals or projects; the list mode is a list of items with information on key dates and progress. | Yes |
| Card View | Display employee goals, business goals or projects using the card mode; the card mode provides details on one item at a time and offers the possibility of editing progress. This can also include employee photos. | Yes |
| Timeline / Gantt | Display employee goals, business goals or projects using the timeline mode; this provides a timeline view of an item's start and due dates. | Yes |
| Org Chart | Managers can access and manage information on their direct reports for all functionalities activated; the organizational chart will provide key data (i.e. risk of loss or most recent performance rating) for each of the manager's direct reports. | Yes |

| Function | Function Description | Response |
| --- | --- | --- |
| Mini-Org Chart | Displays a single analytic data point at a time; the manager can drill down into all layers of his organization and can view key metrics (i.e. performance reviews, goals, succession). | Yes |
| Graphs | Graphical display of various information (i.e. Gap Analysis, goal progress, review completion progress). | Yes |
| Help Links | Online help, FAQs, customer support, product version. | Yes |
| Attach Documents | Ability to attach reference documents to various sections within the system. | Yes |
| Browser capabilities | Supported by general Internet access (works with standard browsers: IE, Safari, Mozilla, Opera). | Yes |
| Mouse-Over Hover | Additional tooltips or descriptions that display when user hovers mouse pointer over various graphics or words within the system. | Yes |
| Web 2.0 | Ability to utilize Web 2.0 functionality, i.e. social networking. | Yes |
| **Security** | | |
| Logging In | Various login options (i.e. manual, SSO, LDAP). | Yes |
| File Transfer | Various file transfer protocol (i.e. FTP, sFTP, vendor-specific transfer import/export tool). | Yes |
| Encryption | Various data encryption ability (i.e. PGP). | Yes |

| Function | Function Description | Response |
|---|---|---|
| Roles / Permissions | Configurable list of permission-based roles with detailed access rights to various organizations, levels, etc. Typically employees only view within their own organization hierarchy. | Yes |
| Integration | Ability to integrate organizational data i.e. HRIS/ATS/ LMS and employee data, including competencies, training, development plans, etc. | Yes |
| **Reporting** | | |
| Standard reports are delivered with the system | System is delivered with a set number of standard reports. | Yes |
| Ad-hoc reporting capability | System is delivered with an ad-hoc report-writing tool so that clients can create their own reports as needed. | Yes |
| Advanced Value metrics | Data analysis of employee review process status, goal progress by hierarchy. | Yes |
| Reporting Security | Ability to enable field-level security and access to report creation, output and distribution. | Yes |
| Reporting UDFs | Able to report user-defined fields. | Yes |
| Exporting reports | Reports can easily be exported to other applications (i.e. .xls, .pdf, .txt) | Yes |

## Succession Planning

| Succession Planning (Manager - Planning of Individual Talent Matched to Critical Roles) | | |
|---|---|---|
| Create and display critical roles for today | Display critical job roles (i.e. title, level, location, division, organization). | Yes |

| Function | Function Description | Response |
|---|---|---|
| Create and display critical roles for future | Display critical job roles (i.e. title, level, location, division, organization) for future (workforce planning-like tools). | Yes |
| Calculate and display performance rating | Performance rating is automatically averaged from various sections of the performance review and displayed (current and past). | Yes |
| Calculate and display performance ranking | High potential employees will be automatically ranked according to order of fit with critical role (i.e. 9-box grid, numeric ranking, high performer, high potential); can be ranked by position, organization, etc. | Yes |
| Multi-dimensional matrix | Matrix that can be configured up to various # of cells (i.e. 9-box, 12-box, 16-box, 25-box); text within grid is configurable. | Yes |
| Various dimensions of matrix | Matrix displays employee performance, potential, number of succession plans for employee, years in management, years in industry. | Yes |
| Navigation from multi-dimensional matrix | Manager can select an employee within the matrix and navigate to his/her information (i.e. performance review, talent profile, employee goals, career plan). | Yes |
| Display employee comparisons | Display comparison of multiple high potential employees according to fit to critical role (i.e. # of employees to compare, comparable data, fit gap analysis, ranking analysis, bench strength). | Yes |
| Create and display role readiness | Manager can create and display high potential employee role readiness (i.e. now, 0-3 months, 3-6 months, 6-9 months, 9-12 months, 12+ months). | Yes |

| Function | Function Description | Response |
|---|---|---|
| Create and display retention risk | Manager can create and display high potential employee retention/loss/flight risk (i.e. high, medium, low, comments). | Yes |
| Create and display role willingness | Manager can create and display high potential employee role willingness (i.e. yes, no, comments). | Yes |
| Create and display willingness to relocate | Manager can create and display high potential employee willingness to relocate (i.e. yes, no, maybe, comments). | Yes |
| Create and display willingness to travel | Manager can create and display high potential employee willingness to travel (i.e. none, 25-50%, 50-75%, 75-100%). | Yes |
| Create and display interest in international assignment | Manager can create and display high potential employee interest in international assignment (i.e. yes, no, maybe). | Yes |
| Create and display interim replacement for critical role | Manager can create and display high potential interim replacement for critical roles. | Yes |
| Display of gap analysis | Automatically calculate and display high potential employees' fit gap analysis to their next position and ranking analysis of each to that next position. | Yes |
| UDFs | Available user-defined fields for succession planning. | Yes |
| **Succession Pooling (Manager - Planning of a Talent Pool for Critical Roles)** | | |
| Display high potential pool | Display nominated and/or approved high potential pool (i.e. employee information, designated nominators, designated approvers, approvals, rejections, role readiness, rejection comments). | Yes |

| Function | Function Description | Response |
|----------|---------------------|----------|
| Calculate and display performance rating | Performance rating is automatically averaged from various sections of the performance review and displayed (current and past). | Yes |
| Calculate and display performance ranking | Pool of high potential employees will be automatically ranked according to order of fit with critical role (i.e. 9-box grid, numeric ranking, high performer, high potential). | Yes |
| Display employee comparisons | Display comparison of multiple high potential employees according to fit to critical role (i.e. # of employees to compare, comparable data, fit gap analysis, ranking analysis, bench strength). | Yes |
| Create and display role readiness | Manager can create and display high potential employee role readiness (i.e. now, 0-3 months, 3-6 months, 6-9 months, 9-12 months, 12+ months). | Yes |
| Create and display retention risk | Manager can create and display high potential employee retention/loss/flight risk (i.e. high, medium, low, comments). | Yes |
| Create and display role willingness | Manager can create and display high potential employee role willingness (i.e. yes, no, comments). | Yes |
| Create and display willingness to relocate | Manager can create and display high potential employee willingness to relocate (i.e. yes, no, maybe, comments). | Yes |
| Create and display willingness to travel | Manager can create and display high potential employee willingness to travel (i.e. none, 25-50%, 50-75%, 75-100%). | Yes |
| Create and display interest in international assignment | Manager can create and display high potential employee interest in international assignment (i.e. yes, no, maybe). | Yes |

| Function | Function Description | Response |
| --- | --- | --- |
| Create and display interim replacement for critical role | Manager can create and display high potential interim replacement for critical roles. | Yes |
| Display of gap analysis | Automatically calculate and display high potential employee's fit gap analysis to position and ranking analysis of employee to position. | Yes |
| UDFs | Available user-defined fields for succession pooling. | Yes |
| **Workflow** | | |
| Succession approval workflow | Ability to: define or edit approvers; add/remove users and roles; change the approval order; reject with comments. | Yes |
| Nominations for succession pool | Ability to nominate, reject and enter comments on nominated HiPo employees. | Yes |
| **Reporting** | | |
| Standard reports are delivered with the system | System is delivered with a set number of standard reports. | Yes |
| Ad-hoc reporting capability | System is delivered with an ad-hoc report-writing tool so that clients can create their own reports as needed. | Yes |
| Advanced Value metrics | Data analysis of high performers / high potential employees, identified gaps, critical roles. | Yes |
| Reporting Security | Ability to enable field-level security and access to report creation, output and distribution. | Yes |
| Reporting UDFs | Ability to report user-defined fields. | Yes |

| Function | Function Description | Response |
|---|---|---|
| Exporting reports | Reports can easily be exported to other applications (i.e. .xls, .pdf, .txt). | Yes |

## Compensation Management

| Compensation Dashboard | | |
|---|---|---|
| Dashboard configuration | Ability to configure dashboard based on user preference. | Yes |
| Create and display a compensation worksheet | Display a compensation worksheet that will provide individual and org planning status and detail. | Yes |
| Create and display reports | Display reports that can be generated, i.e. budget usage by merit, bonus, equity, adjustment and percent of planning completed. | Yes |
| Create and display charts and graphs | Display charts and graphs that are available to show planning actions. | Yes |
| Import and display allocation guidelines | Display compensation allocation guidelines for merit, bonus, equity and adjustments - also refer to the time allocation/ workflow to complete this process. | Yes |
| Import and display eligibility guidelines | Display employee eligibility guidelines for planning, i.e. FT, PT, commission, LOA, new hire, etc. Guidelines are input by compensation department. | Yes |
| Display help and reference tools | Display and view help and reference tools that can be selected by link or mouse hover. | Yes |
| Compensation Budget | | |
| Import and display multiple aggregate planning budget by org | Display multiple approved allocated budgets by diverse business groups on all pages (usually imported from financial system). | Yes |

| Function | Function Description | Response |
|---|---|---|
| Import and display aggregate merit budget by org | Display approved allocated merit budget by diverse business groups on all pages. | Yes |
| Import and display aggregate bonus budget by org | Display approved allocated bonus by diverse business groups on all pages. | Yes |
| Import and display aggregate equity budget by org | Display approved allocated equity budget by diverse business groups on all pages. | Yes |
| Import and display aggregate adjustment budget by org | Display approved allocated adjustment budget by diverse business groups on all pages. | Yes |
| **Employee Information Review** | | |
| Import and display employee Information | Display name, location, photo, org, direct manager (typically imported from PM tool). | Yes |
| Import and display employee position | Display current job title, job code, level/grade. | Yes |
| Import and display employee prior compensation planning period data | Display current hourly rate, annual rate, bonus percent, bonus amount, equity allocation, total compensation. | Yes |
| Import and display employee prior performance rating | Display prior performance rating. | Yes |
| Import and display new employee performance rating | Display new performance rating. | Yes |
| Import and display employee's position salary range | Display employee's salary range. | Yes |

| Function | Function Description | Response |
|---|---|---|
| Import and display salary penetration % based on position salary range | Display % of penetration that employee's salary falls within the range. | Yes |
| **Promotion** | | |
| Display position information | Ability to select and display job titles, job codes, job level/grades. | Yes |
| Import and display corporate promotion guidelines | Ability to display promotion guidelines per position, including salary range and percent increase guidelines. | Yes |
| Promotion amount | Ability to enter promotion percent or amount. | Yes |
| Auto-calculate promotion amount | System to auto-populate promotion amount based on percent increase. | Yes |
| Ability to calculate hourly rate | System to auto-populate new hourly rate based on promotion increase. | Yes |
| Ability to auto-calculate annual rate | System to auto-populate new annual rate based on promotion increase. | Yes |
| Promotion approval chain | TBD. | Yes |
| Develop documentation | Ability to document the promotion justification. | Yes |
| **Adjustment** | | |
| Import and display adjustment guidelines | Ability to display adjustment allocation guidelines, including salary range and percent increase guidelines. | Yes |
| Adjustment allocation | Ability to enter and submit an adjustment percent or amount. | Yes |

| Function | Function Description | Response |
|---|---|---|
| Auto-calculate hourly amount | System to auto-populate new hourly rate based on adjustment percent increase. | Yes |
| Auto-calculate adjustment amount | System to auto-populate new annual rate based on adjustment percent increase. | Yes |
| Adjustment approvals | | Yes |
| Develop documentation | Ability to document the adjustment justification. | Yes |
| **Merit** | | |
| Import and display promotion guidelines | Ability to display merit allocation guidelines, including salary range and percent increase guidelines. | Yes |
| Performance-based recommendations | Merit allocation can be based on performance rating. | Yes |
| Merit allocation | Ability to enter and submit a merit percent or amount. | Yes |
| Import and display proration of merit based on hire date | System to auto-calculate merit increase based on hire date, i.e. less than one year would be calculated by months employed. | Yes |
| Auto-calculate hourly amount | System to auto-populate new hourly rate based on merit percent increase. | Yes |
| Auto-calculate adjustment amount | System to auto-populate new annual rate based on merit percent increase. | Yes |
| Merit approvals | Merit approvals. | Yes |
| Develop documentation | Ability to document the merit justification. | Yes |

| Function | Function Description | Response |
|---|---|---|
| **Bonus** | | |
| Import and display bonus allocation guidelines | Ability to display bonus allocation guide-lines. | Yes |
| Performance-based recommendations | Bonus allocation can be based on per-formance rating. | Yes |
| Bonus allocation | Ability to enter and submit a bonus per-cent or amount. | Yes |
| Bonus adjustment | Auto-Proration of bonus based on hired or leave, i.e. severance date. | Yes |
| Bonus approvals | Ability to obtain appropriate approvals (workflow to select appropriate approv-ers). | Yes |
| Develop documen-tation | Ability to document the merit justification. | Yes |
| **Equity** | | |
| Import and display equity allocation guidelines | Ability to display equity allocation guide-lines. | Yes |
| Performance-based recommendations | Equity allocation can be based on perfor-mance rating. | Yes |
| Equity allocation | Ability to enter and submit equity percent or amount. | Yes |
| Equity allocation adjustment | Auto-Proration of equity allocation based on hire date. | Yes |
| Equity approvals | | Yes |
| Develop documen-tation | Ability to document the merit justification. | Yes |

| Function | Function Description | Response |
|---|---|---|
| **Other** | | |
| Ability to assign a delegate | Ability to assign a delegate to complete compensation planning, i.e. Admin. | Yes |
| Employee Filter | Ability to sort by employee name or data, i.e. first name, last name, employee ID, etc. | Yes |
| Employee Search | Ability to search throughout the tool by employee name or data, i.e. first name, last name, employee ID, etc. | Yes |
| Revert or change functionality | Ability for planning administrators to revert or change submitted data. | Yes |
| Collaborative work-flow | Ability for managers, compensation and HR partners to collaborate on various compensation workflows. | Yes |
| Display out-of-guideline entries | Ability to display out-of-guideline entries made within adjustments, merit, bonus, equity. | Yes |
| **Reporting** | | |
| Standard reports are delivered with the system | System is delivered with a set number of standard reports. | Yes |
| Ad-hoc reporting capability | System is delivered with an ad-hoc report-writing tool so that clients can create their own reports as needed. | Yes |
| Advanced Value metrics | Data analysis of comp gaps based on roles, hierarchy. | Yes |
| Reporting Security | Ability to enable field-level security and access to report creation, output and distribution. | Yes |

| Function | Function Description | Response |
|---|---|---|
| **Security** | | |
| Logging In | Various login options (i.e. manual, SSO, LDAP). | Yes |
| File Transfer | Various file transfer protocol (i.e. FTP, sFTP, vendor-specific transfer import/export tool). | Yes |
| Encryption | Various data encryption ability (i.e. PGP). | Yes |
| Roles / Permissions | Configurable list of permission-based roles with detailed access rights to various organizations, levels, etc. Typically employees only view within their own organization hierarchy. | Yes |
| Integration | Ability to Integrate organizational data with appropriate org system, (i.e. HRIS/Payroll, employee data, including employee salaries, levels, performance rating, etc.) | Yes |
| Reporting UDFs | Ability to report user-defined fields. | Yes |
| Exporting reports | Reports can easily be exported to other applications (i.e. .xls, .pdf, .txt). | Yes |

# ABOUT THE AUTHORS

 **ALLAN SCHWEYER** is a founder and Executive Director of the Human Capital Institute, a Washington D.C.-based think tank and educator in the science of talent management. Schweyer is a past editor of *Leadership Excellence: The Journal of Human Capital Management* and author of the books, *Talent Management Systems* (Wiley & Sons, 2004) and *Talent Management Technologies* (HCI Press, 2009). He is an internationally-renowned analyst and speaker on the topic of transformational human capital management for individuals, organizations, regions and nations. Trained as a labor market economist, Schweyer's contributions include pioneering work on job boards, applicant tracking systems and corporate intranets in the 1990s. In 2000 and 2001, he worked as a management consultant to Reed Business Information in Boston, focusing on career portals for the movie, entertainment and publishing industries. At the same time, Schweyer attended graduate school at Harvard University. Directly prior to joining HCI, Allan was a senior researcher, analyst and consultant with HR.com, editor of the HR.com staffing vertical and author of the industry's most comprehensive guides to HR technologies. Allan's articles and white papers appear in dozens of popular media and industry-specific publications worldwide, including Inc.com, *Future Health* Magazine, *Australia HR* Magazine, *Global Sourcing* Magazine, *The Journal of Leadership Excellence* and many others. He travels the world speaking at conferences and leading workshops on the themes of human capital and talent management.

**ED NEWMAN** is a founder and CEO of The Newman Group, the leading provider of business process and recruiting technology expertise for Fortune 500 and Global 1000 organizations. For the last 15 years, he has provided consulting services to assist major corporations in the area of recruiting and talent acquisition strategy, implementation of recruiting best practices, process assessment and optimization and the effective use of technology. From his experience and deep subject matter expertise, Ed has developed a consulting methodology to quickly assess the effectiveness of recruiting organizations, identify strategic opportunities and deliver a plan of action to attain results. Recent clients include Accenture, Johnson Controls and McKesson. Ed is a frequent contributor of white papers and articles to several online industry forums, such as the Electronic Recruiting Exchange. He has presented at leading industry trade shows and regional chapters of the Society for Human Resource Management (SHRM) and the Employment Management Association (EMA) on topics such as change management and recruiting process re-design, selection implementation and optimization of recruiting technology and maximizing return on investment.

**PETER DEVRIES** is a Consulting Director with The Newman Group. He has proven expertise in talent acquisition business processes and strategy, as well as talent management systems selection and implementation. Over the past six years with The Newman Group, he has developed a notable track record working with various Fortune 500 clients and emerging new economy clients on various projects, including the strategic analysis of talent management processes. In addition, he has served as the project manager for global talent management systems implementations for his clients. Recent clients have included General Motors, Kaiser Permanente and Yahoo! Peter currently acts as the leader of his firm's talent management systems vendor selection and evaluation service offerings.

LaVergne, TN USA
27 January 2010
171321LV00002B/1/P